# Guide to America's Outdoors

# Southern Rockies

# Guide to America's Outdoors
# Southern Rockies

By Gary Ferguson, John Clayton,
and Maureen B. Keilty
Photography by George H. H. Huey

**NATIONAL
GEOGRAPHIC**
WASHINGTON, D.C.

# Contents

*Cover:* Thor's Hammer, Bryce Canyon National Park  *Page 1:* Sunflower
*Pages 2-3:* Wotans Throne at sunset viewed from Cape Royal, Grand Canyon National P
*Opposite:* Summit of Mount Evans, Arapaho and Pike National Forests

# Treading Lightly in the Wild

Blue columbine, Manti-La Sal NF

NATIONAL GEOGRAPHIC GUIDE TO AMERICA'S OUTDOORS: SOUTHERN ROCKIES takes you to some of the wildest and most beautiful natural areas of a region famed for its towering peaks and tundra meadows, its racing rivers and glistening lakes, its red-rock canyons and sandstone arches.

Visitors who care about this spectacular region know they must tread lightly on the land. Ecosystems can be damaged, even destroyed, by thoughtless misuse. Many have already suffered from the impact of tourism. The marks are clear: litter-strewn acres, polluted waters, trampled vegetation, and disturbed wildlife. You can do your part to preserve these places for yourself, your children, and all other nature travelers. Before embarking on a backcountry visit or a camping adventure, learn some basic conservation dos and don'ts. Leave No Trace, a national educational program, recommends the following:

Plan ahead and prepare for your trip. If you know what to expect in terms of climate, conditions, and hazards, you can pack for general needs, extreme weather, and emergencies. Do yourself and the land a favor by visiting if possible during off-peak months and limiting your group to no more than four to six people. To keep trash or litter to a minimum, repackage food into reusable containers or bags. And rather than using cairns, flags, or paint cues that mar the environment to mark your way, bring a map and compass.

Travel and camp on solid surfaces. In popular areas, stay within established trails and campsites. Be sure to choose the right path, whether you are hiking, biking, skiing, or riding. Travel single file in the middle of the trail, even when it's wet or muddy, to avoid trampling vegetation. If you explore off a trail in pristine, lightly traveled areas, have your group spread out to lessen impact. Good campsites are found, not made. Travel and camp on sand, gravel, or rock, or on dry grasses, pine needles, or snow. Remember to stay at least 200 feet from waterways. After you've broken camp, leave the site as you found it.

Pack out what you pack in—and that means *everything* except human waste, which should be deposited in a hole dug away from water, camp, or trail, then covered and concealed. When washing dishes, clothes, or yourself, use small amounts of biodegradable soap and scatter the water way from lakes and streams.

Be sure to leave all items—plants, rocks, artifacts—as you find them. id potential disaster by neither introducing nor transporting non-e species. Also, don't build or carve out structures that will alter the nment. A don't-touch policy not only preserves resources for future generations; it also gives the next guy a crack at the discovery experience.

Keep fires to a minimum. It may be unthinkable to camp without a campfire, but depletion of firewood harms the backcountry. When you can, try a gas-fueled camp stove and a candle lantern. If you choose to build a fire, first consider regulations, weather, skill, and firewood availability. Where possible, employ existing fire rings; elsewhere, use fire pans or mound fires. Keep your fire small, use only sticks from the ground, burn the fire down to ash, and don't leave the site until it's cold.

Respect wildlife. Though they may appear tame, animals in the wild are just that. Watch wildlife from a distance (bring binoculars or a telephoto lens for close-ups), but never approach, feed, or follow them. Feeding weakens an animal's ability to fend for itself in the wild. If you can't keep your pets under control, leave them at home.

Finally, be mindful of other visitors. Yield to fellow travelers on the trail, and keep voices and noise levels low so that all the sounds of nature can be heard.

With these points in mind, you have only to chart your course. Enjoy your explorations. Let natural places quiet your mind, refresh your spirit, and remain as you found them. Just remember, leave behind no trace.

## MAP KEY and ABBREVIATIONS

| | |
|---|---|
| □ National Park | N.P. |
| National Monument | NAT. MON. |
| National Natural Landmark | N.N.L. |
| National Recreation Area | N.R.A. |
| □ National Forest | N.F. |
| State Forest | S.F. |
| ▣ National Wildlife Refuge | N.W.R. |
| ▣ State Park | S.P. |
| State Historic Park | S.H.P. |
| State Recreation Area | S.R.A. |
| ▣ Indian Reservation | I.R. |
| □ National Grassland | N.G. |

| POPULATION | |
|---|---|
| ● DENVER | above 500,000 |
| ● Boulder | 50,000 to 500,000 |
| ● Durango | 10,000 to 50,000 |
| ● Moab | under 10,000 |

### ADDITIONAL ABBREVIATIONS

| | |
|---|---|
| Cr. | Creek |
| DR. | Drive |
| E. | East |
| Fk. | Fork |
| HWY. | Highway |
| L. | Lake |
| MEM. | Memorial |
| Mt.-s. | Mount-ain-s |
| N. | North |
| NAT. | National |
| N.S.T. | National Scenic Trail |
| Pk. | Peak |
| Pt. | Point |
| Ra. | Range |
| RD. | Road |
| Rec. | Recreation |
| Res. | Reservoir |
| S. | South |
| Tr. | Trail |
| W. | West |
| WILD. | Wilderness |

National Wild & Scenic River ... N.W. & S.R.

U.S. Federal or State Highway ─(50)─(12)─

U.S. Interstate ═(70)═

Other Road [118]

Trail - - - - - - - -

Continental Divide ............

### BOUNDARIES

STATE ▬▬▬▬

FOREST     I.R.     N.P.     WILD.

| | |
|---|---|
| □ Point of Interest | � Falls |
| ⊛ State capital | ♀ Spring |
| + Elevation | ⌇ Dam |
| ⤳ Pass | -·⁻ Intermittent River |
| △ Campground | ⌇ Intermittent Lake |
| | ⌇ Dry Lake |

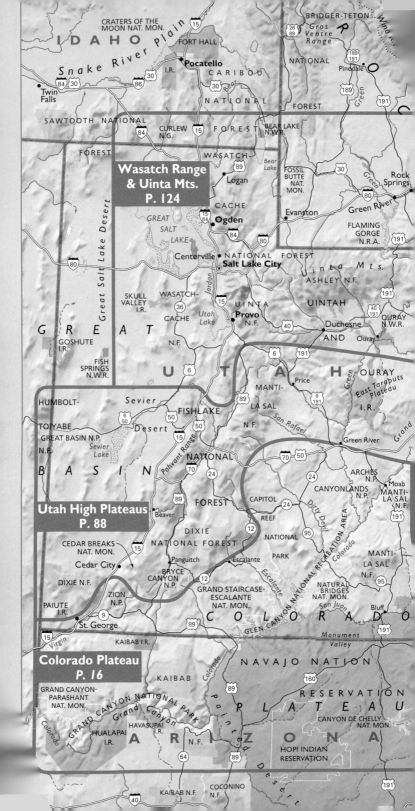

**IDAHO**

CRATERS OF THE MOON NAT. MON.

Snake River Plain

FORT HALL

**Pocatello**

CARIBOU

I.R.

NATIONAL

Twin Falls

Bear

SAWTOOTH NATIONAL

CURLEW N.G.

FOREST

BEAR LAKE N.W.R.

WASATCH-

FOSSIL BUTTE NAT. MON.

**Wasatch Range & Uinta Mts. P. 124**

Logan

Bear Lake

CACHE

Evanston

GREEN SALT LAKE DESERT

GREAT SALT LAKE

**Ogden**

NATIONAL FOREST

Centerville

**Salt Lake City**

Uinta Mts.

ASHLEY N.F.

SKULL VALLEY I.R.

WASATCH-

Jordan

UINTA

UINTAH

CACHE

**Provo**

Utah Lake

N.F.

Duchesne

Ouray

OURAY N.W.R.

AND

GOSHUTE I.R.

N.F.

Price

OURAY

FISH SPRINGS N.W.R.

MANTI-LA SAL

East Tarapults Plateau I.R.

HUMBOLT-TOIYABE

Sevier

FISHLAKE

San Rafael

Green River

**GREAT BASIN N.P.**

Desert

N.F.

GREAT BASIN N.P.

Sevier Lake

NATIONAL

ARCHES N.P.

Moab

MANTI-LA SAL N.F.

**Utah High Plateaus P. 88**

CAPITOL REEF

CANYONLANDS N.P.

FOREST

NATIONAL

Beaver

DIXIE

MANTI-LA SAL N.F.

CEDAR BREAKS NAT. MON.

NATIONAL FOREST

Panguitch

Escalante

PARK

NATURAL BRIDGES NAT. MON.

Cedar City

BRYCE CANYON N.P.

GRAND STAIRCASE-ESCALANTE NAT. MON.

Bluff

DIXIE N.F.

ZION N.P.

**COLORADO**

PAIUTE I.R.

St. George

KAIBAB I.R.

Monument Valley

Virgin

**Colorado Plateau P. 16**

KAIBAB

NAVAJO NATION

GRAND CANYON-PARASHANT NAT. MON.

GRAND CANYON NATIONAL PARK

RESERVATION

PLATEAU

CANYON DE CHELLY NAT. MON.

HUALAPAI I.R.

HAVASUPAI I.R.

Grand Canyon

N.F.

**ARIZONA**

HOPI INDIAN RESERVATION

KAIBAB N.F.

COCONINO N.F.

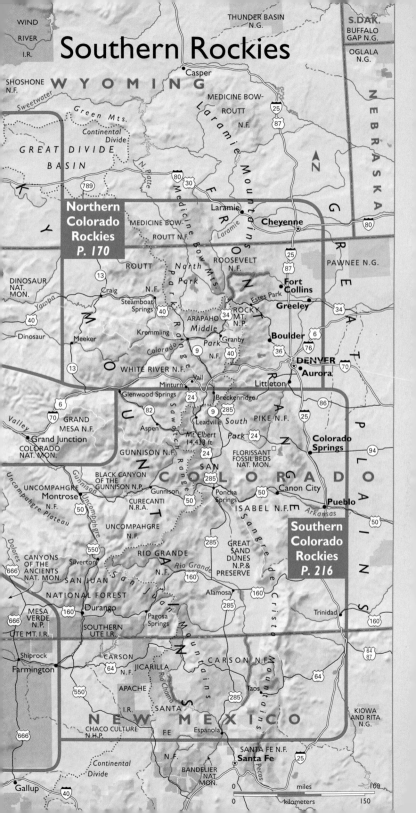

# Southern Rockies

**Northern Colorado Rockies P. 170**

**Southern Colorado Rockies P. 216**

**WYOMING**

**NEBRASKA**

**S.DAK.**

**NEW MEXICO**

**COLORADO**

**GREAT DIVIDE BASIN**

Green Mts.

Continental Divide

Sweetwater

SHOSHONE N.F.

WIND RIVER I.R.

Casper

THUNDER BASIN N.G.

BUFFALO GAP N.G.

OGLALA N.G.

MEDICINE BOW-ROUTT N.F.

Laramie Mountains

Laramie

Cheyenne

MEDICINE BOW N.F.

MEDICINE BOW ROUTT N.F.

North Park

ROOSEVELT N.F.

Fort Collins

Greeley

PAWNEE N.G.

DINOSAUR NAT. MON.

Dinosaur

Craig

Meeker

Steamboat Springs

ROUTT N.F.

Park Range

Kremmling

Colorado

Middle Park

ARAPAHO N.F.

Granby

ROCKY MT. N.P.

Estes Park

Boulder

DENVER

Aurora

Littleton

WHITE RIVER N.F.

Vail

Minturn

Breckenridge

Glenwood Springs

GRAND MESA N.F.

Grand Junction

COLORADO NAT. MON.

Aspen

Leadville

Mt. Elbert 14,433 ft.

South Park

PIKE N.F.

Colorado Springs

GUNNISON N.F.

Sawatch Range

FLORISSANT FOSSIL BEDS NAT. MON.

SAN

Montrose

UNCOMPAHGRE N.F.

Uncompahgre Plateau

BLACK CANYON OF THE GUNNISON N.P.

Gunnison

CURECANTI N.R.A.

ISABEL N.F.

Canon City

Pueblo

Arkansas

UNCOMPAHGRE N.F.

Poncha Springs

RIO GRANDE N.F.

Rio Grande

GREAT SAND DUNES N.P. & PRESERVE

Sangre de Cristo

Silverton

San Juan Mountains

CANYONS OF THE ANCIENTS NAT. MON.

SAN JUAN NATIONAL FOREST

Durango

Pagosa Springs

Alamosa

Trinidad

MESA VERDE N.P.

Shiprock

Farmington

SOUTHERN UTE I.R.

UTE MT. I.R.

CARSON N.F.

JICARILLA N.F.

APACHE I.R.

CARSON N.F.

Taos

SANTA FE

CHACO CULTURE N.H.P.

Espanola

Continental Divide

BANDELIER NAT. MON.

Santa Fe

SANTA FE N.F.

Pecos

KIOWA AND RITA N.G.

Gallup

KIOWA

miles 100

kilometers 150

# Home to the Hills

I'VE OFTEN TOLD THE STORY of meeting the Colorado Rocky Mountains for the first time—when, as a boy of ten, my chin on the back seat of my dad's Studebaker, I stared out the rear windshield with my mouth open and my eyes as big as dinner plates. On returning to our home in the Midwest after that encounter, I informed my parents in unequivocal terms that one day I'd be moving West. And that's just what I did.

Since then, working as both a naturalist and a nature writer, I've had the opportunity to wander thousands of miles of trails and back roads beyond the counting, jumping with great abandon into the mysterious, staggering beauty of Colorado, Utah, Wyoming, Montana, and New Mex-

Valley of the Gods, Utah

ico. Although America has suffered significant loss of truly wild places, we still live in a time when it's possible to visit natural systems big enough to support myriad life forms—sites sufficiently remote, wild, and wind-blasted to free us from the doldrums too often induced by a life detached from grandeur or enchantment.

My fervent wish is that you, too, will find some measure of the unexpected in the mountains, plateaus, rivers, and high desert basins featured in this book. In these unparalleled places, may you awaken to a notion that has been central to the world's nature mythology for thousands of years: that when humans are stuck, sad, or out-of-sorts, they must seek solace in the beauty of nature, finding in wilderness the wonder needed to draw us where we most need to go.

*Gary Ferguson*

# To Have and to Hike

BETWEEN THE WINDSWEPT high plains of Colorado to the east and the lonely, sunbaked Basin and Range Country of Utah to the west lies a gnarled and enchanting puzzle of landscapes. This region, the southern Rockies, fulfills many classic visions of the American West, from cirque basins and cobalt-colored lakes to valleys edged by stark, 1,000-foot walls of stone washed in desert varnish. The area welcomes you all year, whether you're looking to embrace the spring with a ramble through alpine meadows flush with wildflowers; to quench summer's heat in a flash of white water; to make an autumn trek across a mountainside ablaze with golden quaking aspen; or to follow fresh animal tracks across a blanket of newly fallen snow.

These lands owe their unforgettable quality to their position on the North American plate. Beginning about 100 million years ago, the region has been heaving and buckling—getting compressed, pulled apart, thrown up, pushed down, and finally uplifted as a whole—as the plate moves slowly westward to interact with the Farallon and Pacific plates. Many of the rocks you'll see are the mashed remains of ancient seabeds, sculpted by wind and water into great stone labyrinths. Great sheets of ice added the final touches to the high peaks, scouring the uplands into a cluster of U-shaped valleys. Even today, glacial fingers continue to break apart tons of rock, sending it crashing down into the valleys below.

Over the past ten years, an extraordinary amount of work by the Forest Service, the Nature Conservancy, and the U.S. Geological Survey has improved the old system of land stewardship, under which America's natural areas were managed primarily in terms of political boundaries—state lines, for example, or national park borders. This new effort proposes instead to preserve America's outdoors according to ecoregions—that is, natural communities of plants and animals.

Such a bold approach will have a profound ripple effect on future land management. For example, understanding an area on the basis of its ecoregions can help promote biodiversity by focusing attention not on a single endangered species, but on the representative plant communities that support it. This strategy aims to ensure that decisions about everything from proposed timber harvests to housing developments will eventually be based on two things: the immediate effect on the surroundings, and the cumulative effect of a project on all parts of a given natural community.

This outlook has also governed the organization of this book. Sites have been grouped together because they share the same specific plant communities, and support the same myriad life forms that depend on them. As you use the book, see if you can spot the similarities among the various sites in each chapter. By understanding habitat themes, wildlife, climate patterns, and, to a certain extent, even geological characteristics, you will gain a deeper appreciation of where you are. One notable excep-

Asters and lichens, Indian Creek Canyon

tion to the rule is the Colorado Rockies, which we've broken into two separate chapters—north and south of I-70—not for ecological reasons, but simply because doing so makes the book easier to use.

Each of the five chapters that follow begins with a brief introduction explaining a few natural dynamics of the ecoregion in question. Next, the chapter presents noteworthy natural areas, parks, and preserves; all have been chosen for their outstanding natural beauty, their ideal representation of the area, or the range of recreational opportunities they offer. Location, hours of operation and best times to visit, outdoor activities available, phone numbers, website addresses, and other helpful information all appear at the top of each site description.

The guide begins in the southwest corner of the southern Rockies, at the North Rim of Grand Canyon National Park, then heads northeast through the haunting and often overwhelming beauty of the Colorado Plateau. Included in this ecoregion are four lapidary national parks: Zion, Capitol Reef, Arches, and Canyonlands. The book then ventures into the Utah High Plateaus—a long, sweeping arc of uplands that stretch from southeast Utah, near Cedar Breaks National Monument, northeastward across the state to Colorado National Monument and Grand Mesa in northwest Colorado.

Next up are the dramatic peaks of the Wasatch Range and the Uinta Mountains, bordered by the remote, lonely beauty of the Wyoming Basin country. These lands include such treasures as Logan Canyon, Antelope Island State Park, Dinosaur National Monument, and Flaming Gorge National Recreation Area, as well as Browns Park and Ouray National

Wildlife Refuges. The journey culminates in the northern and southern sections of the Colorado Rockies, each of which provides even the most ardent lover of the outdoors a lifetime supply of intrigue in places such as Rocky Mountain National Park, the San Juan Mountains, the high tablelands of White River National Forest, and the dizzying depths of the Black Canyon of the Gunnison.

As you savor these jewels of the American outback, bear in mind that many are fast becoming islands—slices of the natural world impossible to sustain in the face of unregulated growth and development, especially as that change affects wildlife. Like it or not, the intermountain West is no

West Needle Mountains, San Juan National Forest

longer a place where humans can act with impunity. Unless those who love these last wild places make it a priority to protect them—unless we convey to land-management bureaucrats and political leaders precisely what is so precious about these sacred sites, both in this moment and to future generations—much of this enchantment will be lost forever.

By all means, then, celebrate the magnificent nooks and crannies this book is bound to lead you to. Be grateful for each flash of wings, each glimpse of mountain peak, each bracing dip or plunge into snow-cold creek and river. Then, when you return home at last, do everything in your power to keep such magic alive and well in the world. ■

# Colorado
# Plateau

View from the North Rim, Grand Canyon National Park

IF THERE ARE INDEED PLACES WHERE, as novelist Lawrence Durrell claimed, we are but children of the landscape, our behaviors and even our thoughts molded by the power of our surroundings, I suspect that none could manage it more surely or swiftly than the Colorado Plateau. For some, it's the simple beauty of the place—bands of rose to purple rocks cast against an autumn sky, sandstone arches, cottonwood parks huddled along river bottoms. For others, it's the canyons that have linked arms in so

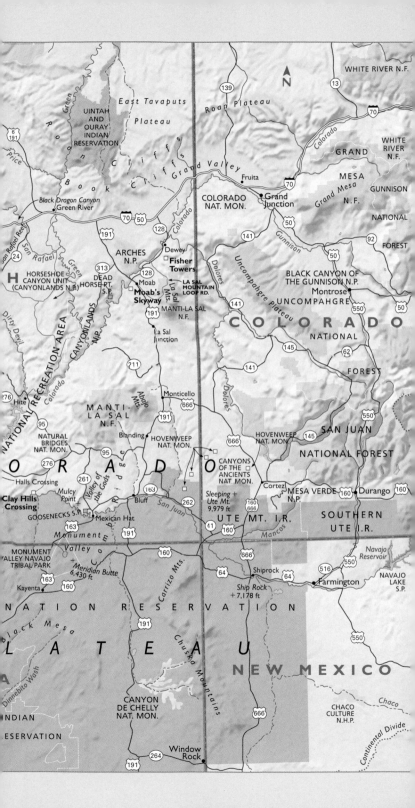

Rainwater-filled pothole, Canyonlands National Park

many places to create nearly incomprehensible mazes—secret, sculpted places of wind and shallow pools and the echo of birdsong. Combine this with the prospect of stumbling across haunting pieces of art or architecture from cultures that flourished here a thousand years ago, and you have a place like no other in the world.

Just as astronomers gazing at the stars can see backward in time, so too can geologists looking at rocks see stories going back millions of years. In few places are those stories more clearly told than on the Colorado Plateau. For all the complex geology hidden in these layers of rock —a puzzle that has intrigued scientists for more than a century— sooner or later it all comes down to one simple condition: a phenomenal period of uplift that is the product of an anomalously hot upper mantle beneath the western United States.

As a result of this action the mighty Sierra Nevada range of California rose, followed by the arresting glory of the Colorado Rockies. But along an arc from roughly northwestern Colorado across the belly of Utah to that state's southeast corner, and on to what is now the North Rim of the Grand Canyon, the rise occurred with far less chaos than in other locations. As you'll see time and again in the aptly named Plateau country, sedimentary rocks lie more or less flat. The uplift was a slow, steady process that raised those rocks without disrupting them.

Over time, wind and water have attacked the rising plateau and cut magnificent canyons, exposing in each layer of rock yet another stunning chapter in the natural history of the world. Layers of Dakota sandstone— once part of a sandy seashore—bear fossils of oysters and clams and countless other marine organisms. The Morrison formation of northeast Utah and northwest Colorado holds a wealth of dinosaur bones. Layers

Pleasant Creek, Capitol Reef National Park

of shale in the Mesaverde formation hint at a time when swamps and warm-water lagoons pockmarked much of the area.

Much of this story is laid bare—and thus easy to spot around any given turn in the trail—because of poor soils and a near-desert climate. Slickrock, the bare surface layer of sandstone that has been worn smooth and slippery by erosion, is forever underfoot. Stream channels are constantly eroding right before your eyes. This starkness makes the Colorado Plateau precious not just on a scientific level, but on a poetic one as well. The experience of beholding life standing in such stark relief offers us reassurance, leaving us attuned to both the fragility and the tenacity of the natural world.

The sites in this chapter have been chosen to highlight this marvelous blend of the spare and the ornate. The massive stone spans of Arches National Park are rendered more dramatic by the fragile blooms of sego lily and evening primrose at their feet. The lower slot canyons of Zion National Park seem less dark and forbidding thanks to a network of groundwater springs, or seeps, that foster violets, monkeyflowers, and orchids, as well as many other plants normally found at higher elevations. And on it goes: Yellow blooms of mules ears nod above the sandy nooks of Capitol Reef; prickly pear flash along the dry bottoms of Canyonlands National Park; and the lavender heads of trailing four-o'clock sway and beckon along the dry, gravelly flanks of the San Rafael Swell.

Exploring the Colorado Plateau demands caution and preparation. Summer temperatures often soar to the 100-degree mark. Water can be hard to come by; take plenty with you on hikes. And a simple rainstorm can send dangerous flash floods careering down desert canyons and arroyos, making clay-based back roads impassable even for 4WD vehicles. ∎

# Grand Canyon's North Rim

■ 1.2 million acres (national park)  ■ Northern Arizona, south of Jacob Lake
■ Best hiking spring and fall  ■ Closed mid-Oct.–mid-May  ■ Hiking, scenic
drives, horseback riding  ■ Adm. fee  ■ Contact Grand Canyon National Park,
Grand Canyon, AZ 86023; phone 520-638-7888. www.nps.gov/grca

MENTION THE GRAND CANYON almost anywhere in the world and people's
eyes will sparkle. The actual experience of the place, or merely a daydream of it, is likely to engender a delightful, even soaring sense of fancy.
From the early Pueblo people to that day in 1540 when Spaniard Garcia
Lopez de Cardenas reached the chasm's edge and fell to his knees in wonder to the modern tableau of families piling out of cars and campers with
mouths agape, there is a timelessness to this place that demolishes all
prior notions of the remarkable. Simply put, superlatives are lost on the
Grand Canyon.

To descend into the canyon from the North Rim is to leaf through the
pages of a remarkable chapter in Earth's history. Moving down from the
lip you'll pass shells and sand dunes from ancient oceans, many of them
complete with the tracks of long-extinct reptiles; later, look around you
to find fossils of ferns and primitive cone-bearing trees. Down farther
await the hardened ripples of still older sea bottoms, and finally the
bedrock—1.7 billion-year-old granite and gneiss.

Despite this wealth of clues, geologists cannot agree on how the
Grand Canyon was formed. Even though the layers of geologic history
are laid out in rather orderly fashion, much of the critical information is
missing: Either it washed away during previous erosional periods or it
still lies hidden beneath layers of rock and debris.

The longest-held theory about the canyon was articulated by geologist
John Wesley Powell, a one-armed Civil War veteran who led the first
party of European explorers through the canyon in 1869. According to
Powell, the Colorado River had been flowing east to west for a very long
time, back when Arizona was flat as a pancake. He theorized that as the
Kaibab Plateau began to rise during the Tertiary period, pushed upward
by violent forces within the Earth, the river began eroding the landscape
at roughly the same rate as the rise. In time the Colorado created a channel located well below the surface of the surrounding landscape.

There are problems with this explanation, however. For starters, geologists have discovered that the western portion of the canyon—the area
roughly marked by the Grand Wash Cliffs—is millions of years younger
than the eastern part. This has led to the notion that two different ancient
river systems ultimately joined—the west-flowing stream "capturing" the
one flowing east—in the area below where the South Rim's visitor center
stands. Ask the age of the canyon today, and many geologists will tell you
it's a youthful five million years. However it was formed, the Grand Canyon is one of the most stirring examples of erosion on this planet.

North Kaibab Trail, Grand Canyon National Park

## What to See and Do

Though clearly a popular destination, the North Rim of the Grand Canyon is best appreciated by those inclined to leave modern comforts behind. At 8,200 feet, it is 1,200 feet higher—and much cooler—than the South Rim, and reaching it entails a long trip across the Kaibab Plateau.

Although a mere 12 miles of open space separates the North Rim from the South, it takes a five-hour, 215-mile drive to get there. Gas stations, grocery stores, and even paved roads are few and far between, as is almost any form of organized tourist diversion. On the other hand, if you're intrigued by wide-open skies and the smell of pinyon, juniper, and ponderosa pine, by long walks leading to staggering views, by Kaibab squirrels and mule deer and goshawks, this is your kind of place.

The **Grand Canyon Lodge** *(303-297-2757)*, located near the southern terminus of Ariz. 67, is a good spot to begin your wanderings, even if you don't happen to be staying there. If you'd like to stay, however, reservations are essential; in most years you'll have to reserve months ahead (rim-view rooms often fill up two years in advance). From the lodge you can get tickets for a three-hour bus tour that will take you to a handful of the most popular vistas along the North Rim.

Because the journey to the bot-

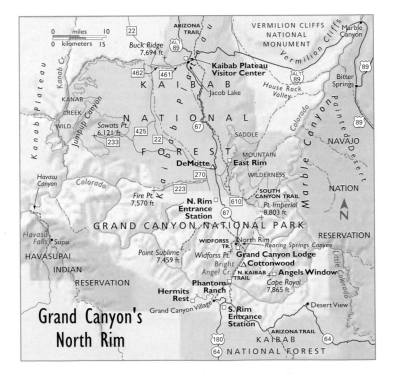

Grand Canyon's North Rim

## Kaibab Squirrel

One resident you're almost certain to meet along the Grand Canyon's North Rim is the Kaibab squirrel, a great fan of the nuts and inner bark of the ponderosa pine. In spring, the squirrel enjoys a special treat: the fruiting bodies, or truffles, of underground fungi that live on the tree's roots. As the squirrels eat this fungi—organisms that are highly beneficial to the tree—the spores pass through the animal's digestive system, spreading the fungi to more pine roots.

The Kaibab squirrel provides a fascinating lesson in allopatric speciation. Before the Grand Canyon took shape some five million years ago, only one tassel-eared squirrel inhabited the area—the one known as the Abert's squirrel that today lives on the South Rim. As the canyon formed, the squirrels living on the North Rim became isolated from the parent population of tassel-eared squirrels. Over untold eons, different conditions in the two environments resulted in the evolution of a distinct subspecies, ultimately rendering the two animal types unable to interbreed.

Although the current major distinction between the Kaibab and Abert's squirrel is tail color (the Kaibab's is all white), these two animals are likely to diverge even more as centuries pass. The Kaibab squirrel serves as a reminder that this plateau is by and large an ecological island; as such, it is remarkably vulnerable to disturbance.

tom of the canyon from the North Rim is far greater than from the South Rim, you won't have the option of traveling there by mule. Grand Canyon Trail Rides does, however, offer one-hour, half-day, and full-day trips down the North Kaibab Trail and along the rim. You can make reservations at the lodge or by calling 520-638-2292 (520-679-8665 in winter).

Pause at the lodge long enough to make the easy quarter-mile trek to **Bright Angel Point,** which offers tumbling views into the canyon across a number of rugged tributaries. The next best place for ogling the scenery is on the **Cape Royal Scenic Drive.** From the lodge head north for 3 miles on Ariz. 67, then turn right onto the drive heading northeast. In 5 miles or so you'll reach a marked intersection, where you make another right turn; proceed 15 miles along the rim to **Cape Royal.** Unlike most overlooks along the North Rim, here you can actually get a view of the Colorado River through a natural arch called **Angels Window.** A 1-mile self-guided interpretive trail begins at the overlook parking lot and carries you across the arch to a magnificent promontory. The forest at this overlook is made up of pinyon and juniper trees—ideal habitat for a variety of birds, including the scrub-jay, juniper titmouse, and common bushtit.

## Canyon Hiking

One of the most heavily used trails along the North Rim is also one of the most arduous. Known as the **North Kaibab Trail,** it begins at

Roaring Springs Canyon, Grand Canyon National Park

Roaring Springs Canyon 2 miles north of the lodge and drops off the forested rim in a hurry, ultimately bound for the Colorado River, 5,841 vertical feet and 14.5 miles away—twice as far as the river is from the South Rim. The round-trip, appropriate only for experienced hikers, is best done over three or four nights. If you're in very good shape and in far more of a hurry than you ought to be, it's possible to make it with two overnights, both spent at Cottonwood Camp about 7 miles from the trailhead *(backcountry permit required, 520-638-7875)*.

It's also possible to enjoy a day's outing on the Kaibab trail without taking it all the way to the bottom. **Roaring Springs picnic area**—a roughly 4.5-mile walk one way with more than 3,000 feet of elevation change—is a fine destination. This beautiful springs, the largest tributary of Bright Angel Creek, exits from a canyonside cave containing more than 11,000 feet of passages.

### Rim Hiking

Of similar distance but far easier to negotiate is the beautiful 9.8-mile (round-trip) **Widforss Trail,** which crosses a gentle landscape peppered with meadows and ponderosa pine forests before terminating at **Widforss Point.** To reach the trailhead, drive 2.75 miles north of the Grand Canyon Lodge, turn left, and continue for roughly a mile down a dirt road.

Another good choice is the 5-mile walk on the **Uncle Jim Trail.** This path takes off at the North Kaibab trailhead and leads to a wonderful rimside view of **Roaring Springs Canyon.** (Uncle Jim, by the way, was James T. Owens, first warden of what was known as the Grand Canyon National Preserve in the early 1900s. A celebrated mountain-lion hunter, Owens eventually became a buffalo rancher.)

No matter what your ultimate destination, hiking the Grand Canyon remains a very different experience from trekking in other places. For starters, the weather fluctuates wildly, going from chilly mornings to sweltering afternoons; indeed, summer temperatures inside the canyon often soar to well over 100° F. Carry plenty of water with you; don't count on finding it along the trail.

The extremes of steep downhill and uphill walking can be tough. Take moleskin for blisters and an elastic wrap for knee strains. A good over-the-counter anti-inflammatory medication can alleviate swelling. The hardest part of the trek will be at the end of the day, when you're most tired. Many walkers have been drawn down by the enchantment of a canyon trail, only to find themselves tripping over rocks in the dark trying to get out. Finally, be aware that summer afternoon thunderstorms and lightning are common. More than a hundred fires are started in this region in an average summer, 75 percent from lightning strikes. ■

# Kaibab National Forest

■ 1.6 million acres ■ North-central Arizona ■ Best months April-Nov. Ariz. 67 from Jacob Lake to North Rim of Grand Canyon closed from mid-Oct.–mid-May ■ Camping, hiking, fishing, hunting, biking, mountain biking, horseback riding, bird-watching, scenic drives ■ Contact North Kaibab Ranger District, Kaibab National Forest, Box 248, Fredonia, AZ 86022; phone 520-643-7395

A MAGICAL PLACE, KAIBAB NATIONAL FOREST is tossed with sweeps of aspen, phalanxes of ponderosa pine, and soaring views—including several that teeter near the edge of the Grand Canyon. It also offers plenty of solitude for those willing to park the car and walk or bike along a network of forest roads and trails. The northern unit of the Kaibab—pronounced KY-bab, after a Paiute word that means roughly "mountain lying down"—covers some 1,000 square miles, a great many of them wonderfully quiet and remote. The Kaibab Plateau is the highest of the five that make up the North Rim of the Grand Canyon; its southern third is contained within Grand Canyon National Park, but much of its northern two-thirds lies within the borders of Kaibab National Forest.

This national forest is one of the few places on the continent with large expanses of old-growth ponderosa pine. The forest is also home to a sizable number of northern goshawks—the remaining members of what may have been the densest population in North America. Commercial logging over the last 20 years—a practice that remains extremely controversial—has degraded the goshawk habitat, mostly through the loss of a solid tree canopy. Turkey, coyote, and elk are also fairly common here, while mountain lion, black bear, and bobcat have been seen on occasion.

The main north-south route across the Kaibab Plateau, Ariz. 67, connects Jacob Lake to the North Rim of the Grand Canyon. The early miles are steeped in a blend of aspen and ponderosa pine forest; as the road climbs, this yields to a mixed Douglas-fir and spruce woods dappled with meadows—perfect places to spot red-tailed and Swainson's hawks.

Jumpup Canyon at sunrise, Kanab Creek Wilderness, Kaibab National Forest

## What to See and Do

Any visit to the North Kaibab Ranger District should begin with a stop at the Kaibab Plateau Visitor Center *(520-643-7298)*, located at the junction of Ariz. 67 and Ariz. 89A; here you can pick up maps and check current conditions of roads and trails, some of which were damaged during the serious wildfires of 2000.

### Hiking

One of the more noteworthy paths in the North Kaibab Ranger District is a portion of the **Arizona Trail,** originally the dream of a Flagstaff teacher named Dale Shewalter. When completed, it will be a 750-mile route closed to motor vehicles, running the length of the state through an extraordinarily diverse collection of habitats.

In 1988, the 50-mile-long **Kaibab Plateau Trail,** starting 2 miles east of Jacob Lake on US 89A, became the first segment of the Arizona Trail to be dedicated. It offers hikers an intriguing mix of fairly easy walking through stands of Douglas-fir, as well as

spruce and ponderosa pine, broken here and there by exquisite meadows.

The **East Rim**—reached both by a trailhead for the Arizona Trail 4.5 miles off Ariz. 67 and by Forest Road 611—offers outstanding views of Marble Canyon, House Rock Valley, and the Vermilion Cliffs, as well as **Saddle Mountain Wilderness.** The biggest challenges for long-range hikers on the Arizona Trail are the lack of water along the route and the likelihood of inclement weather.

A much shorter walk, though still long on scenery, is the **South Canyon Trail.** This lovely hike of 2.5 miles (round-trip) over undulating terrain leads to both a fine weave of forest and splendid views of Marble Canyon. To reach the trailhead, go south on Ariz. 67 for just over 26 miles, then turn east onto Forest Road 611 less than a mile past the entrance to DeMotte Campground. Drive 1.4 miles, and turn right (south) onto Forest Road 610; follow this for 7.5 miles to the trailhead sign.

Kaibab limestone, Saddle Mountain Wilderness

## Bird-watching

The North Kaibab Ranger District offers some extremely enjoyable bird-watching, both for diversity of species and for the outstanding settings. At 8,000 feet, **DeMotte Campground** *(on Ariz. 67, 4 miles N of entrance to Grand Canyon NP)* is a favorite staging ground for birders. It's also a good place to spot red-breasted nuthatches, wild turkeys, Williamson's sapsuckers, mountain and western bluebirds, golden-crowned kinglets, and three-toed woodpeckers.

**Fire Point,** just outside the National Forest boundary with views of the Grand Canyon from the North Rim, is located on For-est Road 223 on the west side of the plateau. It is among the very best birding locations in the forest. You'll find extraordinary variety, from black-headed grosbeaks and downy woodpeckers to black-throated warblers, red crossbills, and even the occasional pygmy owl. Also in the neighborhood are ash-throated flycatchers, rufous and broad-tailed hummingbirds, lesser goldfinches, and spotted towhees.

In the plateau's aspen groves look for warbling vireos, mountain chickadees, and brown creepers. The canyon's forested edges bring chances to see the Cassin's finch, green-tailed towhee, band-tailed pigeon, and hairy woodpecker.

## Mountain Biking

Many routes on the Kaibab are suitable for mountain bikes, varying from narrow dirt paths to forest roads that must be shared with the occasional vehicle. A 30-mile stretch of the Arizona Trail runs south from alt. US 89, just east of the Kaibab Plateau Visitor Center, to East Rim (see p. 29). From here follow Forest Road 611 for roughly 6 miles to Ariz. 67. This is ideal for those with a shuttle vehicle.

Another good ride is the easy, 4-mile trek along Forest Road 264 to **Buck Ridge Viewpoint,** which offers excellent views across broken, soaring country all the way to Bryce Canyon and Zion National Parks. To reach the trailhead, follow Ariz. 67 south from the visitor center for a third of a mile to Forest Road 461, and turn right. Continue for roughly 4 miles to Forest Road 264, and park.

Finally, consider the 18.6-mile round-trip along Forest Road 233 to **Sowats Point** on the edge of Grand Canyon. To reach the trailhead, turn right off Ariz. 67 onto Forest Road 461, one-third mile south of the Kaibab Plateau Visitor Center. Follow this for 5.5 miles to Forest Road 462, turn right, and go 3 miles; turn left onto Forest Road 22 and drive 12 miles, then turn right onto Forest Road 425. Go another 8 miles to Forest Road 233, turn right, and park. (Forest Road 233 is open to vehicles.) ■

### Pipe Spring National Monument

This 40-acre monument, on Ariz. 389 near the town of Fredonia, is primarily a historical site, established around an early Mormon fort. However, a half-mile-long nature trail climbs a small set of cliffs (part of the Kayenta formation—not Chinle, as the sign says) for a panoramic view to the south of the Arizona Strip—that area of the state lying between the Grand Canyon and the Utah state line.

The beautiful oasis of Pipe Spring is located at the base of the Grand Staircase (see pp. 40-41). Water percolates through Navajo sandstone and then hits a layer of less permeable Kayenta; at that point it travels horizontally, gathering along the Sevier Fault before finally escaping to the surface at Pipe Spring. One of the few natural springs on the entire Arizona Strip, it has long slaked the thirst of deer, pronghorn, and bighorn sheep, as well as a wide variety of reptiles, including colorful desert spiny lizards, whiptails, and gopher and king snakes. Also fond of Pipe Spring are such avian migrants as orioles, flycatchers, bluebirds, and Say's phoebes.

This dry, empty country was fairly rich grassland before the settlers arrived. Overgrazing in the 1880s and 1890s changed all that, turning much of the area into the desert scrub you see today. The walk continues through a pinyon-juniper plateau, featuring live oak, roundleaf buffaloberry, greasewood, rabbitbrush, four-wing saltbush, prickly pear, and creeping beavertail.

For more information, contact Pipe Spring National Monument (HC65 Box 5, Fredonia, AZ 86022; 520-643-7105. www.nps.gov/pisp).

# Zion National Park

- 147,551 acres ■ Southwest Utah, near Kanab, St. George, and Cedar City
- Best seasons spring and fall. Kolob Terrace Road closed in winter ■ Camping, hiking, backpacking, rock climbing, tubing, mountain biking, horseback riding
- Adm. fee ■ Contact the park, Springdale, UT 84767; phone 435-772-3256. www.nps.gov/zion

A LUSH COTTONWOOD VALLEY topped by dramatic red cliffs, Zion is one of the crown jewels of the American national park system. You could spend endless days lazing on the lawn in front of the lodge, wandering aimlessly along the North Fork Virgin River, or lingering after sunset on breathtaking Watchman Viewpoint. Zion National Park's sheer cliffs—at more

Angels Landing Trail, Zion National Park

than 2,000 feet, they are the tallest sandstone escarpments in the world—
soar thousands of feet above the valley, exuding a sense of awesome
strength and peace.

The Navajo sandstone that constitutes the cliffs was deposited 200
million years ago, when the area was a desert larger than today's Sahara.
Blowing sand piled into dunes, which later hardened into rock. Throughout the process, the wind did a remarkably good job of sorting: Each
grain of sand resembles its neighbors in both weight and dimension.

Though some areas held pockets of water that became mudstone, desert dunes generally produce far more "pure" sandstones than do river-
beds or even beach dunes, where water leaves deposits of mud or sand
grains of varying dimensions. This purity created the beautifully uniform
texture present in mile after mile of cliff face in the park.

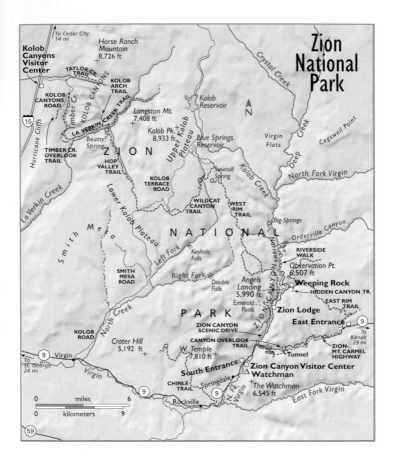

Enter Zion from the east (the most dramatic entrance) and you'll see clear evidence of the old dunes cemented in place. Layers are found in diagonals going one way and then another; this pattern, known as crossbedding, reveals that the dunes piled up on one another as the winds changed direction. Over hundreds of millions of years, the weight of additional sediment layers turned the dunes to rock, glued together by calcium carbonate (lime, which yields white rocks) or hematite (iron oxide, which yields reddish rocks). Because sand grains are relatively large, there's a lot of space between them to admit such cement, making the rocks stronger than those made of smaller clay particles. This is why sandstones form strong, vertical cliffs, whereas clay-based siltstones and shales more often result in slopes and ledges.

You can see the difference right here in Zion. As the Colorado Plateau rose, the North Fork Virgin River cut through natural fractures in the rock, slicing them off to form vertical cliffs. At this point the river has cut through the Navajo sandstone into the lower Kayenta formation; the Kayenta is softer, mixed with more easily eroded mudstone. As the Virgin

River erodes the Kayenta from below the Navajo, it undermines the Navajo and tumbles it into the canyon walls along vertical fractures. Thus does the valley widen.

It may surprise you that such a seemingly small river as the Virgin can continue to sculpt any sort of canyon. Two factors are responsible. The first is the gradient: The Virgin River drops more than 4,000 feet in just 145 miles on its journey to Lake Mead. The second has to do with the steep, thinly vegetated sandstone cliffs, which do not absorb rain when it falls; water quickly runs off in violent, scouring flash floods powerful enough to carry small boulders in their arms, which they pound like battering rams against the valley walls and floor.

The river also creates enticing environments at the base of the cliffs. Reliable water has given rise to a striking array of plants. Even though Zion National Park covers less than 2 percent of Utah's surface area, it contains roughly 35 percent of the state's plant species; these in turn support a wonderful array of wildlife. May and June bring a riot of wildflower blooms, including slickrock paintbrush and prickly pear cactus. Late October paints the leaves of the Fremont cottonwood yellow and the bigtooth maple red. Mule deer are plentiful, but Zion harbors dozens of other animal species as well, including gray rock squirrels, pocket gophers, beavers, and numerous lizards. More than a hundred bird species breed in the area—from hummingbirds to peregrine falcons.

## What to See and Do

In May 2000, Zion implemented a new shuttle bus system for its crowded main canyon during peak visitation months. In addition to alleviating parking shortages and traffic hassles and curtailing auto pollution, the buses sport big windows and skylights that afford far better views than you can get from most cars.

Shuttles run regularly from the new **Zion Canyon Visitor Center** *(435-772-3213)* at the park's South Entrance, near Springdale. If you are staying in Springdale, a free shuttle will take you from your hotel to the visitor center.

The buses roll up the Zion Canyon Scenic Drive, and you can get on and off wherever you like. They operate from early April through the end of October. Dur-

ing that time, cars are banned from the spur road up Zion Canyon, but you can still drive Utah 9 east to Mt. Carmel Junction, as well as anywhere in the Kolob area. At other times of the year cars can travel freely on the Zion Canyon Scenic Drive. If you're staying at the park's Zion Lodge *(435-586-7686)*, you will be issued a permit to drive as far as the lodge.

Plan to spend some time at the visitor center. In addition to providing valuable information about your visit, it is an impressive example of sustainable architecture: The structure takes advantage of shade from the cottonwoods, passive solar heat, and a low-tech swamp cooling system to regulate building temperatures.

The Narrows on the North Fork Virgin River, Zion National Park

## Self-guided Hikes

Two short interpretive hikes provide excellent introductions to Zion's natural history. The **Canyon Overlook Trail** starts at the east entrance of the long tunnel on the Zion-Mt. Carmel Highway (Utah 9); a 1-mile round-trip, the route takes you to an overlook of the Pine Creek and lower Zion canyons. If you entered Zion from the east, this will be your first view of the sheer canyon walls. An interpretive trail guide, available at the trailhead, introduces you to some plants typical of this pinyon-juniper forest, including Utah serviceberry, manzanita, and narrowleaf yucca.

The **Weeping Rock Trail,** located in the main canyon (two shuttle stops beyond the lodge), is likewise a well-interpreted introduction to local ecology. This half-mile paved walk meanders along the bottom of a wet, shaded side canyon, offering a vastly different plant community from the one you'll find in other areas of the park. Numerous trailside signs identify and discuss the plants, including hackberry, box elder, and bigtooth maple. Toward the end of the trail, you'll pass through a "desert swamp": Despite the area's low rainfall, nearby springs produce consistent water here, saturating the earth and creating suitable habitat for plants such as scouring rush and golden columbine.

This trail ends at a lovely "dripping cliff." Groundwater trickling down through the Navajo sandstone has reached a less permeable layer, halting its downward progress and forcing it to seep side-

ways to emerge from the face of this cliff. Plants that need lots of water but little soil—in this location, maidenhair fern plus several mosses and flowers—thrive in these conditions, creating a wonderful weave of hanging gardens. Though Zion is home to hundreds of hanging gardens, **Weeping Rock** boasts some of the most attractive, best interpreted, and easiest to see close-up. In addition, you can look back to the top of the mountain directly across from you, to magnificent Angels Landing.

## Short Day Hikes

Weeping Rock is the starting point for some ambitious hikes. The 2-mile (round-trip) **Hidden Canyon Trail** climbs to a hanging valley off to one side of the main canyon. The maintained portion of the path follows a steep grade for about a mile to the mouth of Hidden Canyon; there are several drop-offs along the way. Stamina and the elements permitting (check at the visitor center if thunderstorms are expected anywhere in the area), you can hike past the "Trail Not Maintained" sign into the canyon itself—a beautiful slot canyon where the side walls are cross-bedded like crazy quilts and bird calls ring out against the rock.

The **Observation Point Trail** also starts at Weeping Rock, though it does not qualify as a short hike. This strenuous 8-mile round-trip leads hikers to the top of the East Rim, where they get stunning views up and down the main canyon.

Though nearly always crowded, a true highlight of a Zion visit is the **Riverside Walk,** which begins at the north end of the canyon road. This easy 2-mile round-trip is great for kids, as well as for those in wheelchairs, though you may need to be careful of flooding after storms. You could walk this trail a hundred times over and see something different every time. The delightful hanging gardens on the cliff faces, for example, may cause you to miss the Fremont cottonwood trees strung along the river. The river and the trees, in turn, are so serene that you may forget to take in the sheer upper cliffs, which are so spectacular that you may have to pause on a rock sooner or later and admire them.

Note how the canyon narrows as you reach the end of the trail. At this higher elevation the river is still cutting the Navajo sandstone, having not yet reached the softer Kayenta that allows for a more rounded valley floor. The trail ends at **The Narrows,** where the canyon is wide enough only for the river itself.

Another popular hike is the **Emerald Pools Trail,** starting directly opposite the Zion Lodge. You can access three separate pools by a variety of easy routes through box elder, Gambel oak, and shrub live oak, or include all three in a 2.3-mile round-trip. This trail is extremely popular, especially at midday, so don't be surprised if you end up in a human traffic jam or two. After rainstorms, waterfalls pour off the cliffs into the pools, where algae thrive and produce that emerald color. In drier weather the colors are not nearly as spectacular.

If you'd like to learn more about the park and its environment, join one of Zion's seasonal ranger-led hikes. These interpreted peregrinations, offered morning and afternoon, are short—most of them less than 2 miles long. Some of the hikes may require preregistration at the visitor center; afternoon walks in particular tend to fill up fast.

For all Zion's popularity, it is still possible to find a bit of solitude here. At most shuttle stops, for example, unmarked but well-trod trails lead 50 or 100 yards to the edge of the **North Fork Virgin River,** where you can enjoy the breeze and the riffles, listen to birdsong, and generally recapture what it felt like to be a kid without a care in the world.

### Cycling

Bikes are allowed only on developed roads, as well as on the 3.5-mile (round-trip) **Pa'rus Trail,** which begins at the visitor center and runs upstream for about 2 miles. Clearly, implementing the shuttle system has made Zion's biking experience far more enjoyable than it once was. The Pa'rus (which also makes a pleasant evening walk) parallels the auto-accessible part of the road; at the end of the trail you can bike the scenic drive. You can also transport bikes on the shuttle buses, though each vehicle has room for only two. Bike rentals are available in Springdale.

### Backpacking

Backcountry camping in Zion requires a permit *(Zion Canyon Visitor Center 435-772-0170),* which is usually issued the day before your hike. Many routes

Great White Throne at the mouth of The Narrows, Zion National Park

require a shuttle; you can make arrangements at the lodge. Remember that summer weather at Zion can be extreme. Hiking and camping in the backcountry demand careful planning. Let a ranger's office know your intended route. Permits for hiking the Narrows are given only at certain low-water levels, usually in late summer. Most other trails are on top of the plateau; Zion Canyon itself, with its crowds and tourist facilities, makes for less than ideal backpacking.

## Kolob Canyons

The far northwestern corner of the park, located just east of I-15, contains sheer sandstone cliffs that are every bit as colorful and spectacu-

lar as those in the main canyon—they're simply a bit smaller and lack a lush river valley at their base. Most of them were formed by small creeks flowing east to west; a scenic drive runs north to south across the mouths of several.

At the end of Kolob Canyons Road, the mile-long **Timber Creek Overlook Trail** offers a chance to stretch your legs and get additional cliff views (not to mention far-reaching vistas to the west and south). If you have more time, you can take Kolob Canyons Road 2 miles east of the visitor center and head into the canyons themselves on the **Taylor Creek Trail** (5 miles round-trip). Another 2 miles up the road is the **Kolob Arch Trail** (14 miles round-trip). ■

# Grand Staircase-Escalante National Monument

■ 1.7 million acres ■ Southwest Utah ■ Best months April-June and Sept.-Oct.
■ Camping, hiking, backpacking, fishing, hunting, mountain biking, horseback riding, scenic drives ■ Contact the Escalante Interagency Office, 755 W. Main St., Escalante, UT 84726; phone 435-826-5600. www.ut.blm.gov/monument

GRAND STAIRCASE-ESCALANTE NATIONAL MONUMENT stretches across a vast area of southern Utah, from Capitol Reef National Park in the east to Bryce Canyon National Park in the west and from Utah 12 in the north to the Arizona border in the south. This controversial new monument—created over strident local opposition—is the first to be administered by the Bureau of Land Management, whose commitment to working with neighboring communities may defuse the charged atmosphere. In this harsh, remote country, large pockets of hardy folk remain uneasy about any degree of tourism, to say nothing of hordes spilling over from heavily developed parks nearby.

Ecologically, the monument consists of three main components. From west to east they are the Grand Staircase area southeast of Bryce, the Kaiparowits Plateau south of the town of Escalante, and the Escalante Canyons surrounding the river of the same name. When geologists talk about the Grand Staircase, the word "grand" is no exaggeration. This

series of huge cliffs is easily visible from the air, miles above the Grand Canyon. Each colorful face represents a different layer of rock, so climbing the **Grand Staircase** toward the north will take you on a trek through 200 million years. The Vermilion Cliffs are made of Moenave sandstone, the White Cliffs of Navajo sandstone, the Gray Cliffs of younger shales, and the Pink Cliffs of limey siltstone.

The **Kaiparowits Plateau** is a high, arid, desolate plateau of very young rock from the late Cretaceous period. Some places contain soils that are poisonous to plants; elsewhere underground coal fires have stained the rock red. In the **Escalante Canyons** area, water has carved Navajo sandstone into a maze. The monument contains an almost endless (and often surprising) rendition of a few basic themes: a lush valley, a mass of slickrock, a complicated web of crazy slot canyons.

As for traditional tourist offerings, there are few. Only one developed trail exists: the beautiful **Lower Calf Creek Falls Trail.** The trailhead, with free interpretive brochures, is located at Calf Creek Campground, 16 miles east of Escalante on Utah 12. This 5.5-mile (round-trip) trail runs up a side canyon of the Escalante River, through Gambel oak, juniper, and prickly pear. Though the trail is easy and quite flat, it can be extremely hot, especially at midday, when even the high cliffs toward the end of the trail provide little shade. The falls themselves open up in the last 100 yards of the trail as a series of delightful discoveries. From spring through autumn, this trail receives heavy use.

Utah 12 through the monument is a stunning drive, especially the famed stretch between Escalante and Boulder. If you have a 4WD vehicle, you could combine this stretch with drives on some of the area's rough-and-tumble dirt roads, including **Hells Backbone** (see p. 109), **Dixie National Forest** (see pp. 108-110), **Hole-in-the-Rock** (see p. 54), or **Cottonwood Canyon.** People who love this area clearly believe that the best way to see it is to stop at some random point on a road, get out, and walk (bikes are limited to developed roads). In a sense, that's the whole point of the monument: It's a vast and rugged place, surprisingly unexplored, its greatest benefits attainable only through first-hand experience.

The shortest drives require at least half a day; longer excursions can take a week or more. Maps for unpaved roads and brochures with guidelines for safely navigating them can be obtained from the Escalante BLM office *(P.O. Box 225, Escalante, UT 84726; 435-826-5499).* Alternatively, start by stopping in at one of the monument's four tiny visitor centers in Escalante *(435-826-5600),* Kanab *(435-644-2672),* Boulder *(435-335-7382),* or Cannonville *(435-679-8981).*

Nearby state parks also offer interpretive trails. **Kodachrome Basin State Park** *(435-679-8536),* 7 miles south of Cannonville, was named by a National Geographic exploration team in 1949. It features a series of short trails through colorful rock formations. Also worth a visit is **Escalante State Park** *(435-826-4466)* for its 1-mile loop through the remains of a petrified forest. ■

Grosvenor Arch at sunset, Grand Staircase-Escalante National Monument

# Capitol Reef National Park

- 241,904 acres ■ Southern Utah, near Torrey ■ Best seasons spring and fall
- Hiking, backpacking, mountain biking, auto tour, petroglyphs, fruit picking
- Adm. fee ■ Contact the park, Torrey, UT 84775; phone 435-425-3791.
www.nps.gov/care

STRETCHING ONE HUNDRED MILES across south central Utah is an impressive geological structure called the Waterpocket Fold—a huge buckling of rock. One section of the fold, containing particularly brilliant colored cliffs and domes, was named Capitol Reef. When the park was established, this spectacular area became its namesake.

The cliff faces along Utah 24 leading into Capitol Reef from the town of Torrey (8 miles west of the park) are extraordinary, especially in the low light of late afternoon. They are part of the Moenkopi formation, whose age of 200 million years makes it far older than—and thus normally buried beneath—the Navajo sandstone that covers so much of southern Utah. The Moenkopi is a reddish siltstone, laid down by streams. Many of the Moenkopi's small ledges show ripple marks, hinting at the rock's origin in an aquatic environment. As you drive east through the park on Utah 24 in the direction of Hanksville, you'll be progressing forward in time at a remarkably quick pace, passing through layers of Chinle, Wingate, Kayenta, and Navajo sandstones. Even though the east side of the park is lower in elevation, it's made up of much younger rock; this includes the Morrison formation—only 100 million years old—which contains fossilized dinosaur bones.

The Waterpocket Fold is like an angled board, one end propped up on a chair. The lower part lies to the east, while the upper part is largely level because of erosion. Kaibab formation rocks found on the surface in the western part of the park are 8,000 feet below ground in the east (around Hanksville). The fold occurred some 65 million years ago; it may have resulted from fault activity far below the Earth's surface, a process so slow that it bent these rock layers rather than breaking them.

Capitol Reef's appearance is chiefly the result of erosion. To the west, younger rocks have eroded away; likewise, within the diagonal portion of the fold itself, the tops of each layer have been eroded. Every rock layer possesses a different hardness and thickness, yielding a wide variety of erosional formations. And because the fold is uneven—the rocks more tilted in some places than in others—the cliffs and valleys exhibit different characteristics in the park's north, central, and southern areas.

The Waterpocket Fold takes its name from the way depressions in the rock hold water. Picture hard boulders being washed down a sandstone slope after a storm; at a flat spot or depression the cascading water swirls them around, using them like drill bits to bore into the softer sandstone. Some of these pockets, called tinajas, may end up 8 or 10 feet deep, though shallower ones are far more common. A few hold permanent

Hikers on the Grand Wash Trail, Capitol Reef National Park

water, supporting tadpoles, frogs, and various plants as well as providing drinking water for larger animals such as bighorn sheep.

The radical differences in elevation and soil chemistry at Capitol Reef engendered a multiplicity of microhabitats. Much more than other national parks, this is a center of endemism—biotic communities native to a very small region only. Many of the plant species found in this park do not fit neatly into existing categories, leading scientists to speculate that entirely new species may lurk here. Capitol Reef is home to eight endangered species, including the Wright's Fishhook cactus and Maguire's daisy, as well as about 30 others that are rare.

## What to See and Do

Capitol Reef's "front country" is less dramatic than its backcountry—and less indicative of what exists in it. One way to experience the park is to drive through on Utah 24, stop at the **visitor center** *(435-425-3791)*, which features small exhibits on natural and cultural history, a slide show, and a bookstore, then take a scenic drive, followed perhaps by a short day hike.

## Scenic Drive

Leaving from the visitor center, the paved **Scenic Drive** winds southward along the Moenkopi cliffs for 9 miles, offering a series of dramatic red-rock vistas *(free guide available at the visitor center)* and access to some stunning hikes.

The trailhead for the 5-mile (round-trip) **Grand Wash Trail** is 4 miles south of the visitor center. The trail winds along a narrow wash canyon, whose see-worthy sights include some amazing rock formations and erosional features.

Continue to the end of Scenic Drive to reach **Capitol Gorge,** a tall, narrow slot canyon that provided the only route through this country until 1962. The shorter trail through this canyon offers similar attractions to those found along the Grand Wash Trail.

**Capitol Gorge Trail** is a flat, 2-mile (round-trip) path that winds past well-marked petroglyphs. Also along this trail you will find exhibits on the exploration and settling of the area. The natural arches, cliffs, domes, and waterpockets—bowl-like depressions in the rock—are stunning. Adventurous hikers can take the 2-mile extension beyond Capitol Gorge to the base of the **Golden Throne,** with views of the cliffs and outcroppings.

## More Hikes

Two popular—though more subdued—short day hikes start in the campground area at Fruita, less than 1 mile past the visitor center on Scenic Drive. (If not camping, park in the pullout across from the large barn.) The **Fremont River Trail** is a 2.5-mile round-trip hike with interpretive brochures available in a box at the trailhead; it follows the river bed for an easy half mile, then climbs 800 feet to an overlook of the valley. The more strenuous, 3.5-mile (round-trip) **Cohab Canyon Trail** climbs a steep quarter mile to the head of a gentle canyon, then follows it for another mile and a half through prickly pear, serviceberry, and Mormon tea to Utah 24.

The **Hickman Bridge Trail** is a worthwhile 2-mile round-trip, ascending from a trailhead on Utah 24 about 2 miles east of the visitor center to a natural bridge hidden above the valley. One of this trail's most fascinating features is the black boulders scattered about the valley. These are basalt—young volcanic rocks, roughly 44 million years old—washed down from the top of Boulder Mountain in glacial floods some 12,000 years ago. You'll find them only in the valleys of the Fremont River, Pleasant Creek, and Oak Creek.

Plant life along this trail includes single leaf ash, snowberry, mountain mahogany, wallflower, and skunkbush. If you're not too tired on the way back, take the **Rim Overlook Trail**—a brisk 4-mile round-trip providing great views from a perch 1,000 feet above the visitor center.

## Backcountry Drives

Several dirt roads, suitable for high-clearance vehicles but impassable when wet, give access to some of the best of Capitol Reef's backcountry. The 58-mile

*Following pages: A slot canyon, Capitol Reef National Park*

**Cathedral Valley Loop** starts 12 miles east of the park boundary on Utah 24 at River Ford (this is indeed a ford of a river, which is the reason why you need a high-clearance vehicle).

An interpretive guide is available at the visitor center and at the beginning of the road. The route passes through a stark crumple of multicolored bentonite hills. This bentonite, part of the Morrison formation, is some of the youngest rock in the area. Overlooks offer views into the South Desert—a long, empty valley with only a sparse layer of vegetation.

From here you can see the "hinge" of the Waterpocket Fold: The depositional layers in the rocks around you are flat, whereas those across the valley tilt into the fold. The road soon turns into the Cathedral Valley, populated with freestanding monoliths composed of Entrada sandstone.

As on all of the Colorado Plateau, this rock is amazingly consistent in color and texture. Occasionally, however, the Entrada sandstone is veined with dikes and sills of intruded magma that crept along fractures. Some of the cliffs, spires, and walls are topped by harder rocks of the Curtis formation; these caps kept the underlying stone intact while the rock around it washed away.

Turn south on Utah 24 just before Cathedral Valley Loop to take the **Notom-Bullfrog Road.** It follows the hinge east of the Waterpocket Fold from the Fremont River Valley south all the way to Lake Powell. Several unmarked trails—**Cottonwood Wash** and **Sheets Gulch** among them—offer experienced hikers access to the fold itself.

For a loop drive, follow the Notom-Bullfrog Road 29 miles south from where it turns off

### Don't Bust the Crust!

Throughout this region you're sure to notice a dark, somewhat lumpy crust on the ground; this so-called cryptobiotic soil—a mix of lichens, mosses, green algae, cyanobacteria, and microfungi—covers nearly 80 percent of the Colorado Plateau.

Cryptobiotic soil is a living web that literally holds the ground in place. The pioneering member of the mix, cyanobacteria, sends out thin filaments surrounded by sticky sheaths that cling to soil particles. Microfungal bodies move in next, tapping nutrients from plant roots and increasing the root system of their host tenfold. Green algae set up shop in the pores of the soil, collecting nitrogen from the air, as do various lichens. Together, the members of this living mulch create the characteristically spongy look and feel of cryptobiotic soil.

Dormant during drought, this layer springs to life again after rain. If your visit to canyon country coincides with recent moisture at the end of a long dry spell, you may witness a remarkable sight: the spongy crust swelling with water. Despite the ability of cryptobiotic soil to withstand temperatures 50 degrees higher than the surrounding air, it is still quite fragile. A single footstep or tire track can destroy this crust.

View of Henry Mountains from Sunset Point, Capitol Reef National Park

Utah 24, then head west on the **Burr Trail Road.** This road is rough, especially through the spectacular switchbacks of the Burr Trail Pass. The payoff is the **Strike Valley Overlook,** a 2-mile walk off a rather bone-jarring spur road in upper Muley Twist Canyon. The overlook gives you a wonderful view of the Waterpocket Fold. Complete the loop by taking the Burr Trail Road (paved once you leave the park) west to Boulder, then follow Utah 12 over Boulder Mountain back to Torrey. The Burr Trail Road passes through a particularly scenic portion of Grand Staircase-Escalante National Monument (see pp. 40-41) known as **Long Canyon,** which is surrounded by dramatic red cliffs of Wingate sandstone.

## Cycling

Bikes are permitted only on park roads. Most back roads see little auto traffic; they can also be hot and dusty, with no water available. The visitor center distributes a free handout on mountain biking that covers the two loops discussed above, as well as the road that descends off Boulder Mountain in Dixie National Forest (see p. 110).

## Interpretive Activities

Rangers offer guided walks, talks, and evening programs from the Fruita area during summer. Capitol Reef has some cultural history, mostly relating to early Mormon settlement of the area. Visit the historic Gifford Farmhouse *(on Utah 24 in the center of Fruita);* fruit picking is permitted in season. ■

Padre Bay on Lake Powell

# Glen Canyon National Recreation Area

■ 1.3 million acres ■ Southeast Utah, stretching 186 miles to Lees Ferry in northern Arizona ■ Best months March-Oct. ■ Camping, hiking, boating, houseboating, swimming, fishing, horseback riding, scenic drives ■ Adm. fee ■ Contact the recreation area, Box 1507, Page, AZ 86040; phone 520-608-6404. www.nps.gov/glca

STEP OFF YOUR HOUSEBOAT onto the sandy shore of a slender canyon hours from the marina, and you're apt to utter a single one word: "Wow!" It might come from wandering beneath these soaring pink, buff, and cinnamon walls, or from discovering some delicate hanging garden hugging a slickrock seep, or from finding a stone arch in a remote canyon that few people have ever seen.

Centerpiece to this magnificent recreation area is Lake Powell, the world's second largest man-made reservoir. The crown jewel of that lake, Rainbow Bridge, stands 290 feet tall with a span of 270 feet—the largest natural bridge in the world, and a sacred site to the Navajo Indians. Completed in 1963 by the Bureau of Reclamation, Glen Canyon is the nation's second highest dam; behind it sprawls 186-mile-long Lake Powell with 1,960 miles of crenellated shoreline, offering more water frontage than the entire west coast of the United States.

Glen Canyon was named in 1869 by explorer Maj. John Wesley Powell, who delighted in its "curious ensemble of wonderful features—carved walls, royal arches, glens, alcove gulches, mounds and monuments." Despite the fact that small groups of people traveled here in the years following Powell, much of the landscape remained virtually unexplored until the 1950s, when the bureau proposed the dam—one of many intended to serve the parched, landlocked Southwest. Although the project succeeded on one level, Glen Canyon Dam also became a tragic tombstone: It flooded the Colorado River's least known canyons, burying in a watery grave sites that had been spectacular beyond words.

The controversy continues. A 1997 proposal to restore Glen Canyon by partially emptying Lake Powell sparked strong public reaction. While proponents push for the canyon's restoration, opponents point to the lake's recreation, water storage, and power-generating capacities.

## What to See and Do

Conflicts aside, it remains the pleasure of many to steer a rental houseboat along a quiet pocket of Lake Powell, pausing for a swim before motoring up yet another canyon. All boaters should follow a detailed map of the lake, preferably one by Stan Jones *(available at Glen Canyon Visitor Center)*, which is updated annually.

Rental houseboats are available for groups of 2 to 20; you can easily spend three days to three weeks cruising places where few speedboats bother to go. Each craft comes with linens, kitchen utensils, and a set of navigational charts to get you out and back safely. The lake's four marinas all offer boats and supplies: Wahweap,

near Page, Arizona; Halls Crossing, 47 miles west of Natural Bridges National Monument; Bullfrog, a ferry ride across the river from Halls; and Hite, the most northern. For information call the concessionaire, Lake Powell Resorts and Marinas *(800-528-6154)*.

Lake Powell is also a popular fishing destination. Anglers avoid the summer crowds by renting a boat in late spring or early fall. Fishing is best during these times for northern pike, walleye, large- and small-mouthed bass, crappie, striped bass, and catfish.

### Rainbow Bridge

Rainbow Bridge—the largest natural rock span in the world—can be reached via a tour boat leaving from Wahweap, Bullfrog, or Halls Crossing. The boat delivers you to a 0.7-mile trail leading directly to the span.

When author Zane Grey visited here early in the 19th century, he inscribed his initials on a rock near the base of the bridge. In Grey's day, only an intrepid few undertook the strenuous hike to Rainbow Bridge; today thousands visit each year. *(For a permit to reach the bridge, contact the Navajo Nation Parks & Recreation Department, Box 9000, Window Rock, AZ 86515; 520-871-6647.)*

The bridge itself is a splendid sight—a mighty sweep of fine-grained, cross-bedded Navajo sandstone soaring 300 feet above the sandy bottom of Bridge Canyon. Rainbow Bridge started out as a hole punched in a rock fin by a vigorous, sediment-laden stream known as Bridge Creek. The stream's erosional power, combined with constant weathering of the Navajo and Kayenta formations, turned a modest hole in the rock into the remarkable span seen today. As for the elegant curve of the span, Navajo sandstone tends to drop off its parent rock in graceful curves as it erodes.

### Hikes

In the Wahweap area you'll find the 0.4-mile **Horseshoe Bend View Trail,** which gives a good look at the spot where the Colorado River cuts a horseshoe-shaped bend through layers of sandstone. Parents must keep a close eye on children; there are no guardrails at the viewpoint. The trailhead is at the end of a dirt road 5 miles south of the Carl Hayden Visitor Center at Glen Canyon Dam.

### Space Invaders

Two non-native species are choking out native plants—including the venerable cottonwoods—that have graced Southwestern waterways for centuries. Tamarisk was introduced a century ago to control erosion, while Russian olives were brought in as ornamentals. Unfortunately, both arrived without native pathogens and predators, letting them crowd out indigenous species.

Growing fast into dense thickets, the roots of "tammies" consume massive quantities of water each day. Cottonwood seedlings, dependent on gravel bars along rivers to sprout, often cannot best this fierce competitor. In the long run, many cavity-nesting birds—including woodpeckers, bluebirds, and owls—will have to move on in search of more favorable locations. Without cottonwood regeneration, beavers, which are dependent on the tree for food, gnaw down many of the old giants that they previously would have ignored.

Russian olive—easily identified by silver green leaves hiding 2-inch-long spines—often mingle with tamarisk, creating a nearly impenetrable thicket along stream banks.

Control of both species is difficult, since the plants can spread by seeds, cuttings, or roots. Land managers are currently experimenting with biological control agents.

Wahweap Bay, Lake Powell, Glen Canyon National Recreation Area

Arches, balanced rocks, and natural bridges await along the 3-mile **Wiregrass Canyon Trail** to Lake Powell. You'll find the trailhead 6 miles east of the town of Big Water. On this route you'll be following a wash rather than a trail, occasionally climbing around pour-offs—that is, steep drops created by flash floods. About a mile from the trailhead is a small natural bridge, formed when flood waters from the canyon parallel to Wiregrass cut through the narrow canyon wall. Look for small arches high in the canyon wall, and don't hesitate to explore the side canyons along the way.

Desert canyons can become ovenlike in summer, making fall, winter, and spring the best times to hike. (In summer, set out just after sunrise.) To get to Wiregrass from Page, drive north on US 89 to Big Water, Utah, turning right between signposts 7 and 8. At 0.3 mile turn right again onto Smoky Mountain Road, then continue 4.6 miles to the "Wiregrass Canyon Backcountry Use Area" pullout.

### Hole-in-the-Rock Road

Though most visitors to Lake Powell have water-based recreation on their minds, some find driving the region's back roads to be a grand adventure. The 62-mile Hole-in-the-Rock Road takes you along the once grueling route used by the 1879 Mormon expedition, which consisted of 250 people, 83 wagons, and 1,000 head of livestock.

Seeking a shortcut to the San Juan River, where they hoped to establish settlements, the missionaries spent the winter chipping and blasting to enlarge a crack in the rim above the Colorado River. The resulting path dropped 2,000 feet, with a grade of 25 to 45 degrees. John Hall, one of southern Utah's earliest pioneers, built a boat for the missionaries that ferried them across the river. For ten years he operated the ferry until people found an easier crossing 35 miles upstream, the present site of Halls Crossing. This road is accessible for high-clearance passenger cars, but the last 10 miles are suited to 4WD vehicles only. ■

# Natural Bridges National Monument

■ 7,636 acres  ■ Southeast Utah, 42 miles west of Blanding  ■ Best months March-June and Sept.-Nov. Visitor center open May-Sept.  ■ Hiking, scenic drives  ■ Day-use fee; camping fee  ■ Contact the monument, HC 60 Box 1, Lake Powell, UT 84533; phone 435-692-1234. www.nps.gov/nabr

BACK IN 1883, PROSPECTOR CASS HITE spent his days wandering the wild, trackless canyons of the Colorado River in search of gold. Although he never hit pay dirt, he did discover a wealth of natural beauty. Hite's precious treasure included three river-carved bridges located within an easy walk of one another.

Today, **Bridge View Drive,** a 9-mile loop, takes visitors past 220-foot-tall **Sipapu,** the world's second largest natural bridge, 210-foot **Kachina,** and the delicate 106-foot **Owachomo.** Short trails lead from parking areas to bridge viewpoints; especially worthwhile is the one-third-mile trail to the overlook for **Horse Collar Ruin,** a uniquely shaped prehistoric structure. The 9-mile **Natural Bridges Loop Trail,** accessible from any of the overlook trails off Bridge View Drive, takes you under all the bridges and past lush desert oases to a canyon bottom etched with the markings of ancient cultures. Watch for white-throated swifts in the skies above the canyon; they also hover along the sheer faces of the rock wall, tending their nests of mud and twigs.

A video and exhibits at the solar-powered **visitor center** located on Utah 275 just inside the monument entrance explain how meandering streams cut through Permian age Cedar Mesa sandstone to carve the natural bridges. Many of the fascinating ranger-guided walks and evening

Sipapu Bridge, Natural Bridges National Monument

programs focus on the region's early human occupation in the period from 7000 B.C. to A.D. 500.

To learn about the area's native plants, including desert sage, pinyon, and juniper—and how they were used as food, tools, and medicine by the Ancestral Puebloans—follow the short self-guided interpretive trail located just outside the visitor center.

Natural Bridges holds the distinction of being Utah's first National Park Service area. Theodore Roosevelt established the monument four years after the area was featured in a 1904 issue of NATIONAL GEOGRAPHIC.∎

# Bluff Area

- Southeast Utah, at the intersection of US 163 and US 191 ■ Best months April-Nov. ■ Camping, hiking, rafting, biking, scenic drives, petroglyphs, Ancestral Puebloan ruins ■ Contact Bluff Visitor Information Center, Hwy. 191, Bluff, UT 84512; phone 435-672-2220. www.go-utah.com/bluff

There's a restful air about Bluff (population 340), a shady little community tucked into the southeast corner of Utah along the San Juan River. Century-old stone homes reflect the town's Mormon beginnings. Cottonwoods line the streets. Surrounding the town is a rich weave of redrock formations, enticing locals and visitors alike to explore the area on foot and by raft, bike, or car.

## What to See and Do
### Rafting

Without question, the area's biggest attraction is rafting the San Juan River. The silt-laden waters of this major artery of the Colorado River flow past ancient cliff dwellings and through dramatic rock layers that record some 300 million years of geology. River permits are required; call the Bureau of Land Management office in Monticello *(435-587-1532)* to arrange your trip. An easier option is to sign on with Wild Rivers Expeditions *(800-422-7654)*, the oldest educational adventure outfitter in the Southwest. This family-owned company's popular one-day, 26-mile trip from Bluff to Mexican Hat is a good introduction to the river's geological and archaeological treasures.

San Juan River, Goosenecks State Park

Every rafter will want to stop at spectacular **Butler Wash Petroglyph Panel** for a glimpse of the life-size, broad-shouldered human-shaped figures, as well as at **River House Ruin**—a well-stabilized, 800-year-old Ancestral Puebloan dwelling. Later in the day, look to the left for **Mules Ear** diatreme, a rubble-strewn eruption of rocks sticking up from **Comb Ridge.** Forming an 80-mile-long monocline, the ridge remains one of the most unusual natural barriers in the West. Lunch under the cottonwoods, or try any number of short hikes into the plunge pools and hanging gardens of the surrounding canyons.

Visitors with more time can arrange four- to eight-day trips to **Clay Hills Crossing.** Longer floats include a stop at the world's best preserved Pennsylvanian Age marine fossil outcrop (290 million years old), as well as a visit to the stone cabins used during Bluff's gold rush of 1892-93. Deep in the sinuous canyons of the Goosenecks, the **Honaker Trail** climbs 1,200 feet, yielding one of the most incredible views of the Four Corners region to be found anywhere. Colorado's Sleeping Ute Mountain, New Mexico's Ship Rock, and Arizona's Carizo Mountains are among the landforms visible from this delightful viewpoint. The tight twists of the river ease at Clay Hills Crossing, which serves as the end for extended trips.

## Goosenecks State Park

Begin your land-based explorations of the area at Goosenecks State Park *(435-678-2238),* located on Utah 316. The park is famous for its striking view of the entrenched meanders of the San Juan River. Here the river travels through a 1,500-foot chasm, winding 6 miles to advance no more than a mile and a half as the crow flies; photographers will want to break out the wide-angle lens. From Bluff, drive west 24 miles on US 163, climbing a pass on Comb Ridge, then turn northeast and go 1 mile on Utah 261 to Utah 316; turn left to reach the park. A brief detour to **Mexican Hat Rock,** a signature sandstone sombrero, can be made by going 1 mile past Utah 261 on US 163.

## Muley Point

To soak up some of southern Utah's fabulous desert landscape, drive back to Utah 261 and head north 5 miles up the steep graded switchbacks. At the top, turn left onto the 3-mile dirt **Moki Dugway.** ("Moki" is a Mormon word for the Anasazi; "dugway" is a geologic term for carving or digging.) This road climbs 1,200 feet up a sandstone cliff to reach **Muley Point Overlook.** Visible below is the Valley of the Gods, as well as the distant buttes of Monument Valley (see pp. 60-61).

Consider the challenges of traveling this forbidding country in horse-drawn wagons, a feat accomplished by some 250 Mormons over six months in 1879–1880. During the torturous 260-mile-long passage from eastern Utah to what is now Bluff, not one death occurred (there were even three healthy births). Driven by the words of their church—"This forbidden corner must be colonized"—the missionaries did just that, only to abandon Bluff four years later in the face of floods and financial hardship. Their crossing of the Colorado River resulted in the now famous **Hole-in-the-Rock** (see p. 54), a pass three-quarters of a mile long to the river, 2,000 feet below. At Clay Hills they met similar challenges and wound up using hand tools to build passages around several deep canyons (their dynamite had long since run out).

### Leapin' Lizards

Dashing across the sandstone, whiptail lizards are as common to the Southwest as campground squirrels are in the Rocky Mountains. In a bid to keep their body temperature at 102° F, these slender, three- to six-inch lizards dash back and forth from sun to shade. Whiptails are also frenetic foragers, running, climbing, and probing with their snouts for ground-dwelling insects and spiders.

Helping the whiptail elude predators such as birds, snakes, and coyotes is its ability to sprint at speeds up to 15 miles per hour, then suddenly dive into the protection of a bush; if snagged by the tail, the lizard relinquishes it in the getaway.

Half of the southern Rockies' 12 whiptail lizard species are unisexual—that is, capable of reproducing without mating. Because their progeny are genetic replicas of the mother, they are prone to disease and inherited weaknesses. On the plus side, whiptails can reproduce twice as fast as other lizards, enabling them to inhabit areas such as floodplains where other populations are routinely eliminated.

Whiptail lizards vanish from October to April. During this period they hibernate in shallow burrows, waiting for the air to warm again.

Climber on Mexican Hat Rock, Valley of the Gods

### Valley of the Gods

End your day's travel at Valley of the Gods, located off US 163 east of the access road to Muley Point. A level, 17-mile loop road winds through sandstone formations resembling Monument Valley in miniature. Bicycle touring—rentals are available—and photography are popular here.

### Hovenweep National Monument

On another day, consider a walk through the pinyon and juniper trees to the remote archaeological sites of Hovenweep National Monument *(970-562-4282. www.nps .gov/hove)*. The six Ancestral Puebloan villages in Hovenweep's canyons were built in A.D. 1200, positioned around the area's few precious water resources. To reach Hovenweep, head east from Bluff on Utah 262. Pass historic Ismay Trading Post, then turn left on the monument's marked entrance road. Camping facilities and ranger-guided tours are available. ■

Totem Pole and Ye B Chai Rock, Meridian Butte

# Monument Valley Navajo Tribal Park

■ 30,000 acres ■ Arizona-Utah border between Kayenta, Arizona, and Mexican Hat, Utah ■ Best months April-Nov. Visitor center open year-round; campground open summer only ■ Guided hikes, auto tour ■ Adm. fee ■ Contact the park, P.O. Box 93, Monument Valley, UT 84536; phone 801-727-3287

YOU'VE SEEN IT IN a hundred Westerns (and twice that many car commercials), but to stand in Monument Valley is a truly unforgettable experience. Along the park's 17-mile **loop drive** you'll come face-to-face with spectacular sandstone formations in vibrant, almost shocking hues of red and orange, rising 1,000 feet from the sandy, windblown landscape.

Above the occasional solitary Navajo herdsman trailing his flock of sheep into a nearby arroyo, the sky seems to go on forever.

Thanks to the encouragement of trading-post owner Harry Goulding, director John Ford immortalized the valley with his 1938 film *Stagecoach*. Countless Westerns have been shot here since then, and the film industry remains fascinated with the landscape to this day.

Long before cowboys galloped across Monument Valley, the scene was one vast sweeping dune. For 250 million years the forces of wind and water scalloped the edges of this plateau into mesas. Over more time still, the mesas were whittled into buttes, then spires, and finally into the grains of sand at your feet.

Today Monument Valley is home to Navajo families, many of whom continue to craft traditional pottery, silver jewelry, baskets, and woven rugs. Much of this work is available at trading posts and tribal cultural centers throughout the region. The valley is just one part of the **Navajo Indian Reservation**—at 17.5 million acres the largest in the nation.

The drive affords great views as it heads southeast from the visitor center, winding among such well-known features as **Elephant Butte, John Ford's Point, Camel Butte, Artist's Point,** and **The Thumb.** If you plan to explore beyond the road, you'll need both a permit and a Navajo guide *(801-727-3287)*. Tours of Monument Valley typically include a stop at a Navajo hogan—a traditional one-room wood-and-mud dwelling—as well as close-up looks at some of the region's many arches. Tour operators located outside the visitor center offer offer a variety of excursions, including moonlit, wildlife, and special photography tours, departing from the predawn hours through late afternoon. For guided tours of Monument Valley and its environs, contact Totem Pole Tours *(P.O. Box 360579, Monument Valley, UT 84536; 435-727-3313 or 800-345-8687)*.

If southwestern sunsets top your list of favorite things, Monument Valley is the place to be. Ensconce yourself on a rock facing west and watch the lengthening shadows stretch across the desert floor. The ever changing light intensifies the hues of the red rock, then fades, yielding in time to spires silhouetted against a star-studded sky.

Complete your visit by sampling some frybread, a Navajo taco, or a mutton sandwich, available at any of the family-owned food stands along the park entry road. As a courtesy, always ask for permission before photographing the local inhabitants. ■

## Prickly Pear Cactus

In spring you'll delight at this cactus's brilliantly colored, 2- to 3-inch-diameter blooms, while in summer the plants will sport red to purple fruit, called tuna. Take a close look at the thorns of a prickly pear. More than offering protection, each needle reflects light, acting as a kind of air conditioner that cools the flesh of the cactus by almost 20 degrees. Bristly hairs at the base of each spine trap air next to the stem, further insulating the plant from heat.

# Mesa Verde National Park

MASTERS OF MASONRY, the Ancestral Puebloans (formerly known as the Anasazi) left remarkable examples of their skill in stonework scattered all across the Colorado Plateau. Thousands of multistory dwellings, watchtowers, granaries, and ceremonial underground rooms called kivas still dot the landscape—enduring evidence of a population that may have numbered 30,000 at its height.

Mesa Verde National Park *(P.O. Box 8, Mesa Verde National Park, CO 81330; 970-529-4465. www.nps.gov/meve. Adm. fee)* is a 52,122-acre preserve located in southwest Colorado that contains some of the most pristine Ancestral Puebloan ruins found anywhere. The park—accessible from US 160, some 36 miles west of Durango, or 10 miles east of Cortez—is a stunning reminder of this amazing culture, which began settling in the region around A.D. 500 and thrived until A.D. 1300.

During the 800 years in which they flourished in this harsh, unforgiving terrain, the Ancestral Puebloans evolved from a hunting-gathering existence to a society of farmers, weavers, potters, and stonemasons—a feat they accomplished without benefit of a written language, wheeled vehicles, pack animals, or metal tools.

In the late 1200s, the Ancestral Puebloans completely abandoned the cliff dwellings at Mesa Verde and the surrounding canyons in the notably brief span of only two generations. Archaeologists speculate that this cultural diaspora may have been prompted by resource depletion,

Cliff Palace, Mesa Verde National Park

drought and famine, or perhaps even a change in religious beliefs.

Archaeologists, however, are no longer the only ones contemplating Mesa Verde's past. Interpretation of the park's buildings, artifacts, and legacy now also reflects the opinions of the 24 Native American tribes that claim a cultural affiliation with the Ancestral Puebloans.

While enjoying a guided tour, for example, you may watch an interpretive ranger—a Hopi from Arizona—demonstrate how his people first planted corn with a digging stick. Then you'll hear him outline a recent study indicating that the same corn may have been redistributed to a distant needy population—a theory refuting some long-held assumptions that the Puebloans lived in isolated villages independent of outside contact.

Included in the training of park interpretive staff—10 to 20 percent of whom are Native American—are visits to tribal elders in the modern-day pueblos of Arizona and New Mexico. The rangers listen to the elders' stories—the same tales passed down for many generations—then convey them to visitors during ranger-guided explorations of sites in the park.

Interpretations are always evolving at Mesa Verde, with each tour promising visitors new insights into this ancient culture. As one Navajo interpretive ranger describes the shift in emphasis, "Years ago, when I first started working here, I talked about room numbers, the chemistry of rocks, window size. Today I'm telling my native legends about this place and its past. And the visitors are listening."

Unoccupied for centuries, these dwellings were well known by later nomadic Native American tribes that

Long House, Weatherill Mesa

roamed the area. But not until a snowy afternoon in 1888—when a couple of cowhands named Weatherill chasing down stray cattle came upon an ancient city of stone asleep in a canyon—did the Mesa Verde story become known to the world. As the fame of these spectacular cliff dwellings spread, Congress acted to prevent their destruction or exploitation. Established in 1906, Mesa Verde became the first national park dedicated to preserving the works of an indigenous culture.

Each year more than 650,000 visitors travel to Mesa Verde. The park is open year-round, with some lodging, food, and camping facilities operating on a seasonal basis. A large percentage of guests opt to take guided tours of some of the park's best known sites—**Balcony House, Cliff Palace,** and

**Long House.** The best way to choose which tours to take during your half-, full-, or multiday stay is to start at the visitor center, 15 miles from the park entrance, where rangers are on hand to help you plan your visit. Or contact the park's concessionaire, ARAMARK *(970-529-4421),* for information on its half- and full-day tours. You can purchase tickets one day in advance on a first-come, first-served basis. The tours to Balcony House, Cliff Palace, and Long House last one hour and are still a remarkable bargain, but be aware that the hikes are strenuous; they entail a good deal of climbing at elevations from 6,000 to 8,500 feet.

Before embarking on a guided tour, you may want to stop at the **Chapin Mesa Museum,** about 20 miles from the park entrance. Featuring the video

*Legacy of Stone and Spirit* as well as exhibits of original artifacts ranging from yucca fiber sandals to intricately painted ceramic mugs, the museum is a gem. Lifelike dioramas display miniature vignettes of Ancestral Puebloan life as it advanced over the centuries.

A short, steep walk down to **Spruce Tree House**—the park's third largest and most visited cliff dwelling—gives a sampling of life on this parched plateau during Mesa Verde's classic period, A.D. 1100 to 1300. Interpretive signs on **Petroglyph Point Trail,** a 2.8-mile loop that begins along this walk, help you understand how the prehistoric people fed, clothed, and housed themselves in these high desert canyons.

To view the cultural progression of the Ancestral Puebloans firsthand, head to **Mesa Top Loop Road,** a 6-mile circuit located just past the park headquarters and museum area. Short hikes from the road to the interpreted pit house and surface pueblo sites show examples of the earliest dwellings on the mesa. **Square Tower House,** the park's tallest dwelling, and **Sun Temple** are both accessible from this road. You can also walk to overlooks of both Balcony House and Cliff Palace, though only those holding tickets for a specific tour are admitted to these structures.

On your way out of the park, take the time to stop at the **Far View Sites,** about 4 miles north of the museum. Trails lead to the village, tower, and dwellings of this extensive farming community. Nearby is **Mummy Lake,** a large, circular depression that may have functioned as a man-made reservoir. ■

# Canyonlands National Park

■ 337,598 acres ■ Southeast Utah, northwest of Monticello and Moab ■ Best seasons spring and fall. Spring storms often make roads impassable ■ Camping, hiking, rafting, mountain biking, jeep tours, pictographs ■ Adm. fee. Camping, backcountry, and rafting permits required; reservations recommended ■ Pets not permitted on park trails or in backcountry, even in vehicles ■ Contact the park, 2282 S.W. Resource Blvd., Moab, UT 84532; phone 435-719-2313, 435-259-4351 (permits). www.nps.gov/cany

CANYONLANDS NATIONAL PARK, in the north of the Colorado Plateau, preserves a maze of canyons sliced by two powerful rivers, the Colorado and the Green. Within this enormous rock wilderness visitors can hike, raft, bike, and camp—or, better yet, simply sit and listen to the songs of canyon wrens dripping off the sandstone walls.

With yearly visitation at Canyonlands National Park nearing the half-million mark, the site has gained considerable currency since 1859, when Capt. J. N. Macomb of the U.S. Topographical Corps wrote: "I cannot

Shafer Canyon with La Sal Mountains in the distance

conceive of a more worthless and impractical region than the one we now find ourselves in."

The Green and Colorado Rivers meet at the heart of the park to form a Y-shaped confluence, which has been used to divide Canyonlands into three districts. The Island in the Sky District is the northern section, a 1,000- to 2,000-foot-high mesa bordered by the Green River on the west and the Colorado River on the east. Paved roads, hiking trails, and 4WD roads thread the Island, providing easy access to spectacular views.

The Needles District, located in the park's southeast corner, is dominated by red and orange spires of Cedar Mesa sandstone. Popular with hikers, the Needles District is also known for such features as the Confluence Overlook, Chesler Park, and Elephant Hill. The Maze District, as its name suggests, remains the park's least accessible section. Travel in the Maze requires time—at least three days—as well as a high degree of backcountry route-finding skill.

The vast scope of Canyonlands cries out for an extended visit, but if you're pressed for time, you'll need to focus your attention on a single district; no roads link them together. And come prepared—grocery stores and gas stations are a long drive away.

## What to See and Do

### Island in the Sky District

The Island in the Sky District *(435-259-4712)* is reached 4 miles past the turnoff on Utah 313 to Dead Horse Point State Park. It is the easiest district to visit because it requires the shortest amount of time. In a single long day you can drive or take short walks to scenic viewpoints, as well as hike to a natural arch and a stunning 1,000-foot-deep, mile-wide depression.

If vast, uninterrupted landscapes unleash your inner poet, bring a pen and paper to **Grand View Point,** 12 miles south of the visitor center on the main park road. Inhale the sweeping vista of the surrounding red rock of the Maze and Needles Districts, and the deep shadows where the Green and Colorado Rivers flow. There's also the distant, sometimes ethereal blue humps of the La Sal, Abajo, and Henry mountain ranges. If time allows, take the easy 2-mile round-trip trail that starts at the parking area at Grand View Point and follows the rim. Other splendid overlooks, all of them well marked, await you at **Buck Canyon, Candlestick Tower,** and **Green River;** all three are located just off the park road, 2 to 6 miles north of Grand View.

### Hikes and Drives

The easy half-mile **Mesa Arch Trail** loops through the sand and leads to Mesa Arch, a stone win-

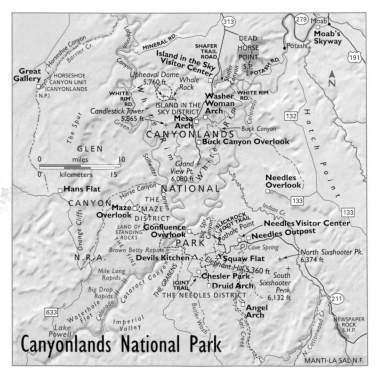

Canyonlands National Park

## Potholes

Gems of the desert, potholes are scattered all across canyon country. They come in all sizes and shapes, from the baby bathtubs that dimple Canyonlands' Pothole Point Trail to the giant catchments of the Waterpocket Fold in Capitol Reef National Park. Potholes begin as slight dents in the rock surface. Over time, erosion deepens them enough to hold airborne dust and insect larvae. Add water and you have an aquatic ecosystem.

All life forms in a pothole are exquisitely adapted to this delicate existence. Ounce per ounce, there's more life in a pothole pool than almost any other place in canyon country. At a newly filled pothole you may see mosquito larvae rise to the surface, then sink back down again. Bloodworms resembling lengths of red thread snap and loop in a pulsating rhythm. Gnat larvae, having lost up to 92 percent of their body weight to dehydration, will swell to life again when water returns to the potholes.

Tadpoles, too, can survive in these temporary pools, which may last only a matter of weeks. Tiny horseshoe crab-shaped crustaceans called fairy shrimp tolerate months of drought before a rain shower precipitates their egg production.

---

dow framing a fabulous portrait of canyon country. The trail begins at the park road, 5.75 miles south of the visitor center. Sadly, foot traffic has destroyed much of the cryptobiotic crust along this popular trail, but prickly pear cactuses remain.

The spectacle of Mesa Arch begins with a 500-foot drop to Buck Canyon, with the White Rim and La Sal Mountains looming in the distance. Look here for the distinctive butte called **Washer Woman Arch** with an "eyehole" window. Watch your children at this unguarded viewpoint.

To see Canyonlands' most spectacular geological formation, drive 5 miles northwest on the park road to the **Upheaval Dome trailhead,** where trail guides describing the structure of the formation, as well as the many competing theories on its origins, are available. As you walk along the quarter-mile path, notice the rocks along the trail.

The Navajo and Kayenta sandstone rocks, ranging in color from a light cream to a brownish-red, tilt away from the dome as a result of either an impacting comet or perhaps the dissolution of a salt dome. The geologic controversy burns on.

Approaching the dome (and the first viewpoint), you'll see **Syncline Valley** as a depression between the trail and **Whale Rock** to the east; in reality, the valley encircles the dome. Those with children should use extreme caution at this viewpoint.

Also consider making a trek on a finger of slickrock leading to the **White Rim Overlook.** On a clear day, this easy, three-quarter-mile trail beyond the Upheaval Dome Trail includes views of the russet brown pinnacles of Monument Valley, most of them topped with caps of White Rim sandstone. The Totem Pole is the tallest and most impressive of these pinnacles.

Chesler Pauls Trail in the Needles District, Canyonlands National Park

The **White Rim Road** is a 4WD road 100 miles long and of moderate difficulty. It takes two or more days to drive the entire length; permits (which can be reserved ahead of time) are required. A number of adventure companies based in Moab (including Navtec Expeditions, *801-259-7983 or 800-833-1278*) offer guided tours of this beautiful area.

Mountain bikers can join Holiday Expeditions *(801-266-2087 or 800-624-6323)* for a vehicle-supported four-day bicycle tour of the rim in spring and summer. Private tours can be reserved beginning in mid-July.

## The Needles District

**Newspaper Rock,** located on Utah 211, is a wonderful midway stop on the 49-mile drive from Monticello to the Needles District. This 200-square-foot chunk of Wingate sandstone cliff appears to have been a bulletin board for several ancient cultures, beginning roughly 1,500 years ago. Animals, broad-shouldered human figures, and the occasional snake or river shape are among the hundreds of images scratched into the desert varnish. Across the highway, among the cottonwoods, sits a pleasant picnic area and campground. No potable water is available.

En route to the Needles District you'll pass through such Western movie formations as Sixshooter Peaks—buttes made of Wingate sandstone. Just before the park entrance, a side road on your right leads to the Needles Outpost, your last chance for food and basic auto needs. Just inside the park entrance, stop at the Needles Visitor Center *(435-259-4711)* for free maps and information brochures. Given the size of the Needles District, you'll need a full day for a general tour and walks to spectacular viewpoints.

### Hikes and Drives

Begin at the quarter-mile **Roadside Ruin Nature Trail** *(on the left, just past the visitor center)*, where you'll find an Ancestral Puebloan granary, as well as plants that furnished food, medicine, and tools for the native peoples who lived here from A.D. 500 to 1200.

From here, drive 0.6 miles to the first road on your left, then turn left again on the next dirt road and follow it 1.1 miles to the parking area and trailhead for the highly engaging, self-guided **Cave Spring Trail.** The cave near the trailhead holds the remains of a cowboy line camp, used as recently as 1975, when the last cattle were removed from the park. Wonder why coffee cans are wrapped around the table legs here? It's to prevent rodents, especially pack rats, from crawling up them. (Pack rats have their backers, mind you. Ecologists and geologists have long studied pack rat nests—some of which have been occupied for hundreds of thousands of years—

to determine historic weather and vegetation patterns.)

Just past the cowboy camp, look for a seep—a groundwater spring—at the base of the canyon wall flanked by a set of pictographs. Evidence suggests the flat area behind you was farmed by the Ancestral Puebloans. Watch for maidenhair ferns hanging from tiny seeps in rock overhangs beside the trail. Two wooden ladders provide an easy route up and over the rock to a slickrock plateau; from here a set of rock cairns will lead you back to the trailhead.

**Pothole Point Trail,** an easy 0.6-mile loop, starts from the park road, 5.8 miles from the visitor center. Rock cairns mark the path over slickrock pocked by a series of potholes (see sidebar p. 69).

Access to four exciting viewpoints highlights the **Slickrock Foot Trail,** a mile north of Pothole Point Trail on the main park road. For kids, following cairns along a 2.4-mile loop across a slickrock plateau can become a fast-paced game that leaves their parents behind. Everyone will gather at the trail's four viewpoints, however, to enjoy features such as Sixshooter Peaks, the La Sal and Abajo Mountains, and the Needles Overlook. Watch for a mini-arch (it's only 10 inches high) peeking over the right edge of the trail shortly after Viewpoint 1. At Viewpoints 3 and 4 you may lose sight of the cairns and wind up marooned on a high point; in such a predicament, simply retrace your steps until you find the last cairn. The trail rejoins the neck of the loop before returning to the trailhead.

*Following pages:* Mesa Arch at sunrise

Those who prefer a less strenuous way of enjoying the scenery need only drive another mile beyond Slickrock Foot Trail to the end of the park road at **Big Spring Canyon Overlook.** Here canyons ripple the landscape in all directions. The 5.5-mile (one way) **Big Spring Canyon Overlook Trail** ends at Confluence Overlook, 500 feet above the junction of the Green and Colorado Rivers.

From Squaw Flat Campground, 4 miles from the visitor center, both walkers and car tourists have numerous options for trips. The 3-mile Elephant Hill access road gives those driving a 2WD car a look at what many consider to be the ultimate test for four-wheelers: **Elephant Hill.**

From here, a network of trails will take you to **Chesler Park**— a meadow surrounded by tall, spindly sandstone monoliths, or needles—and to Devils Kitchen Camp, another base camp for hikes to 200-foot-tall **Druid Arch.** Or try the mile-long **Joint Trail,** which passes through a sandstone slot canyon. Permits are required for backcountry camping through-

Mountain-biking the White Rim Road, Canyonlands National Park out the park; reservations are almost de rigueur in spring and fall.

## The Maze District

Canyonlands' least visited district, limited to primitive roads and lengthy trails, is perhaps best sampled at **Horseshoe Canyon.** This remote section of the park, located west of the Island in the Sky, is known for its **Great Gallery,** one of the finest displays of ancient rock images in the Southwest. Plan a full day for the **Great Gallery Trail,** a 6.5-mile (round-trip) hike to the canyon bottom, and don't forget to bring plenty of water.

If possible, join a ranger-led trip to this area, offered on weekend mornings in the spring and fall. For more information call the Hans Flat Ranger Station *(435-259-6513)*. Getting to the ranger station is a challenge in itself. From Green River, take Utah 24 south off I-70 and travel 24 miles; turn east at the junction with a dirt road. Drive 25 miles to the next junction and turn left, then travel 5 miles to the next gravel road and turn right; finally, proceed 1 mile to the parking area. ■

# Goblin Valley State Park

■ 3,654 acres ■ South-central Utah, near town of Green River ■ Camping, hiking ■ Best seasons spring and fall ■ Adm. fee ■ Contact the park, Box 637, Green River, UT 84525; phone 435-564-3633. www.parks.state.ut.us

REDDISH BROWN, GOBLIN-LIKE rock creatures lure hikers into this geologic showplace. Many people simply wander around the whimsical formations, stopping now and then to peer through a goblin's "eyehole." Others prefer to hike the two easy trails that traverse the small park.

Goblin Valley's elves rise up from an easily eroded siltstone known locally as Hoodoo Entrada, cousin to the tawny-colored stone that forms the arches around Moab. The russet-colored formations in the park are part of the San Rafael Reef; like the backbone of a giant stegosaurus, it forms the eastern edge of the San Rafael Swell (see pp. 86-87), a 130,000-square-mile uplift. When you drive into the park on Goblin Valley Road, taking note of the impenetrable barrier of the reef's "bones" on your left (west) and the arid, featureless landscape on your right (east), you'll understand why this area went virtually undiscovered until well into the 20th century.

Miner and amateur geologist Arthur Chaffin wandered into the remote rock valley in 1921, reconnoitering an oil exploration road. He scratched the location on a rough map, naming it "Valley of the Mushrooms," then forgot about it until 1949. In that year Chaffin began guiding clients there who wished to see something out of the ordinary.

The park's largest concentration of goblins can be viewed from a sheltered picnic area near the campground. For a closer look, try the 1.5-mile

Eroded sandstone formation

**Carmel Canyon Loop Trail,** located 1 mile past the park campground, where the paved road ends. The trail begins by bending left through a badlands area, offering views of a prominent butte called **Mollys Castle,** then winds through a narrow canyon before climbing back to the road about 200 yards from the trailhead. The 2-mile (one-way) **Curtis Bench Trail** begins on the road near the campground, then heads south through a variety of formations before arriving at an impressive view of the Henry Mountains—the last mountain range in the continental United States to be explored by Europeans. From here, the trail winds east to the observation area.

The crumbly sandstone surrounding the goblins erodes with each rainstorm, causing them to appear taller every year. As you explore this area, take care not to tread on the goblins' fragile pedestal rocks. ■

Colorado River, Dead Horse Point State Park

# Dead Horse Point State Park

■ 5,362 acres ■ Southeast Utah, near Moab ■ Camping, hiking, bird-watching
■ Best seasons spring and fall ■ Adm. fee ■ Contact the park, Box 609, Moab,
UT 84532; phone 435-259-2614. www.parks.state.ut.us

A WIDE-ANGLE LENS and plenty of film will help capture the far-reaching
and beautiful views from this slender promontory, poking 2,000 feet
above the serpentine meanders of the Colorado River. By foot or car it's
a short 1.5 miles to the famous site, which served as a natural corral for
early cowboys in the region. The **Canyon Rim Trail,** a 4.25-mile loop
from the visitor center that keeps a safe distance from the precipitous
edges, offers remarkable views. Along the way you'll notice turquoise-
colored ponds in the valley below, where potassium-rich groundwater,
pumped up in wells, is evaporated to concentrate potash, an ingredient
of most garden fertilizers.

Check out the fence of entwined juniper trees as the trail and road rejoin at the narrow neck before **Dead Horse Point.** Park personnel erected this barrier to mimic the type used by 1880s cowboys, who roped and broke wild mustangs on this finger of land, preparing them for sale to buyers nationwide. One legend says the park was named for a doomed herd of horses: Left to roam free, the animals somehow died of thirst. From the viewpoint you can see another possible source of the park's name: a sandstone formation that looks like a horse lying on its side.

The overlook offers fine views of the Colorado River. The rock layers visible from here—a sprawling wash of color, from red and gray to buff and salmon—are, from the top, named as follows: Entrada, Navajo, Kayenta, and Wingate sandstone layers, followed by the Chinle, Moenkopi, Cutler (look here for the recumbent horse), and Honaker Trail formations. Much of this area is unfenced; those with young children will want to keep their visit short.

Hikers may extend the walk back to the visitor center by following the 2.75-mile trail along the far side of the promontory. If you still haven't had enough, take the quarter-mile **nature trail** outside the visitor center. In summer, rangers lead walks and evening programs for families.

Sitting at 6,000 feet but belonging to a desert (the park receives only about 8 inches of yearly precipitation, most of it in the form of snow), Dead Horse Point is a good place to observe plants common to southern Utah. Many of the shrubby plants here, including cliffrose and mountain mahogany, sport small, somewhat waxy leaves—qualities that minimize water loss. Sagebrush sends out long taproots to reach underground water supplies; the prickly pear cactus stores moisture in its spongy tissues. Many flowers have evolved to maximize moisture, usually after spring rains or midsummer showers: They rapidly bloom and set seed, then remain dormant for much of the rest of the year. ∎

### Sharp-eyed Hunters

From Dead Horse Point you're likely to spy two well-known birds of prey: the golden eagle and the peregrine falcon. With its 7-foot wingspan and broad chest, the golden eagle soars the desert thermals, dropping to open grasslands to snatch jackrabbits with its sharp talons. Golden eagles mate for life, often returning annually to the same cliff-ledge aeries. In flight, goldens appear mostly brown; the bird's golden nape is visible only at close range.

The peregrine falcon, on the other hand, swoops through the sky at tremendous speed, slamming into its feathered prey—often the white-throated swift. Poisoned by DDT, peregrines were on the brink of extinction in the mid-1960s. An aggressive breeding and reintroduction program, combined with a ban on the pesticide, proved so successful that peregrine falcons were removed from the endangered species list in 1999. Peregrines are slate gray, with a pale throat and breast.

North Window, Arches National Park

# Arches National Park

■ 76,519 acres ■ Southeast Utah, northwest of Moab ■ Best seasons early spring and fall. Wildflowers peak in April and May ■ Hiking, rock climbing, wildlife viewing, scenic drives, petroglyphs ■ Adm. fee. Backcountry permit required; hiking permit required for Fiery Furnace ■ Contact the park, P.O. Box 907 Moab, Utah 84532; phone 435-259-8161. www.nps.gov/arch

AT ARCHES NATIONAL PARK, a slickrock wonderland perched on a plateau high above the Colorado River, stone meets sky in ways you never dreamed possible. Over hundreds of millions of years, the forces of nature have created a sandstone masterpiece: wildly shaped towers, fins, balanced rocks, and petrified sand dunes.

And, of course, arches. The park contains the world's largest concentration of them—some 2,000 arches, ranging in size from 3 to 300 feet (measured base to base); included is Utah's signature formation, Delicate Arch. A 22-mile paved road traverses the park, providing access to a variety of trailheads and viewpoints.

Some 300 million years ago, inland seas covered the large basin that formed this region. The seas refilled and evaporated—29 times in all—leaving behind salt beds thousands of feet thick in places. Later, relentless weathering attacked the surrounding mountains, especially to the northeast. Streams carried sand and boulders from the uplands and deposited them on the salt layer. Because the salt layer is less dense than the overlying thick blanket of rock, it rises up through it, deforming it into domes and ridges, with valleys in between. Faults deep within the earth have also contributed to the morphology of the area. One visible result is the 2,500-foot vertical displacement of the Moab Fault, which can be seen from the visitor center.

When the Colorado River cut its deep canyon through the Colorado Plateau, groundwater flowing toward it dissolved the salt beneath the domes; they then collapsed into today's northwest-heading Salt and Moab Valleys. This also created a sequence of parallel cracks in the sandstone. Water and erosion pried these cracks open over time, forming parallel fins of rock like those seen at Fiery Furnace and Devils Garden. Weathering attacks the fins to create hollows on each side. As these hollows deepen, they eventually merge to form an opening, or natural arch. Arches increase through weathering, erosion, and rockfalls from their roofs. In 1991, for example, a 60-foot-long slab fell from the underside of Landscape Arch—at 306 feet, the park's biggest. No arch is eternal, however. Occasionally an entire arch roof will collapse, leaving paired towers in its wake.

## What to See and Do

Begin your tour of Arches at the visitor center, located just past the park entrance, where you'll find a wide selection of maps, pamphlets, and books to acquaint you with the park's layout and geology. Ask the ranger about guided walks and special events; the popular **Fiery Furnace** outings often fill up during peak season (*mid-March–Oct.*), but you can call the visitor center to make reservations for this 2.5-hour hike 48 hours ahead of time.

When you're ready, head out on the park road, switchbacking past a golden cliff wall to the first stopping point, **Park Avenue.** This is nature's version of a city street edged by skyscrapers. Sandstone fins 150 to 300 feet high line the area. The easy 1-mile **Park Avenue Trail,** which begins at the marked pullover, offers close-up views of these stony high-rises. If your driver is willing, ask him or her to meet you at trail's end, on the road near views of the **Three Gossips.**

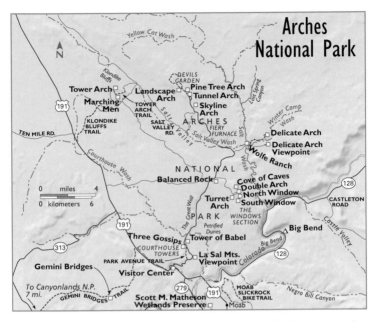

## Arches National Park

Eight miles beyond Park Avenue, the park road passes the **Petrified Dunes Viewpoint,** then **Balanced Rock,** finally arriving at a turnoff on the right leading to the **Windows,** where four large arches frame distant panoramas. From the parking lot, an easy jaunt to the right leads you to the North and South Windows; a short walk to the left heads to **Turret Arch.** Across the road is **Double Arch,** where the **Cove of Caves** offers a cool respite on a hot, sunny day.

### Delicate Arch

After the Windows, return to the main park road; the next turnoff to the right is for Delicate Arch, a must-see. As nature writer Edward Abbey put it in *Desert Solitaire: A Season in the Wilderness,* "If Delicate Arch has any significance it lies, I will venture, in the power of the odd and unexpected to startle the senses and surprise the mind

out their ruts of habit, to compel us into a reawakened awareness of the wonderful—that which is full of wonder."

If time is limited or you plan to do a number of hikes, consider viewing this famous treasure from the **Delicate Arch Viewpoint,** 1 mile beyond the turnoff for Wolfe Ranch. The viewpoint is an easy 100-yard stroll from the parking area at the end of the road.

The 1.5-mile one-way hike to Delicate Arch begins at the remains of pioneer John Wesley Wolfe's ranch, which include a weathered corral and a tattered log cabin. Follow the bridge across Salt Wash to the cliff on the left, where Ute Indians left petroglyphs. The Ute, who once roamed from the eastern slope of the Colorado Rockies to the canyonlands of southern Utah, camped here, probably trading with Wolfe for provisions.

Balanced Rock at sunset, Arches National Park

The trail is ingeniously designed to hide Delicate Arch from view until your very last step. From the valley floor the trail threads patches of cryptobiotic soil (see p. 48) before reaching flat slabs of sandstone, where cairns mark the route. The final third of a mile is a teaser. As the path climbs, it hugs a sandstone fin, then edges along a steep bowl that bars all view of the famous arch. The last few steps require some nerve, but you will be rewarded with a marvelous look at Delicate Arch straddling the edge of a slickrock basin.

Standing 45 feet tall at its highest point, Delicate Arch frames the La Sal Mountains, a fact that gave this extraordinary structure its original name—Landscape Arch. A cartographer's error, however, mislabeled Delicate Arch as Landscape Arch, and vice versa; the oversight was never corrected. The best time to photograph Delicate Arch is near sunrise or sunset. Time your evening hike for the full moon and you may have the thrill of seeing the moon rise above the arch—though the return trip in dim light can be tricky.

## More Arches

If you ache for more arch encounters, follow the main park road 6 miles north of the Delicate Arch turnoff to Devils Garden. This end-of-the-line destination offers one of the best hikes in the park. Seven arches, including the famous **Landscape Arch,** lie within walking distance on trails that will delight both neophyte and seasoned hikers.

The easy 0.8-mile trail to Landscape Arch begins on a wide gravel path, then bisects a pair of sandstone fins. Along the way, short side trails lead to **Tunnel** and **Pine Tree Arches.** Follow a steep spur trail for a heads-up look at Landscape Arch. At your feet will be large chunks of the rock that cascaded down from the underside of the arch in 1991.

## Tower Arch

Sensational sights await those hiking the 1.2-mile (one-way) **Tower Arch Trail** in the park's remote Klondike Bluffs area. To enter this intricate upthrust of weird sandstone formations, drive 1 mile south on the main park road from the Devils Garden parking lot, then turn west on the 2WD, high-clearance road just past Skyline Arch. (This unpaved road may be impassable during or after storms.) Follow the road 7.7 miles through Salt Valley to the turnoff on the left for Tower Arch Trail.

Cairns direct you from the parking lot up a steep rock ridge to a fine view to the east of the Fiery Furnace and the La Sal Mountains. That long, dark ridge on the north horizon is Book Cliffs. The trail crests another ridge, with **March-ing Men** looming on the left as a towering crowd of human-shaped rocks. These formations stand sentry to your gradual descent to the trail's low point, a land littered with fantastical fins and pinnacles.

After you cross the wash, cairns guide you through a sea of fins and sand to Tower Arch, which takes its name from the pinnacle standing nearby. Look closely at the right abutment of this arch for an inscription carved by Alexander Ringhoffer. Deemed a founding father of Arches Park, Ringhoffer ran a mine in Salt Valley during the 1920s. From Tower Arch you could explore this labyrinth of fins and pinnacles for days and still not see them all. When it's time to return, retrace your steps. ■

### One Hump or Two?

You haven't traveled through canyon country until you've done so on a camel. The concept is not as wonky as it sounds: Paleontologists believe that camels originated in North America 40 million years ago, so the animals once likely roamed these high desert plateaus. Some camel species migrated to South America, where they evolved into today's llama and vicuña. Larger species crossed the land bridge to Asia and developed into two distinct species—the single-humped Arabian dromedary and the double-humped Bactrian of central Asia. Today you can enjoy a dromedary ride through the red-rock bluffs of Hurrah Pass courtesy of Camelot Lodge (435-259-9721. www.camelotlodge.com).

# Moab Meanders

Moab, near the confluence of the Green and Colorado Rivers, is outdoor recreation central. Stop first at the Moab Information Center *(805 N. Main Street; 435-259-8825 or 800-635-6622)* to talk with seasoned Moabites or pick up publications covering all aspects of canyon country. Outfitters, bookstores, and sporting-goods stores line Main Street; their staff can suggest biking and hiking trails and loop tours.

## Mountain Biking

It's hard to resist Moab's two-wheeled trails: Cycling options range from tours of mountain meadows to descents down rolling slickrock to passages through narrow slot canyons.

The challenging **Moab Slickrock Bike Trail** *(2.3 miles E of town, up Sand Flats Rd.)* is a rite-of-passage for fat-tire fanatics, yet it's not for zealots alone: You can sample slickrock touring on the 2.5-mile practice portion before continuing on the trail's 10.5-mile loop. With plenty of diversions to scenic viewpoints of the Colorado River, Moab, and the La Sal range, the normally four- to six-hour ride can easily expand to an all-day adventure.

The 14-mile (one-way) **Gemini Bridges Trail** offers views of Arches National Park, the La Sals, and a pair of rock spans, called Gemini Bridges, hundreds of feet long. This easy to moderate ride starts on US 191 roughly 1 mile south of Utah 313, on the way to the Island in the Sky District of Canyonlands National Park.

For the ultimate in backcountry biking, consider a multiday trip with vehicle support. A 4WD vehicle accompanies most guided tours, carrying food, gear, and the occasional bruised or breathless biker. The **White Rim Road** offers a classic tour of canyon country. The three- to seven-day trip follows a jeep road along the mesa top of Island in the Sky, dropping 1,000 feet to a bench of White Rim sandstone. A maze of canyons lines one side of the trail; towering over your head on the other side are rock walls up to 1,500 feet tall.

If time (and your endurance for steep climbs) is limited, pedal the 21-mile **Shafer Trail Road** with Tag-a-Long Expeditions *(435-259-8946 or 800-453-3292)*. This half-day trip descends 1,200 feet of switchbacks through a corner of Island in the Sky. The trip ends at the Colorado River, where the outfitter will meet you for a scenic return to the trailhead.

## Scenic Drive

If you prefer four wheels to two, drive all or part of the 60-mile-long **La Sal Mountain Loop.** Starting just north of Moab on Utah 128, this route follows the Colorado River Gorge for 19 miles before rising 4,000 feet into the foothills of the La Sal Mountains. At the start, on the west side of the river, is the high rim of Arches National Park; after this the views broaden to include beautiful valleys spiked with stone monuments, including Priest and Nuns, Castle Rock, and the Fisher Towers. These comparably soft spires are remnants of a valley wall; water and other erosional forces widened the vertical cracks in the wall, gradually separating sections into independent towers.

The loop turns southeast through Castle Valley for 11 miles, passing Round Mountain—a solidified plug of magma that pushed up from the surrounding sandstone. Turn right on La

Moab Slickrock Bike Trail

Sal Mountain Loop Road, driving south along the La Sal Mountains' western flank. The air is cooler here—about three degrees for each 1,000 feet of elevation gain. Detour down unpaved spur roads to visit tucked-away alpine lakes. The loop drive turns west about 7 miles before reaching US 191 south of Moab.

## Matheson Wetlands Preserve

A refreshingly green refuge in a sprawl of red-rock desert, the 890-acre Scott M. Matheson Wetlands Preserve (435-259-4629) attracts nearly 200 species of birds and a wide number of mammals. The preserve is named for a late governor of Utah, who was a tireless champion of conservation. Today it is the only high-quality wetland along the Utah shores of the Colorado River.

Habitats within the preserve change dramatically from day to day and from season to season. The best times to visit are spring, fall, and winter, when birds flock to the site. The 1-mile, wheelchair-accessible loop trail has boardwalks to wildlife-viewing spots and a path to the river.

## Moab's Skyway

Across the street from the Matheson preserve is Moab's Skyway (435-259-7799. www.moab-utah.com/skyway). This chairlift ascends nearly 1,000 feet of red rock in less than 12 minutes. At the top, a wheelchair-accessible board-walk leads to a viewpoint and several foot trails. A short trail accesses the Colorado Vista Overlook, perched above the river gorge far below. Follow the signs to Panorama Point, which offers a grand toss of red-rock spires and sandstone walls. Cliffrose, saltbush, rice grass, and rabbit brush are scattered across the rock. Riding back down, look for the petroglyphs between Towers 6 and 7, and 2 and 3. (You can also hike down via a 7-mile trek on the Moab Rim and Hidden Valley Trails, which begins just south of the skyway's upper terminal.) ∎

San Rafael River

# San Rafael Swell

■ 65 miles long, 40 miles wide ■ East-central Utah, near the towns of Price and Green River ■ Best seasons spring and fall; best months to float the San Rafael River May-June ■ Rockhounding, boating, rafting, biking, horseback riding, scenic drives, petroglyphs ■ Contact the Bureau of Land Management, P.O. Box 99, Hanksville, UT 84734, phone 435-542-3461; or BLM, P.O. Box 7004, Price, UT 84501, phone 435-636-3600. www.blm.gov/utah/price/default.htm

LIKE A GIANT BOWL INVERTED, the San Rafael Swell bulges out of the Colorado Plateau, exposing a wonderland of spires, buttes, and contorted canyons. The rock formations here, rivaling those of Canyonlands and Arches National Parks to the east, posed a massively insuperable obstacle to the crossing of southern Utah for 200 years. Today I-70 bisects the swell, giving motorists an easy route over this remarkable uplift.

The swell was clearly an impediment in 1776, when the Dominguez-

Escalante expedition (see pp. 106-107) set off in search of a route to connect the Spanish settlements of New Mexico with southern California. Their efforts opened up the territory, and traffic through the swell increased; tragically, much of it was Indian slaves. Traders met in this area to sell Paiute, Goskute, and Ute women and children as servants in Spanish New Mexico and California. Even though this odious practice had been outlawed by Spain in 1650 and by Mexico at its independence in 1821, it continued into the early 1850s.

Famous western scout Kit Carson carried mail and military dispatches across the swell, while Butch Cassidy escaped into a rock maze here after one of his robberies. Later on, generations of enterprising cattlemen rounded up and sold off the swell's wild horses; their cattle drives then trampled wide the paths that eventually became the first roads. During the 1950s, miners bumped along these same routes in search of uranium and natural gas.

Today it's four-wheelers kicking up the dust along the swell, plying a tangled network of roads that baffles the best of navigators. Please honor the signs prohibiting motorized travel in the swell's wilderness study areas. The most popular drive is **Wedge Overlook** and **Buckhorn Draw Road,** which leads to dramatic views of the **Little Grand Canyon** of the San Rafael River. To access the Wedge from I-70, head north 20 miles on Ranch Exit 129 to a sign for Wedge Overlook. Turn left at the intersection and drive 6 miles to the parking area. The road drops from the overlook into a narrow slot of sandstone shaded by cottonwoods before reaching Fullers Bottom, the put-in for float trips on the San Rafael River. This 15-mile, 5- to 6-hour river run is swift but free of rapids; the trip follows the high cliff walls of the canyon you saw at the overlook and ends at San Rafael Campground. Don't continue beyond the campground unless you are very experienced; the rapids are quite dangerous. The river is best floated during spring runoff in May or June. Side-canyon explorations can extend the trip into an overnighter.

A few of the swell's earliest hunters passed through **Black Dragon Canyon,** where they etched a dragonlike image in the walls, along with geometric shapes and animorphic forms. To get there from I-70, drive 14 miles west of Green River, Utah; turn north on a dirt road just past Milepost 145 and follow it for 1 mile. Turn left up a streambed to the canyon mouth; to see the petroglyphs, walk a quarter mile up the canyon.

Goblin Valley Road follows the San Rafael Reef, a saw of stone spires that rise 2,000 feet out of the desert and peak at Temple Mountain. The road ends at the state park of the same name (see p. 76). A walk through **Little Wild Horse Canyon**—a delightful day hike through a twisting sandstone ravine—begins near the park. Bone-dry most every day, the swell's canyons flash flood with reddish brown torrents of water during sudden rainstorms. Do not enter *any* of them when rain threatens. Before venturing into the swell, be sure you have the "Trails Illustrated San Rafael" map, or the "USGS San Rafael Desert" topographic map. Carry at least a gallon of water per person per day. ∎

# Utah High Plateaus

Pine Valley Mountain Wilderness, Dixie National Forest

THE FABULOUS DESERT WASHES and folded layers of sedimentary rock that mark much of Utah and western Colorado appear all the more inviting when viewed from the cool sweep of the high plateaus. Indeed, only from the elevated vantage point of the plateaus—the flanks of the Tushar Mountains and Thousand Lake Mountain, the precipitous edge of Grand Mesa—can you get the deepest, most inspiring sense of the surrounding dry lands. Both visually and biologically, this edge country is one of

America's most fascinating landscapes. (Edges are sometimes referred to as ecotones—places where two different environments meet.)

The Utah High Plateaus encompass an astonishing diversity of environments and terrain. Stretching in an arc from Utah's southwestern corner across the central part of the state and into west-central Colorado, the region embraces several plateaus that rise along the edge of the Colorado Plateau. Among them are the Markagunt, the Paunsaugunt, and the Sevier. This is the locus of such wilderness meccas as Bryce Canyon National Park, Dixie National Forest, and Grand Mesa National Forest.

Geologically speaking, the high plateaus have a fairly simple structure:

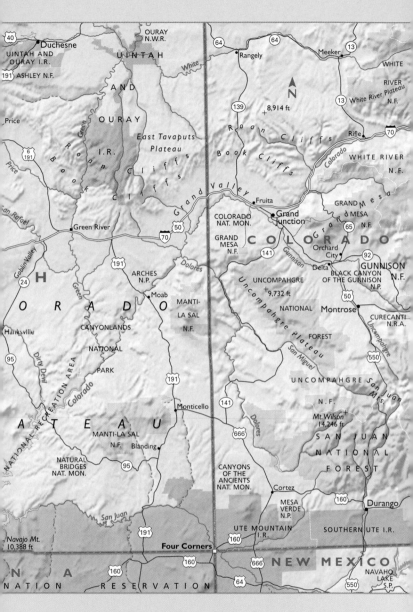

Layer upon layer of sedimentary formations were uplifted more or less intact, then preserved by their caps of hard, erosion-resistant volcanic rock. Remnants of volcanic craters are scattered here and there; one such place is Utah's tiny Ferguson Roadless Area, north of I-70.

Elsewhere in the high plateaus, however, erosion has made significant headway: The slow, horizontal eroding of Tertiary deposits at the edges of tablelands has sculpted such topographic delights as Cedar Breaks National Monument, as well as the dramatic rock scallops on the eastern edges of Fishlake National Forest.

Because of their height, these plateaus snag the lion's share of the

Prickly pear cactus in bloom, Dixie National Forest

region's moisture, much of which falls in the form of snow. The beautiful Pahvant Range in Fishlake National Forest, for example, gets its name from a Ute word meaning "much water."

That moisture, in turn, gives rise to beautiful forests of aspen, Douglas-fir, and spruce fir, as well as grassy nips and tucks that furnish tasty summer range for deer and elk. Lower elevations, which receive less precipitation, host stands of pinyon, juniper, Gambel oak, mountain mahogany, and sagebrush. The lowest regions of the high plateaus spawn raging, snowmelt-fed watercourses in spring; many of these swell into boulder-choked rivers that plunge headlong through the canyons of the Colorado Plateau, scouring them into new landscapes.

One environment you'll frequently encounter while exploring the high plateaus is the Douglas-fir forest. The easiest way to tell a Douglas-fir is by its cones: They bear small, trident-shaped bracts between the scales. These trees tend to be closely spaced, forming a dark, moody woods that keeps very little light from reaching the forest floor. Moss, common juniper, and the kinnikinnick are among the few species able to take root in this shrouded understory. Beautiful, pale green fronds of a lichen known as Old Man's Beard hang from the fir branches. Hairy woodpeckers and great horned owls make their homes here, as do mountain chickadees.

How far down the plateaus Douglas fir reaches depends a great deal on how much moisture the soil contains. You may find yourself hiking through fine stands of fir on the north-facing side of a mountain, only to emerge on a south-facing slope utterly bereft of trees.

A ramble across these high plateaus will almost certainly be a source of surprise and delight. Here are scenery, solitude, and a perfect perch for surveying some of the most intriguing Western lands of all. ■

Queens Garden, Bryce Canyon National Park

# Cedar Breaks
# National Monument

■ 6,155 acres ■ Southwest Utah, near Brian Head and Cedar City ■ Best
months late May–mid-Oct. (many services and roads closed in late fall and
winter) ■ Camping, hiking, backpacking, guided walks, scenic drives ■ Adm. fee
■ Contact the monument, 2390 W. Hwy. 56, Suite 11, Cedar City, UT 84720;
phone 435-586-9451. www.nps.gov/cebr

CEDAR BREAKS IS AN AMPHITHEATER of sculpted rock formations called
hoodoos (see sidebar p. 98). These colorful pillars are composed of limestone, eroded in the same ways and at roughly the same time as nearby
Bryce Canyon (see pp. 97-105). Clearly, however, Cedar Breaks has its
own unique character. For one thing, many visitors find the colors more
dramatic here than at Bryce. The amphitheater is also bigger and deeper.
Moreover, the gradient at Bryce is about 1,000 feet over 10 miles; at
Cedar Breaks it's a whopping 2,500 feet over just 3 miles.

The plateaus of this area are tilted blocks, which create a landscape
that rises and falls in a pattern like a series of breaking waves. Cedar

Cedar Breaks National Monument at sunset

Breaks lies on the upside of the Hurricane fault—the steep edge where the wave breaks. Bryce, on the other hand, is on the more gradual back side of its plateau.

Cedar Breaks' Markagunt Plateau is higher than Bryce's Paunsaugunt (the visitor center at Cedar Breaks sits at more than 10,000 feet elevation), and it supports more of an alpine ecosystem. Snow lingers until late June; wildflowers such as Indian paintbrush, lupine, yarrow, and penstemon peak in mid to late July. Meadows atop the plateau get more moisture and suffer less heat than the surrounding areas, resulting in an explosion of plant life. The old-growth Engelmann spruce forest here fell victim to a beetle epidemic in the late 1990s; as a result, you will occasionally see dead trees standing amid healthy subalpine fir and bristlecone pine.

Only 20 percent of the monument—the area atop the plateau with views down into the amphitheater—contains the usual visitor services; the rest has been proposed as wilderness. A remote area nearby, located roughly below the amphitheater, is already a Forest Service-administered wilderness known as Ashdown Gorge. Unlike most of southern Utah, this untrammeled land was never grazed by cattle or sheep, making it a rich region for research on so-called relic vegetation—species of flora that predate the arrival of pioneers.

## What to See and Do

The steepness of the amphitheater makes it difficult to hike among the hoodoos, but overlooks at the **visitor center** and at turnouts along the road provide glimpses of these amazing formations, along with excellent vistas to the west. From these view spots, you'll stand at the very edge of the Markagunt Plateau, looking out upon the Basin and Range ecoregion.

It's worth your while to walk two trails along the rim. The 2-mile **Alpine Pond Loop,** which has an interpretive guide, leads to a forest glade and pond; the 2-mile **Ramparts Trail,** on the other hand, leads past a grove of bristlecone pines at **Spectra Point** to a viewpoint of the amphitheater. Both trails begin at parking areas along the monument road.

Backpackers who are willing to make the hard, 9-mile hike down into the wilderness can start from **Rattlesnake Creek Trail,** just north of the park boundary. Be sure to check with the visitor center before you go; this path is not regularly maintained. Camping is forbidden in the amphitheater, so you'll need to set up your camp in the **Ashdown Gorge Wilderness,** then day-hike back up into the monument.

During the summer season rangers offer hourly geological talks, as well as evening campground programs on wildlife, bristlecone pines, and Native American cultural history. On weekends they lead guided morning hikes to the bristlecone pine stand at Spectra Point. ■

Alpine Pond, Cedar Breaks National Monument

Natural Bridge, Bryce Canyon National Park

# Bryce Canyon National Park

■ 35,835 acres ■ Southwest Utah, near Hatch, Panguitch, and Tropic ■ Best
months April-Oct. (some spur roads closed in winter) ■ Camping, hiking, backpacking, guided walks, cross-country skiing, snowshoeing, bird-watching ■ Adm.
fee ■ Contact the park, P.O. Box 170001, Bryce Canyon, UT 84717; phone
435-834-5322. www.nps.gov/brca

FIRST-TIME VISITORS TO BRYCE CANYON NATIONAL PARK may be excused for
thinking they've stumbled into an alien phantasmagoria. A geologic oddity, the canyon is composed not of the sandstone common to this area,
but of very soft limestone known as the Claron formation. Whereas most
limestones developed in ancient shallow seas, this one formed in a landlocked system, the Tertiary Lakes of 63 million to 40 million years ago.
Like today's Great Salt Lake, this body of water had no exit, so the sediments washing in from nearby mountains settled on the lake bed.

The variety of sediments produced Bryce's brilliant colors: Reds and yellows come from iron in various stages of oxidation; pinks and purples from manganese; greens from copper. This particular limestone has plenty of impurities, including silts, clays, cobbles, and sand. Because these particles are poorly cemented together, the resulting rock is weak—and therefore highly prone to erosion.

The depth of the ancient Tertiary Lakes varied over thousands of years, changing the deposition patterns of the streams that entered them. When the lakes were deep, a stream would dump sediments right at its mouth; the iron that produced red rocks concentrated there, whereas the lighter sediments that settled out toward the middle of the lakes were pure limestone, nice and white. When the lakes were shallow, however, the force of streams would push even the heavier sediments farther out into the middle. This is why the rock appears today in alternating bands of red and white.

Occasionally the lakes' level fell so low that it acted like a tidal flat, pushing water dozens of miles back and forth every day. The chemistry of this process concentrated magnesium in the sediments, producing a much harder form of carbonate called dolomite. Today you can often see this oatmeal-colored dolomite capping a hoodoo, forming a sort of hard hat that protects the lower, softer rock from erosion.

Speaking of erosion, because Bryce Canyon lies near the top of its watershed, the chief sculpting agent today is frost—water freezing and thawing inside the cracks of rocks. Thanks to its high elevation, Bryce undergoes more than 200 freeze-thaw cycles every year. Not only that, but the park sits at the intersection of two fault zones: the Paunsaugunt fault, running north-south, and the Rubys Inn overthrust fault, running east-west.

When these faults move, weak rocks such as Claron limestone tend to break along fractures called joints. The perpendicular nature of these fault lines means the joints—composed of a lot of deep, short fractures—tend to appear in checkerboard formation. Snow melts into the joints, freezes, and

## Hoodoos: Who Knew?

The term "hoodoo" originated at Bryce, though its derivation is shrouded in conjecture. It could be a variation of "voodoo" or perhaps an attempted translation of the Paiute term for the formation. Interestingly, a similar-sounding word in ancient Hebrew means "aboriginal person." Because the region's first white settlers included Mormon scholars versed in ancient Hebrew, some people speculate that Mormons may have coined the odd term.

You can see hoodoos in other places, but almost nowhere are they as dramatic as those found at Bryce. The Goblin Valley (see p. 76) north of Hanksville, for instance, sports fatter, more rounded sandstone hoodoos—features that die-hard Bryce fans refer to as "couch-potato hoodoos."

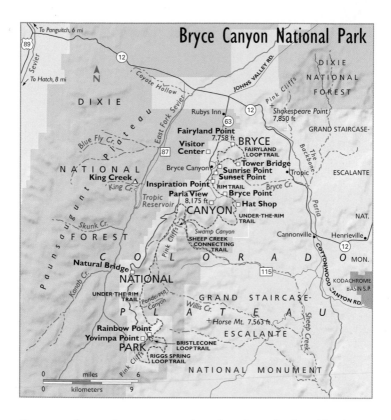

Bryce Canyon National Park

then expands, popping out square-shaped sections of rock and leaving behind hollowed-out blocks in the substrate. As erosion continues on the ridges, windows—holes—develop in these hollowed areas; layers of rock get sloughed off, creating vertical columns known as hoodoos (see sidebar opposite). These rock spires look so eerily human that Paiute legend referred to them as ancient people turned to stone.

The park's main road is an 18-mile-long spur along the top of the Paunsaugunt Plateau, which gains elevation as you move south. Near the visitor center you'll be surrounded by ponderosa pine forest that may harbor mule deer or great horned owls. To the south are stands of spruce, white fir, and aspen inhabited by elk, goshawks, and the occasional southern spotted owl.

Bryce's unique wildlife includes one of the largest colonies of the endangered Utah prairie dog. This species, found only in southern Utah, carries bubonic plague, which wipes out 70 to 80 percent of its population every five years. In very rare instances you may also spot California condors or nesting peregrine falcons. More than 200 species of birds have been sighted in the park; spring is an especially good time to see them. Finally, Bryce is an excellent place to admire venerable bristlecone pines—the senior tree in the park is believed to be some 1,700 years old.

Horseback rider below the rim, Bryce Canyon National Park

The Park Service plans to implement a shuttle bus system to alleviate traffic and parking problems during the busy May to September season. The shuttle will be optional, but you'll have to pay a fee—in addition to the entrance fee—to drive your car into the park. Park plans also call for a new visitor center. In the meantime, the current facility offers geology programs, campfire talks, children's programs, and guided walks on a daily basis throughout the summer.

Dramatic evening hikes are scheduled during the three nights of the full moon *(seasonal)*. These are very popular and fill up quickly; register early in the day. During the new moon you can catch an astronomy program—especially appealing given the clear air and lack of light pollution.

## What to See and Do

Spur roads off the main park road just south of the visitor center offer several breathtaking overlooks of the main amphitheater: **Sunrise, Sunset, Inspiration,** and **Bryce Points,** as well as **Paria View.** Of these, Bryce Point is the most impressive. Indeed, despite the names, Bryce Point is the best place to watch either sunrise or sunset. The 17-mile drive along the main park road to **Rainbow Point** presents several additional turnouts with panoramic views to the east and small sets of hoodoos in the foreground. If pressed for time, however, spend it on a hike in the park's central area.

### Hiking

The highlight of a visit to Bryce is hiking in the amphitheater, marveling at the hoodoos. The **Navajo Loop** and **Queens Garden Trails** make a popular 3-mile round-trip. You can walk the route in either direction, but by parking at Sunset Point you can descend the Navajo's steep switchbacks and then regain elevation more gradually on the Queens Garden side. The switchbacks take you down in a hurry,

passing into a narrow canyon surrounded by two ridges, or fins. A couple of Douglas-fir grow in the shade, but as the canyon opens out the plant community expands, with juniper and ponderosa pine joining in. In three-quarters of a mile you'll reach the valley bottom, filled with ponderosa pine. From this point, less ambitious hikers head straight back up the Navajo Loop Trail, though it's an easy jaunt along the valley floor to the Queens Garden complex, where you begin to ascend again.

Note how jagged and jointy the rock is here compared with the slickrock in much of the rest of southern Utah. This is the impure Claron limestone—a rock that bears the characteristic pebbles-in-cement look of a conglomerate. Take the short spur to view the formation known as the Queen, a hoodoo that evokes Queen Victoria sitting on her throne.

Of greater interest is the **Queens Garden,** a wonderful array of white, pink, gray, and brown rock layers. With head-on views of both the fins and the hoodoos, it's easy to imagine the layering and

*Following pages: Hiker on the Navajo Loop Trail, Bryce Canyon National Park*

faulting that created them. Follow the trail to the rim, then walk half a mile back to Sunset Point. This stretch of the hike allows both close-up and distant views of hoodoos, as well as a fine panorama falling away to the east.

Another excellent hike is the 8-mile **Fairyland Loop Trail.** If time is limited, do the 3-mile jaunt from Sunrise Point down to Tower Bridge and then return. This trail gives good glimpses of bristlecone pine—better, in fact, than those on the **Bristlecone Loop Trail** at Rainbow Point, though the latter trail features interpretive signs.

### Under-the-Rim Trail

No greater pleasure awaits the backpacker than the 22.5-mile Under-the-Rim Trail, a one-way, two-day trek best taken north to south from Bryce Point to Yovimpa Point. Stop at the visitor center to obtain a backcountry permit *(fee)* and register for primitive campsites you intend to use.

### Gambeling About

An accomplished young ornithologist, William Gambel served as assistant to Thomas Nuttal, the author of the first field manual on birds in America. In just a few years of roaming the West in the 1840s, Gambel discovered more than a hundred new species of birds. Along with the Gambel oak, four species of birds and a genus of lizard were named after him. At age 28, he died in California, only to have his bones washed from their hillside grave during a gold mining operation.

This hike displays a staggering array of geologic wonders, from the fine cross-bedding of Claron limestone fins and hidden springs flush with wildflowers to the unforgettable **Pink Cliffs.** Though some stretches of the trail are rather rugged, an early morning departure will allow you to make the 10 miles to Sheep Creek or Swamp Canyon, passing through the erosional fantasyland of the **Hat Shop** en route. Along here anyone will appreciate a comment often attributed to pioneer rancher Ebenezer Bryce, for whom the park is named: "It's a hell of a place to lose a cow." The latter portion of the trek climbs rather sharply over several miles to an elevation of 9,100 feet, offering magnificent views to the north and south, from the Pink Cliffs all the way to Navajo Mountain.

Although this hike is renowned for its uncanny rock formations and soaring vistas, there are woodlands to savor as well: ponderosa pine peppered with manzanita and bitterbrush; aspen groves dappled with columbine and Oregon grape; huddles of spruce, fir, and bristlecone pine. Portions of the trail also pass by thickets of Gambel oak, a favorite browse of mule deer and a tree celebrated as one of the few Rocky Mountain species to turn red in the fall.

Along the trail look for a variety of bird life; Steller's jays, Cooper's Hawks, northern flickers, violet-green swallows, pygmy nuthatches, vesper sparrows, and broad-tailed hummingbirds. You'll also be sharing the trail with tiger salamanders, as well as tree, sagebrush, and short-horned lizards. ∎

View near Inspiration Point at dawn, Bryce Canyon National Park

# Men with a Mission

FROM MANY OF THE VISTAS in the central portion of Dixie National Forest—in particular, those afforded by the Brian Head Ski Area and others along the Markagunt Plateau  visitors can look westward to the edge of the Great Basin, where in the fall of 1776 an expedition plodded southward on an altogether astonishing journey.

On July 29 a ten-man group led by Spanish priests Francisco Atanasio Dominguez and Silvestre Vélez de Escalante set out from Santa Fe, New Mexico, to pioneer an overland trail to newly founded Spanish missions in California. The reasons for the journey were varied. Besides offering a more economical means of reaching California, an overland route would help protect the Spanish missions in California from the Russians, who were thought to be moving down the West Coast. Some of the men hoped to make their fortunes in California.

The expedition failed to reach California, and the men seeking their fortunes were fortunate to return to Santa Fe with their lives. In the course of its trek, however, the party traversed an enormous slice of present-day Utah. And even though these intrepid explorers were probably not, as once believed, the first Europeans to enter the state—that honor may belong to a traveler named Rivera, who apparently made it into the Moab region around 1765—their diaries, natural and cultural history notes, and an array of maps introduced the world to this spectacular area. The fathers, for example, made the first known written description of a prehistoric Ancestral Puebloan ruin.

Although their destination was Los Angeles, west and slightly south of Santa Fe, the expedition first headed north into southwestern Colorado. They traveled on a zigzag course toward present-day Grand Junction, fording the Colorado River about 30 miles west of where that city stands today. Near Rangely, Colorado, the expedition finally began to head westward, following a line roughly parallel to modern US 40. The men and animals pushed all the way to the mouth of the Provo River, where they startled bands of Ute Indians.

The western slope of the Wasatch Range, where the Provo winds its way to Utah Lake, thrilled the padres, who had little doubt that rich, agriculture-based settlements could be built. These, they felt, would rival anything that had been established up to that time in New Mexico. As might be expected, the leaders missed no opportunity to share their religion with the native peoples they encountered, promising the potential converts that "if they consented to live as God commands," the fathers would return within a year, bringing crops and cattle with them. This was not to be: Economic and political downturns in Spain sapped support for missionary activities, preventing the friars from making a return visit.

From the Provo area, the men headed southward, blazing a trail slightly west and roughly parallel to I-15. The error of traveling on a large, northwesterly arc through Colorado and Utah soon became apparent. On October 6, west of the Markagunt Plateau near present-day Cedar City in southwestern Utah, an early season snowstorm hit the party, pin-

Pine Valley Mountain Wilderness, Dixie National Forest

ning it down for the next two days. Facing the prospect of more harsh weather—and even starvation—Dominguez and Escalante informed the men that it would be foolhardy to soldier on; they recommended a return to Santa Fe instead.

Some historians believe this decision stemmed primarily from the fathers' eagerness to start preparing for mission construction in the Utah Valley. Whatever its true motivation, the announcement very nearly sparked a mutiny among the civilians in the group. In time, however, they acquiesced. The party started for home.

Only then—having nearly died of thirst, having eaten their mules, and having suffered through a typical early onset of winter in the Utah high plateaus—did the men start to face real difficulties. After negotiating the plateaus and mountains of northern Arizona, the largest obstacle of all proved to be the Colorado River.

Once they had skirted the Vermilion Cliffs, the party descended to the river at present-day Lees Ferry, only to find the crossing impossible. More than a week's trekking over brutal terrain was required to find a suitable river crossing. (This spot, 30 miles below the mouth of the San Juan River, was for many years known as the Crossing of the Fathers.) "We climbed up to the opposite side by a precipitous and rocky ridge-cut," recalled one expedition member, "passing some rock shelves which are perilous and improvable only by dint of crowbars."

The steps that the men carved to climb out of Padre Canyon have survived into modern times. Unfortunately, like so many other natural and cultural treasures, they now lie 500 feet below the surface of man-made Lake Powell. After five months and 2,000 miles of wandering, the entire party safely reached Santa Fe on January 2, 1777. ■

# Dixie National Forest

■ 1.97 million acres ■ Southern Utah ■ Best months April-Oct. ■ Camping, hiking, backpacking, guided walks, rockhounding, boating, canoeing, fishing, mountain biking, horseback riding, wildlife viewing, scenic drives ■ Contact the national forest, 82 N. 100 East, Cedar City, UT; phone 435-865-3700. www.fs.fed.us/outernet/dixie_nf/welcome.htm

THE DIXIE NATIONAL FOREST covers a large area north of Grand Staircase-Escalante National Monument. It consists mostly of the following wooded high plateaus: the Markagunt Plateau surrounding and to the east of Cedar Breaks; the Paunsaugunt Plateau around Bryce Canyon; the Sevier Plateau north of the Paunsaugunt; the Table Cliff Plateau east of the Paunsaugunt; and the Aquarius Plateau north of the towns of Escalante and Boulder. Aquarius Plateau soars to 11,328 feet at Boulder Mountain, making it North America's highest forested plateau.

Rising from desert expanses to high-altitude stands of aspen, spruce, and fir on the Aquarius Plateau, these lands were all formed at the same

Mountain biking in Dixie National Forest

time. Fault lines between them have since eroded into valleys. Traveling this country today is a lesson in how vegetation changes with elevation. On Utah 12 heading south from Torrey over Boulder Mountain, for example, the route climbs from a pinyon-juniper forest through ponderosa pine, then into aspen, Douglas-fir, and Engelmann spruce.

Farther west, Utah 143 from Panguitch to Cedar Breaks National Monument (see pp. 94-96) offers a similar succession, and includes limber pine above Panguitch Lake. You can also experience this shift by driving dirt roads such as the **Hell's Backbone loop** (off Utah 12 between Boulder and Escalante) or by mountain biking the **Wildcat-Cat Creek trails** on Boulder Mountain.

## What to See and Do

The **Red Canyon** area northwest of Bryce invites exploration on numerous hiking and biking trails through red-rock country and Bryce-like hoodoos. If the hoodoos here are smaller in height and girth than those at Bryce, so are the crowds. The mile-long **Pink**

**Ledges Trail,** which starts directly behind the Red Canyon Visitor Center, offers an interpretive brochure. The trails at both **Losee Canyon** (3 miles long) and **Thunder Mountain** (8 miles) are good routes for either bikers or hikers.

Locals enjoy fishing for trout, especially in the many lakes on Boulder Mountain. To the west, **Navajo** and **Panguitch Lakes** are large, natural, high-altitude lakes with well-developed campgrounds and boat ramps. Canoeists must share the waters with powerboaters. In addition to rainbow and brook trout, some areas boast rare Bonneville and Colorado River cutthroat trout.

An almost endless network of backcountry roads and single-track trails suitable for mountain biking winds through Dixie National Forest. Few areas are more astonishing than the **Brian Head** mountain region, northeast of Cedar Breaks National Monument. The terrain does honor to the term mountain biking: Hundreds of miles of trails and roads lead through chilled air and aspen groves, past tumbling streams and 10,000-foot peaks. Indeed, it's possible in this area to begin well above timberline, then make a long, dizzy descent through the woods all the way to the red rock.

Several businesses in the tiny town of Brian Head—at 9,600 feet, one of the highest communities in Utah—offer shuttle services that take you to the top of 11,307-foot Brian Head Peak, allowing long rides down the mountain to pickup sites below. For intermediate riders, a particularly fine route—full of wildflowers and soaring views—is the **Dark Hollow-Second Left Hand Canyon** ride, a 17-mile (one-way) trek from Brian Head Peak to the small town of Parowan.

The small town of Brian Head also sponsors a series of nature walks on Saturdays in July and August. For information on these or other recreational opportunities, call the Brian Head Chamber of Commerce *(888-677-2810. www.brianheadutah.com).* ∎

# Fishlake National Forest

■ 1.4 million acres ■ Central Utah ■ Best seasons summer and fall
■ Camping, hiking, fishing, hunting, mountain biking, horseback riding, wildlife viewing, scenic drives ■ Contact the national forest, 115 E. 900 North, Richfield, Utah 84701; phone 435-896-9233 or 801-638-1033 (Fishlake Discovery information desk during summer). www.fs.fed.us/recreation/forest_descr/ut_r4_fishlake.html

A COOL GREEN ISLAND OF ASPEN and coniferous forest east of the intersection of I-70 and I-15, Fishlake National Forest sprawls across the very heart of southern Utah's high plateaus. This is an especially comfortable place on hot days, when the slickrock and the pinyon-juniper forests of lower elevations are baking in the summer sun.

A number of roads serve as extraordinary gateways into this high oasis, notably the **Beaver Canyon Scenic Byway** (Utah 153), which runs east for 17 miles from I-15 at the town of Beaver, along the Beaver River to Elk Meadows, at the feet of the beautiful Tushar Mountains. This is an especially fine drive in the fall, when aspen and mountain maple stage their riots of color, made even lovelier against the rich, dark green backdrop of the conifers.

Numerous interesting hiking trails thread this area, but most of them must be shared with the whine and rumble of all-terrain vehicles. One notable exception is the **Skyline National Scenic Trail** running along the broad flank of the Tushar Mountains, accessed by following Utah 153 from Beaver for approximately 24 miles; the trailhead is a quarter mile south of the Big Flat guard station. This is a glorious upland hike, with meadows and wildflowers and soaring views into the Circle Valley some 5,000 feet below.

An excellent 10-mile, end-to-end trip can be made from the starting point at Big Flat to a parking area at Big John Flat. To reach the pickup point, take Utah 153 from Beaver for roughly 15 miles, then continue north on Forest Road 123 for approximately 5 miles.

Another worthwhile driving route is found farther to the east, along the 23-mile **Fish Lake Scenic Byway,** which follows Utah 25 from west of the town of Loa, past Fish Lake and Johnson Valley Reservoir to Utah 72. This beautiful route features abundant coniferous woods and lush meadows. Keep a sharp eye out as you drive and you may see deer and both golden and bald eagles.

Fishermen will enjoy many a quiet hour of casting for trout and Mackinaw at either **Fish Lake** or **Johnson Valley Reservoir.** The stacked rock monuments visible near the junction

Sunset at Fishlake National Forest

of Utah 24 and 25 were constructed by hand over a period of four decades by a local sheepherder.

For the hearty walker, a fine hike along this drive takes off a mile beyond Pelican Overlook, just west of Fish Lake. The 4-mile **Pelican Valley Trail** climbs steadily some 2,100 feet to the top of the Fish Lake Hightop Plateau, which can then be traversed in a northerly direction along little-used jeep roads. Once again the views are remarkable, with the island uplifts of the Henry, La Sal, and Abajo Mountains visible far to the east—their feet in the desert, their heads in the clouds. ■

# Manti-La Sal National Forest

■ 1.3 million acres ■ Central and southeast Utah and southwest Colorado ■ Best seasons late spring–fall ■ Camping, hiking, backpacking, mountain climbing, boating, fishing, hunting, mountain biking, scenic drives ■ Contact the national forest, 599 W. Price River Dr., Price, UT 84501; phone 435-637-2817. www.fs.fed.us/r4/mantilasal/

STRETCHING SOUTH AND EAST from central Utah into western Colorado, Manti-La Sal encompasses the diverse ecology of the canyonlands outside Moab and the alpine meadows of the La Sal Mountains. The Manti division, hard against the eastern portion of Fishlake National Forest, embraces the grand, forested sweep of the Wasatch Plateau between I-70 and US 6. A rugged, high-clearance road called the **Skyline Drive** runs across

Medicine Lake in the La Sal Mountains

the plateau from Utah 31 to I-70, through sprawling meadows and huddles of subalpine fir, past limestone towers and indigo-colored lakes. This
80-mile route makes an extraordinary three- to four-day outing for intermediate mountain bikers with access to a shuttle vehicle.

Other roads into the forest include Utah 31, a scenic byway; Utah 29,
which leads to beautiful Joes Valley Reservoir; and a dirt road from Utah
10 at Ferron that heads west across the plateau to the town of Mayfield.

The **Left Fork Huntington Creek National Recreation Trail** begins
near Utah 31 in Huntington Canyon. This 6-mile trail winds along the
creek through spruce-fir forests and meadows laden with lupine, flax,
buttercup, columbine, paintbrush, and wild onion, past narrow canyons
and peaks that top 10,000 feet. For those with a penchant for wetting a fly
line, the Left Fork Huntington, Scad Valley, and Lake Fork Creeks, as well
as Rolfson Reservoir, are all worth a few dozen casts. ■

Canyon Rim Trail, Colorado National Monument

# Colorado National Monument

■ 20,534 acres ■ West-central Colorado, near Grand Junction ■ Best seasons spring and fall ■ Camping, hiking, rock climbing, biking, horseback riding, auto tours, bird-watching, wildlife viewing ■ Adm. fee ■ Contact the monument, Fruita, CO 81521; phone 970-858-3617. www.nps.gov/colm

IN A LAND GORGED ON GEOLOGY, where soaring vistas and secret crannies lie in wait behind clusters of sandstone spires, Colorado National Monument stands out as one of the great destinations of the high plateaus. Located on the northern edge of the sweeping Uncompahgre Plateau, the land here has been eroded into a fantastic collection of towers, spires, and cliffs, all cast in layers of red- to cream-colored rock. This is a place of deep, shadow-laden canyons and sunlit pinnacles, where colors—even moods—ebb and flow with the passing of every sun.

Granted monument status in 1911, this remarkable preserve owes its existence in large part to one extraordinarily enthusiastic booster, an eccentric named John Otto, who devoted a good chunk of his life to saving this unique slice of Colorado. In recognition of his efforts Otto was awarded the post of the monument's first custodian—for which he was paid the whopping sum of $1 a month. Otto was never short on enthusiasm for the entire area; the Grand Valley, he often claimed, was fertile enough to grow pumpkins the size of railroad cars.

After a stop at the visitor center 4 miles inside the monument's west entrance to orient yourself and pick up a printed guide, take time for the **Rim Rock Drive,** a short tour that offers a variety of outstanding views of both the monument and the great sweep of the Grand Valley, some 2,000 feet below. This route is also suitable for bicycling, but watch for vehicle traffic and fallen rocks. There's a wonderful array of wildlife at this monument, from rock wrens, golden eagles, and pinyon jays to mule deer, bighorn sheep, and mountain lions. As always, those who rouse themselves to explore the monument just after first light stand the best chance of capturing these creatures in memory or on film.

Rim Rock Drive is a good overview of Colorado National Monument, but more intimate encounters can be had on a number of walks; some 13 hikes depart from this roadway. One favorite is the half-mile **Otto's Trail,** located 1 mile from the visitor center, on the northeast side of Rim Rock Drive. The path begins among clusters of pinyon and juniper, as well as tufts of a stiff, multijointed plant called Mormon tea. Although this growth gets its name from the early Mormon settlers who quickly took to it, Mormon tea has a much longer history of use. Native people relied on it to relieve congestion caused by colds and allergies. Otto's Trail will also introduce you to the single-leaf ash, a favorite for making tool handles, as well as yucca, which native people put to use in everything from rope to sandals.

This is also a good place to catch glimpses of the rock wren. The small, gray to brownish bird can be identified by the odd crook in its tail and by its habit of bobbing while it walks, as if listening to music that no one else can hear. A busy forager, constantly combing stones and boulders for insects, the rock wren issues a pleasant series of trills at a fairly constant pitch.

Otto's Trail ends at an airy, windswept sandstone perch, offering wonderful views of the Grand Valley and the Book Cliffs; in front of you will be the Pipe Organ formation, while to the right is Monument Canyon and the 550-foot-tall Independence Monument. Many of these spires have not yet fallen to the effects of wind, ice, and water because they are protected by their light-colored, erosion-resistant capstones of the Kayenta formation. This is also a good place to catch sight of white-throated swifts doing a fast dance in and out of the recesses of the canyon, taking insects on the wing.

If Otto's Trail leaves you hungry for more, try the quarter-mile **Window Rock Trail,** which affords wonderful views into Wedding Canyon, or the **Alcove Nature Trail,** a self-guided interpretive walk on the Kayenta Bench. For something a bit more ambitious, try the **Black Ridge Trail**—a 5.5-mile trek, part of it across BLM lands—leads to inspirational views of Grand Mesa and the mighty San Juan Mountains, far to the south. ■

### Digging Dinosaurs

The southern Rockies contain fossil beds that have yielded an amazing assortment of dinosaur bones. If you're a fan of the extremely distant past, visit the Museum of Western Colorado's "Dinosaur Journey" exhibits in Fruita. This facility also offers supervised dinosaur digs, though advance reservations are required. Call 970-858-7282 for more information. The museum's main facility (970-242-0971. www .wcmuseum.org), located in Grand Junction, has a wonderful collection of artifacts, historic photos, and natural history displays.

# Grand Mesa

■ 540 square miles ■ West-central Colorado ■ Camping, hiking, backpacking, boating, fishing, mountain biking, horseback riding, bird-watching, scenic drives ■ Contact the Supervisor's Office, GMUG Forest, 2250 Hwy. 50, Delta, CO 81416; phone 970-874-6600. www.fs.fed.us/r2/gmug

APTLY NAMED, GRAND MESA is one of the largest flat-topped mountains on the planet. But this promontory, lying within Grand Mesa National Forest, is more than just another fine run of high country. Dotted with more than 300 lakes and reservoirs—many of the latter created for irrigation in the late 1800s using horses, wagons, and drag lines—Grand Mesa perches on the edge of both the Colorado Plateau and the Wyoming Basins ecoregions.

Besides spruce-fir and meadow complexes found around 10,000 feet,

Mesa Lake, Grand Mesa National Forest

hints of other life zones are abundant—from rugged alpine peaks to the distant, rockbound world of the Book Cliffs to the orchards and sprawling hay fields of the Grand Valley, many of them watered by artesian wells. Indeed, few places offer such a feast of visual and biological diversity. In the distance between the floor of Grand Valley and the top of the mesa are four different biological zones: the upper Sonoran zone, containing sagebrush, juniper, and pinyon; the transition zone, where Gambel oak is common; the Canadian zone, marked by clusters of aspen; and the Hudsonian zone, with its dark huddles of spruce and fir.

As you stand atop the mesa, savor the long views spread out below that bear witness to the power of erosion. The layers of sandstone and shale that make up the bulk of Grand Mesa are capped by a protective layer of basalt lava flows, vomited up some 25 million years ago as part of a widespread but discontinuous volcanic field covering much of west-central Colorado. Later the region was eroded—in this area by the Colo-

Grand Mesa National Forest

rado River and its local tributaries to the north and the Gunnison River to the south—leaving isolated, flat-topped mesas.

Yet the Grand Mesa story transcends mere volcanics and erosion, for ice also had a hand in sculpting this magnificent landscape. During ice ages—the last one hereabouts occurred 20,000 years ago—Grand Mesa, like the San Juan Mountains to the south and the White River Plateau to the east, disappeared beneath an ice cap. This gelid mantle grew hundreds of feet thick in some places, extending icy fingers in the form of outlet glaciers thousands of feet down stream valleys throughout the region.

## What to See and Do

Grand Mesa offers fine hiking, camping, and sight-seeing. An abundance of dirt roads branching off Colo. 65—a scenic byway running along the top of the mesa from north to south—lead to dispersed camping and challenging mountain-bike routes. Cyclists should keep two fingers on their brake levers because ATVs also use many of these roads. Information

and a variety of books are on hand at the Grand Mesa Visitor Center at Cobbett Lake, located at the junction of Colo. 65 and Forest Road 121. The quarter-mile self-guided **Discovery Trail** starts right behind the visitor center.

### Crag Crest Trail

This national recreation trail is an outstanding 10.3-mile loop, its high points drifting through the rubble of the basalt volcanic cap that covers much of Grand Mesa. The route is accessible from two well-marked trailheads. The western trailhead is located at Island Lake, near Grand Mesa Lodge; the eastern trailhead is reached by traveling east of Island Lake on Colo. 65 and making a left turn onto Forest Road 121, which is marked by signs for Ward Lake. After 1.5 miles, bear left; you'll reach the trailhead in approximately 0.6 mile, just past the Eggleston Lake campground, across from a signed parking area on the shore of Eggleston Lake. The western trail climbs the 1,000-plus feet to the crest more gently, but most hikers will be able to easily traverse the well-graded eastern path at Eggleston Lake.

Starting in the east the trail rises to Bullfinch Reservoir, then begins a more serious climb, offering ever better views of mesa topography—lake after lake littered across the landscape and flashing in the sun. The real gift of this walk is the crest itself: Barely 4 feet across in some places, it has sheer drops on either side and magnificent views all around. In addition to the water, meadows, and woods of the mesa, far to the north are the barren shales of the Book and Roan Cliffs. To the southeast stand the magnificent West Elk Mountains and, roughly 75 miles to the south, the San Juan Mountains, which include a number of peaks above 14,000 feet. Visible to the west is the Uncompahgre Plateau; on clear days you can even see the La Sal Mountains of eastern Utah.

The trail drops to the west through the spruce-fir forest, passing the **Cottonwood Lakes Trail.** Bear left here and continue for another mile, then bear left again, which will return you to Eggleston Lake and your car in another 3.5

## Clark's Nutcrackers

As you walk the Crag Crest National Recreation Trail, be on the lookout for Clark's nutcrackers— a hearty and often raucous black-winged, gray-bodied bird named in honor of Capt. William Clark of the Lewis and Clark expedition. True to their name, nutcrackers—like their relatives the pinyon jays, which are plentiful at lower elevations—are eager consumers of conifer seeds. When the year's nut crop is heavy, these birds collect the seeds by the thousands and store them in communal caches. Not all are consumed, however; many of the seeds end up sprouting into new trees.

One challenge to gathering nuts is that not all shells contain edible seeds. The birds focus their efforts on dark, healthy-looking seeds; you may see nutcrackers rattling seeds in their shells, listening for the distinctive sound of robust seeds over empty or withered ones.

Nutcrackers are members of the family Corvid, which includes crows and ravens; other corvids in and around Grand Mesa are the black-billed magpie and four of the five North American jays. You should also scan this area for flickers, blue grouse, chickadees, and finches.

Eggleston Lake, Grand Mesa National Forest

miles. Though not nearly as dramatic as the upper portions of the walk, this lower stretch still offers some nice brushes with both lakes and meadows.

This walk is extremely popular, so those in the mood for solitude will want to get an early start, preferably by 7 a.m. Also, note that the exposed nature of Crag Crest makes it a dangerous place during summer afternoons, when lightning strikes are common.

**Land O' Lakes Trail**
If you're looking for something less rigorous than the Crag Crest trail, try the much less strenuous half-mile Land O' Lakes Trail, located along Colo. 65 just west of Island Lake. This paved path winds quickly to a splendid overlook, from which you can take in Crag Crest and Ward Lake to the east, as well as the Black Canyon of the Gunnison and the San Juan Mountains to the south.

An interpretive sign at the end of the trail explains that the Ute Indians knew Grand Mesa as Thingunewat, which translates loosely as "home of the departed spirits." Standing at this overlook, on the brink of some of the most remarkable country in the intermountain West, it would be hard

to imagine a more satisfying refuge in which to enjoy the afterlife.

## Scenic Drives

Aside from the Crag Crest trail, perhaps the best way to sample the extraordinary scenery and geology of Grand Mesa is by traveling along **Lands End Road.** This gravel route takes off south from Colo. 65 west of the Grand Mesa Visitor Center.

In 12 miles the road reaches a small stone "observatory" built by the Civilian Conservation Corps on the west rim of Grand Mesa. Originally touted as a fire lookout, its location offers views of the Gunnison and Colorado River Valleys. The building now serves as a Forest Service visitor center, open in the summer from 10 a.m. to 4 p.m., and sports a small collection of books and brochures. Although it's possible to continue on Lands End Road, making a rather steep drop off the mesa all the way down into Grand Valley, most people prefer to descend via Colo. 65.

Before heading back, take 15 minutes to walk the short, self-guided interpretive trail beside the observatory. In addition to magnificent views, this is a good place to spot golden eagles, Swainson's hawks, and peregrine falcons. ■

# Wasatch Range & Uinta Mountains

Paragliding in the Traverse Mountains near Provo, Utah

STEEP-SIDED PEAKS where avalanches rumble through much of the winter; long, dark runs of Douglas-fir, lodgepole pine, subalpine fir and spruce; chains of high meadows that provide critical habitat for wildlife from deer to bear to elk—the rugged high country of Utah's magnificent Wasatch and Uinta ranges offers all this and more. Understandably, these beautiful runs of mountains draw tens of thousands of people a year, making it crucial to refrain from such heedless practices as cutting trails, camping

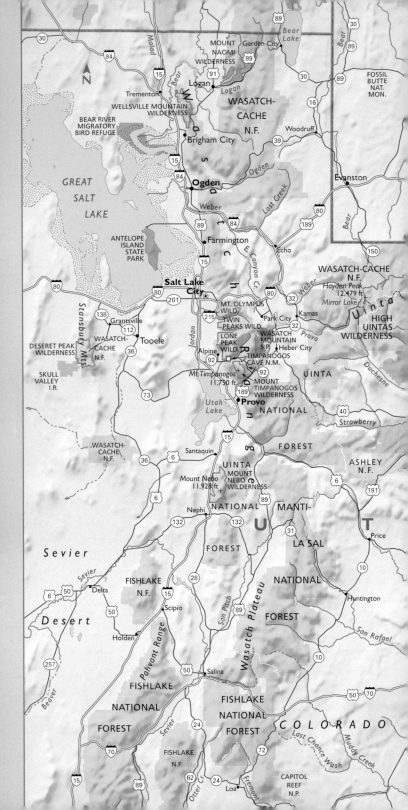

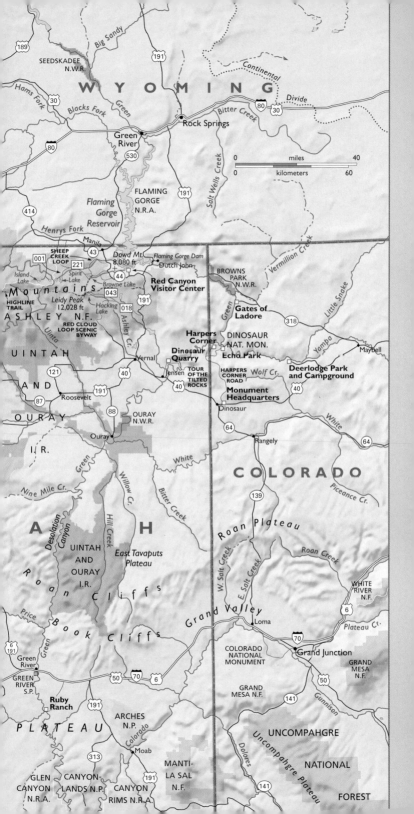

Sunrise at Red Canyon, Flaming Gorge National Recreation Area

next to water, or improperly disposing of waste. When multiplied by current use rates, these missteps can within a few years denude popular streams and lakeshores of vegetation, leaving scars on the landscape that will take centuries to heal.

Above and beyond its breathless views, the most enticing aspect of this ecoregion is the wetlands, lakeshores, and stream corridors that lie tucked among forests and high, rocky folds. There's the enchantment of the water itself, plus the fact that these riparian areas commonly support three times the number of plant and animal species found in nearby uplands. The next time you walk along a streamside trail, note the dramatic difference in the density and variety of vegetation within 10 feet of the water.

This chapter also includes a portion of the Wyoming Basin ecoregion, which lies generally northeast and south of the Uinta Mountains. Unlike the classic Rocky Mountain feel of the Uintas, the Wyoming Basin region is an irregular, tumbling maze of windswept plateaus and high desert, brightened at its heart by the twists and meanders of both the Green and Yampa Rivers. Within this region thrives a fascinating collection of natural areas, including Flaming Gorge National Recreation Area, and Browns Park and Ouray National Wildlife Refuges.

Some visitors, at least on first glance, find the starkness of the Wyoming Basin country overwhelming. But magic can clearly be found here: Pronghorn make fast, floating runs through a gray-green wash of greasewood and sage; deer drift down off the plateaus into the wind-scoured bottoms at the first slap of winter; dough-colored hummocks of Glen Canyon sandstone brood over dark huddles of pinyon and juniper squatting at their feet; ancient lizard petroglyphs stare back from sandstone walls. It's a place of both incomprehensible sweeps of geography and tiny, delicate flushes of life—a place where chaotic jumbles of rock reveal exquisite patterns spinning on a few common themes.

Of all the habitats in the Wyoming Basin area, the dryland shrub community is probably the easiest one to overlook. Yet in this land of marginal soils, extreme temperatures, and near-desert conditions thrive some of nature's most intriguing adaptations. Sagebrush, for example, puts out a web of lateral roots near the surface of the ground to take advantage of the occasional rain shower; at the same time, it sends a cluster of taproots deep into the earth to access groundwater. Sage leaves bristle with tiny hairs, which keep the desiccating winds away from the surface of the leaf.

Animals, too, deploy an arsenal of tactics to combat the heat and drought common to these areas. A kangaroo rat can survive long periods without drinking because its fat-rich diet allows the creature to produce water on a metabolic level during digestion. The large ears of jackrabbits dissipate their body heat. Many birds boast light-colored or semi-reflective feathers. Amid the abrupt beauty of the area's canyons and arroyos, its wild residents flourish through adaptation to this intriguing—and often unforgiving—land. ∎

# Wasatch Front

■ North-central Utah ■ Year-round ■ Camping, hiking, rock climbing, boating, fishing, biking, horseback riding, wildlife viewing, wildflower viewing, scenic drives ■ Contact Salt Lake Ranger District, Wasatch-Cache National Forest, 6944 S. 3000 East, Salt Lake City, UT 84121; phone 801-943-1794. www.fs.fed.us/wcnf

SOME 70 MILLION YEARS AGO, and continuing for some 30 to 40 million more, the westward drift of the North American tectonic plate created enormous strains on this part of the continent. The latter part of this era saw periods of astonishing volcanism—violent frenzies of ash and lava and mudflows. For the last 25 million years an extraordinary horizontal stretch has occurred in this region, and still continues today: The Earth's crust is being broken into the north-south trending, alternate ridges and valleys that we know today as the Basin and Range Country of western Utah, Nevada, and California.

At roughly the same time, there was a slow but certain and continuous rise in Utah and surrounding states: The entire region rose higher by nearly a mile. The strain on the Earth's crust during this movement along fault lines—some areas rising and others sinking—created dramatic inconsistencies in the land. One of the best examples of this phenomenon is the Wasatch Range. Remarkable for its relief—it soars some 7,100 feet above the Salt Lake Valley floor—it also possesses one of the steepest mountain faces in the world.

Steep is a quality that residents and travelers alike understand all too well, having climbed the peaks or witnessed the remarkable number of avalanches and landslides that crash down the mountainsides each year. In addition, earthquakes are common on the faults along which the mountains sit, serving as a reminder that the forces that formed the Wasatch Range are still very active, and that the range is in a constant state of development. This combination of steepness and earthquake activity is sobering, as parts of Salt Lake City lie virtually on top of the Wasatch Fault and a stone's throw west of a range prone to landslides.

The Wasatch Front is cut by a number of exquisite canyons, each one a portal to some of the best natural beauty and outdoor recreation opportunities in the American West. Just to the west, on the other hand, sprawls a north-south valley system laced with wetlands that have long provided hospitable land for wildlife. Hikers in the region's popular wilderness areas enjoy a host of alpine delights, from shimmering lakes to dramatic headwalls and cirques, as well as willow-lined wetlands and meadows thick with buttercups, paintbrush, forget-me-nots, bistort, and Parry clover. The wind-blasted upper reaches of these high-altitude jewels are also where you'll find what ecologists refer to as fellfields (fell is Gaelic for "rock"). Plants in these areas tend to be such low-growing cushion or mat plants as dwarf clover, moss campion, and alpine phlox. Appreciation of their fragile beauty is enhanced by recognizing the extraordinary

Skiing Mount Superior, Wasatch Range

Paintbrush, Wasatch Range

challenges of living in this environment: The soil here offers little in the way of organic material, the weather is often bitterly cold (and normally devoid of protective snow cover), and the wind—which almost never stops—can rob plants of much needed moisture.

## Central Wasatch Front Wilderness Areas

Strung out along the high peaks of the central Wasatch Range are four astonishing wilderness areas totaling roughly 70,000 acres. This is a land of soaring peaks and flower-strewn meadows, of abrupt glacial cirques and icy lakes and streams—all rendered more precious by their proximity to the sprawling urban areas in the valley below.

Northernmost of these wilderness areas is **Mount Olympus,** a name that seems pretentious only until you start roaming this high country. One of the best hikes is the trip to the top of 10,246-foot **Mount Raymond,** which lies just east of the smaller Mount Olympus. This 4,000-foot climb, up and back on the same pathway (a small scramble is necessary to reach the summit), is not a trip to be taken lightly. In summer, start early in the morning to lessen your exposure to late afternoon thunderstorms. To reach the trailhead from Salt Lake City and I-215, head 1.5 miles east on 6200 South to Big Cottonwood Canyon; turn left on Utah 190 and drive 5 miles to the trailhead for **Mill B North Fork Trail.**

Just south of Mount Olympus is the 13,000-acre **Twin Peaks Wilderness,** a magnificent riot of glaciation. A good walk here is the hike along **Mill B South Fork Creek** to a lovely string of alpine lakes: Blanche, Florence, and Lillian. This 5-mile round-trip gains roughly 2,400 feet of elevation. It begins a short distance from the trailhead to Mount Raymond, but on the south side of Big Cottonwood Canyon (Utah 190).

The 30,000-acre **Lone Peak Wilderness** (Utah's first congressionally dedicated wilderness) is next in line, sandwiched between Little Cottonwood Canyon and the beautiful valley of the American Fork. **Lone Peak Trail** leads to the summit of this wilderness's namesake mountain—a challenging overnight trek, requiring a climb of 6,000 feet from the trailheads at either Bells Canyon Reservoir or outside the town of Alpine. Those with a shuttle vehicle can start at one trailhead, hike the 4 miles to the top, and descend to the other past a nearly unbelievable cluster of high peaks, with good chances to see eagles and red-tailed hawks, mountain goats, and (in season) a bevy of outstanding alpine wildflowers.

The final preserve in the central Wasatch is the 10,750-acre **Mount Timpanogos Wilderness,** which takes its name from a rough translation of a Ute word for "rocky stream." (This area and the hike to Mount Timpanogos are described in more detail on p. 138.)

All four areas receive heavy use throughout the summer and early fall. On some trails you may even find yourself packing out the trash of less environmentally aware visitors. The establishment of these (and other) wilderness preserves required years of hard effort by an enormous number of committed and concerned people. Their victory deserves to be honored with the utmost respect and care. ■

# Timpanogos Cave National Monument

■ 250 acres ■ Southeast of Salt Lake City on Utah 92 ■ Best months mid–May–Oct. Year-round temperatures inside the cave are 42°-48° F ■ Hiking, wildlife viewing, cave tours ■ Adm. fee. Closed in winter. Cave visits by guided tour only. Tickets may be purchased up to 30 days in advance; numbers are limited, weekends usually sell out ■ Children under 16 must be accompanied by an adult; no strollers or pets ■ Contact the monument, Rural Route 3, Box 200, American Fork, UT 84003; phone 801-756-5239. www.nps.gov/tica

TO ALL BUT THE MOST ARDENT cave lovers, it may seem like a daunting task to climb three-quarters of the way up the sheer face of a canyon—1,000 feet of elevation gain in a mile and a half—just to get a glimpse of Timpanogos Cave. Yet this is one uphill trip that justifies the effort. And if you think this is steep, consider that the discoverer of this cave blasted a path nearly straight up the face of the canyon, using ropes and tree ladders.

Timpanogos Cave National Monument

In addition to the enchanted beauty of the three caves that make up the monument, the paved, switchbacked path to their mouth provides glorious views of the American Fork Valley—a dramatic, stream-eroded gorge where trees hang by their roots from steep-sided canyon walls. The trek up, along the cave trail, is a marvelous hike through layer after layer of geologic history, from the Tintic quartzite of the Cambrian period (visible about three-quarters of a mile up the trail) to the Deseret limestone of the Mississippian period at the entrance to the cave. Curiously, evidence of roughly 125 million years of that history, between the Maxfield formation and the Mississippian limestones, is simply missing, leaving geologists scratching their heads.

Keep a close eye on the area near the canyon entrance for bighorn sheep; in spring, sweep your binoculars along the upper flanks, toward the Lone Peak Wilderness, for the chance to see mountain goats.

Long before this canyon was sliced open by the westward-flowing American Fork Creek, groundwater laced with carbon dioxide (forming a mild acid) circulated along fractures in the Deseret limestone. Over time the water carved chambers along three separate faults. These became the three caves at Timpanogos. The area around Timpanogos Cave is one of the few examples of karst terrain—landscape where the dissolution of limestone has created an abundance of caves and sinkholes—anywhere in Utah and Colorado. As the American Fork Creek continued to downcut the canyon, it lowered the regional water table, exposing the chambers to air. Ever so slowly, water still trickling down through the soil above has deposited minerals on the walls, floors, and ceilings, forming a wonderland of massive flowstones as the water comes in contact with the cave air. On a tour of the cave you'll see sharp, delicate crystal flowers, sometimes referred to as frostwork; and an impressive array of stalagmites and stalactites, including the 6-foot-long, heart-shaped stalactite known as the Heart of Timpanogos.

Like most developed caves, Timpanogos suffered significant alterations in its early years as a tourist attraction, including new entrances and exits. This led to profound shifts in cave conditions as the increase in air flow lowered the cave's humidity and covered many of its features in dust. A restoration effort began in the early 1990s; its first step was to install double doors, creating a system of airlocks. Since then the humidity has increased, and the delicate processes of cavebuilding have resumed.

## What to See and Do

Although a climb up the **cave trail** is undeniably scenic, the subterranean spectacles awaiting you in the cave should not be neglected. The standard one-hour tour leads visitors through **Hansen Cave, Middle Cave,** and **Timpanogos Cave** before emerging from the cool, moist air; dress accordingly.

Hansen Cave holds the monument's largest column (13 feet), but the most spectacular scenery sparkles in Timpanogos Cave, where fanciful names fit the fantastical formations: The smooth coatings and sculpted flowstone terraces of the **Cascade of Energy** stand in stark contrast to the brilliant white helictites—narrow, twisting columns that can form vertically or horizontally—in the **Chimes Chamber.**

In addition to the standard cave tour, Park Service naturalists offer an excellent half-day program, "Introduction to Caving," which includes portions of Timpanogos not otherwise accessible. The staff also conducts a variety of evening programs in natural history at the cave visitor center and selected campgrounds in **Uinta National Forest,** as well as at **Sundance Ski Area** northeast of Provo.

Just west of the cave visitor center, on the north side of the road, the quarter-mile **Canyon Nature Trail** is keyed to an interpretive brochure *(available at visitor center)*. The path climbs gently from box elder and cottonwood groves into broken oak, juniper, and white fir woodlands. Along the way, notice how exposure to the sun helps determine which plants will grow on a given side of a canyon. Here, the north-facing slope, which receives less direct sunlight, holds tall clusters of white fir; the south-facing slope,

Along the trail to Timpanogos Cave

receiving more sunlight and thus retaining less moisture, manages only smaller, more scattered clusters of trees, including the tenacious Gambel oak.

## Alpine Loop Road

The roads cutting through the steep east-west canyons of the Wasatch Front offer easy access to a string of splendid preserves. Timpanogos Cave National Monument is just one of the treasures located along the stretch of Utah 92 that forms part of a U-shaped route, the **Alpine Loop Road** *(open Mem. Day–Oct.),* with US 189. This 24-mile seasonal road connects the town of Highland, on the American Fork drainage, with the town of Provo to the south. (Because the Alpine Loop Road is both narrow and winding, it is unsuitable for vehicles more than 30 feet long.)

Continue east along Utah 92 from Timpanogos Cave to the Timpooneke Campground, beside which the **Timpanogos Trail** beckons up mighty **Mount Timpanogos.** In that long, soaring line of summits along the Wasatch Front, Timpanogos is the most prominent, rising 7,000 feet above the valley floor. The trek to this magnificent summit—at 11,750 feet the second-highest (after Mount Nebo at 11,928 feet) in the Wasatch Range—is a great place for views and for close encounters with remarkable runs of remnant snowfields, alpine wildflowers, and cirque basins.

Like most trails along the Wasatch Front, this has long been an extremely popular hike with locals; if you go, count on having lots of company. (For years, an annual community day hike was held to the summit of Timpanogos. In time the event drew so many hikers that officials had to discontinue it in order to protect the resource.) Those with a shuttle car may make this a one-way hike, heading up from the Timpooneke trailhead (cooler, with more shade), then descending past Emerald Lake to a trailhead near the small community of Aspen Grove, roughly 6 miles by road from the Timpooneke Campground.

Also on the Alpine Loop Road, 8.5 miles east of Timpanogos Cave, Forest Road 114 breaks off and in 7 miles reaches a delightful interpretive area known as **Cascade Springs.** Here you'll find three short loops (together measuring barely 1 mile of trail) along a marvelous series of springs pouring out of the thin glacial till. Clearly, this water has at some point in its underground journey flowed through various limestone caverns. It deposits minerals at these springs that create a type of rock known as travertine. Over time, the one million gallons that flow from the spring each day have fashioned a thoroughly enchanting cluster of travertine pools and terraces, most of them framed by gardens of monkeyflower, monkshood, cattail, and yellow columbine.

That quilt of vegetation in turn helps support a fine array of bird life. From hummingbirds to dippers to red-tailed hawks, these winged visitors fly against the backdrop of Cascade Mountain and Mount Timpanogos, which climbs heavenward some 7 miles away in great waves of stone. ■

Rock climbing, Logan Canyon

# Logan Canyon

■ 274,785 acres  ■ Northern Utah, northeast of Logan on US 89  ■ Year-round
■ Camping, hiking, rock climbing, boating, canoeing, fishing, mountain biking,
horseback riding, skiing, wildlife viewing, scenic drives  ■ Contact Logan Ranger
District, Wasatch-Cache National Forest, 1500 E. Hwy. 89, Logan, UT 84321;
phone 435-755-3620. www.fs.fed.us/wcnf

US 89, WHICH RUNS NORTH from Arizona to Montana, is one of the most
enticing roads in the West. Rarely is it in better form than when it leaves
the city of Logan to enter the nearly vertical limestone walls of Logan
Canyon. Slicing through the abrupt, towering high peaks of the Wasatch,

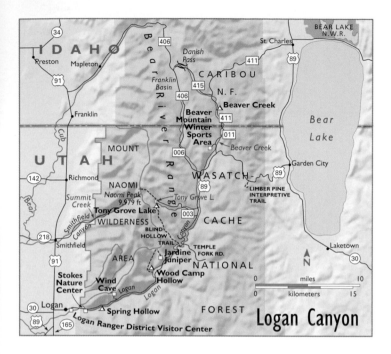

Logan Canyon

it follows the clear, fast-moving Logan River. The drive from Logan to Bear Lake takes about an hour, but the various views and trails accessible along Logan Canyon could keep you occupied for days. This route, 41 miles of which were among the first to be accorded scenic byway status by the Forest Service, offers an amazing array of scenic and recreational opportunities: bike rides on dirt roads and riverside paths; easy walks through classic riparian zones; and ambitious hikes through a wild tumble of peaks capped with subalpine and Douglas-fir.

Your first stop should be the Logan Ranger District Visitor Center at the east end of the city of Logan, where you'll find a fine collection of books and maps, hiking and camping information, and interpretive displays chronicling local history. Next to the visitor center, an outdoor interpretive stop is a great place to appreciate some of the many wonderful views—west to the Wellsville Mountains (at 5,000 feet one of the steepest inclines from base to summit of any mountain range in the world) and east to the spectacular Bear River Range.

Budding naturalists of all ages should plan a stop at the small but extremely user-friendly **Allen and Alice Stokes Nature Center** (*US 89, E of Logan 1 mile past canyon entrance. 435-755-3239. www.logannature.org*). This walk-in facility has displays of everything from plants to snakes to birds, as well as many common native plants labeled for your easy identification. There are even comfortable chairs in which to relax and peruse the center's fine collection of identification books, to help locate and name your more unusual finds.

## What to See and Do

A number of hiking and biking trails branch out from the lower portion of Logan Canyon. Two miles east of the visitor center (and accessible from the Stokes Nature Center), the hard-packed hiking-biking **Red Bridge-River Trail** winds 4.2 miles along the south side of the Logan River. Or try the 1.5-mile **Riverside Nature Trail** *(hiking only)*, located 4.3 miles east of the visitor center, on the east side of Spring Hollow Campground. This walk—a wonderland of bird life, stitched through with maple, virgin's bower, and plenty of box elder—is lush almost beyond belief. (Box elder, long appreciated by settlers for its shade, as well as by photographers for its fall colors, takes its name from its light-colored wood, which resembles boxwood. Its leaves also look somewhat like those of the elder. In some parts of the country, native people tapped box elder trees and made a sweet syrup from the sap.)

Five miles from the mouth of the canyon, the trailhead for **Wind Cave** starts a 1,000-foot climb over 1.5 miles to a beautiful set of arches with staggering views of the canyon. Looking for something longer? Try the 10-mile trek to the massive **Jardine Juniper.** The hike begins next to the Wood Camp Hollow Campground *(10.4 miles E of the Logan Ranger District Visitor Center)* and leads first through a series of open meadows bedecked with flax, scarlet gilia, fireweed, balsamroot, and penstemon. It then makes a modest climb through a forest of spruce and Douglas-fir,

skirting the edge of **Mount Naomi Wilderness.** Finally, at just under 5 miles, it arrives at the base of the giant Jardine Juniper. This stunning sweep of twisted trunk and branches is thought to be close to 1,200 years old; that would make it a seedling around the time that Charlemagne was crowned Holy Roman Emperor.

Some of the junipers in this area display pale foliage in places, with silvery white berries mixed among the normal dark blue-green berries (actually cones) of the juniper. This is mistletoe, a parasitic growth found in junipers throughout the region.

The latter portion of the trail offers grand views into Logan Canyon. You can see how the north-facing side of the cut is wrapped in thick blankets of spruce and fir, whereas the drier, more exposed south-facing slopes are home to only scattered clusters of juniper and bunchgrass.

Additional enjoyable day hikes include the **Blind Hollow Trail** *(trailhead on US 89, 14.9 miles E of visitor center),* which leads in 4 miles to the upper reaches of the Bear River Mountains. Six miles farther east on US 89, turn west on Forest Road 003, which leads in 7 miles to **Tony Grove Canyon Recreation Area.** Its centerpiece is the small but beautiful **Tony Grove Lake,** where you can canoe, picnic, fish, and camp. ("Tony" refers to the site's popularity with wealthy adventurers of the late 1800s when trendy upper-class types were known as "tonies.") Visitors can stroll around this beautiful glacial

Butterfly on thistle, Logan Canyon

lake on a self-guided nature trail. More serious hikers can set out for Mount Naomi Wilderness on any of four excellent trail systems. From the parking area at Tony Grove Lake, the trailhead is the portal for the trek to the top of **Naomi Peak,** at 9,979 feet the highest peak in the northern Wasatch. To reach it requires a climb of a little less than 2,000 feet in the course of 4 miles.

Some 11 miles farther east along US 89, shortly before Bear Lake *(about 31 miles E of visitor center),* the **Limber Pine Interpretive Trail** serves as a fine introduction to various plants and natural processes of the Utah-Wyoming Rocky Mountains ecoregion. (Take full advantage of the interpretive signs by walking this loop trail in a counterclockwise direction.) Besides the occasional delightful view, the trail offers a wonderful mix of aspen, spruce, fir, mountain mahogany, and of course limber pine, broken here and there by grassy meadows and spires of dolomite (a relative of limestone common throughout much of Logan Canyon).

The massive limber pine on the back side of the trail—once believed to be the largest limber pine anywhere—actually consists of five trees growing together, roughly 550 years old. Limber pines are exactly that: extraordinarily flexible, able to withstand the brutal winds and heavy snow loads common to the high places where this tree is most at home.

## Mountain Biking

Like so much of Utah, this northern reach of the Wasatch is ideal terrain for mountain bikes. For an excellent intermediate ride of just under 30 miles, drive 23 miles east of the Logan Ranger District Visitor Center to the turnoff for **Franklin Basin Road** (Forest Road 006). Park here, then ride roughly 3 miles up US 89 before turning left on Utah 243. Continue past the entrance of the Beaver Mountain Winter Sports Area, following Forest Road 011 across the Idaho border (it becomes Forest Road 411 at this point) toward Beaver Creek Campground. Two miles past the campground, turn left onto Forest Road 415. This will carry you through Egan Basin and across Danish Pass. Continue bearing left through Franklin Basin, turning due south on Forest Road 406 (this becomes Forest Road 006 in Utah), for a fast descent to your car.

Another good biking road (though heavy with recreational riders on weekends) is the **Temple Fork Road,** so named because much of the wood for Logan's Mormon Temple came from here. It is located off US 89, just over 15 miles east of the Logan Ranger District Visitor Center.

An excellent outing for those with eyes and ears for birds is the easy, 6-mile round-trip **River Trail,** an unimproved road that takes off from the first road on the right in Logan Canyon, half a mile above First Dam.

Though Smithfield Canyon is a magnificent entry point for hikers heading for Mount Naomi Wilderness, the 8-mile gravel road along **Summit Creek** also makes a fine, moderately strenuous bike ride *(trailhead in Smithfield, at jct. of Center St. and 300 East).* ■

# Bear River Migratory Bird Refuge

■ 74,000 acres ■ North Utah at northeastern tip of Great Salt Lake ■ Year-round ■ Hiking, fishing, hunting, biking, wildlife viewing, auto tour ■ Contact the refuge, 58 S. 950 West, Brigham City, UT 84302; phone 435-723-5887. www.r6.fws.gov/bearriver

LIKE SO MANY OF AMERICA'S great parks, preserves, and refuges, Bear River Migratory Bird Refuge was born out of the anxiety that often comes from having long turned a blind eye to the needs of other species. Two decades into the 20th century, less than 10 percent of the original marshland along the Bear River Delta remained, victim of various water diversion projects to serve the growing needs of agriculture. In 1928 Congress approved the establishment of the Bear River Migratory Bird Refuge.

Some time later, during the 1980s, unusually heavy snowmelt caused water in Great Salt Lake to rise 7 to 11 feet above its normal level, breach-

Avocet, Bear River Migratory Bird Refuge

ing the refuge's dikes and destroying much of the valuable habitat. Important food sources such as pondweed were wiped out, while migrating shorebirds lost the shallow feeding habitats they relied on. When the waters receded at the end of the decade, it took a Herculean effort—much of it by volunteers—to move more than one million cubic tons of earth and restore the refuge to a semblance of its former value to migrants and seasonal nesters.

The refuge, worth a visit at any time of year, becomes downright spectacular during the spring and fall migrations. American avocets, marbled godwits, great blue herons, and white-faced ibises arrive in great numbers, as do some half million ducks and geese. In November tundra swan flocks may swell to 35,000 birds, while December through March bald eagles, northern harriers, and rough-legged hawks are common. A 12-mile self-guided **auto tour** provides excellent wildlife-viewing opportunities *(call for road conditions Jan.-March)*. In addition to driving, bicycling and walking are also permitted along the route. ■

# Antelope Island State Park

■ 28,022 acres ■ Northern Utah, on Great Salt Lake ■ Year-round
■ Camping, hiking, swimming, boating, biking, horseback riding, bird-watching,
wildlife viewing, scenic drive ■ Adm. fee ■ Contact the park, 4528 W. 1700
South, Syracuse, Utah 84075; phone 801-721-9569. http://parks.state.ut.us/
parks/www1/ante.htm

A LANDLOCKED BODY OF WATER such as Great Salt Lake harbors the potential for wildly fluctuating water levels. Indeed, in the spring of 1983, when
the Wasatch Range unleashed an unusually heavy deluge of melted snow,
water levels rose so much that the 7.2-mile-long causeway to Antelope
Island flooded, closing the park for ten years.

In truth, fluctuating water levels had a lot to do (though indirectly)
with the name of this preserve. Low water levels allowed explorer John
Fremont and a young guide named Kit Carson to ride their horses to the
site in 1845. After dining on the plentiful pronghorn antelope they found
here, the pair named the island in thanks.

Clearly, this is one of the best places anywhere for savoring the strange
beauty of Great Salt Lake. The largest natural lake in America west of the
Mississippi River, Great Salt Lake currently measures about 1,600 square
miles. Since the water level was first measured in the mid-1800s, the lake
depth has varied some 20 feet—enough to change the location of the
shoreline by 15 miles in some places. These profound shifts are caused by

Great Salt Lake at Antelope Island State Park

the lake's lack of an outlet, which also makes Great Salt Lake six or seven times saltier than the ocean. Exactly how salty the lake is in any given year depends on how much moisture it receives, as well as how much evaporation takes place. During low water in 1963 the lake reached a salinity nine times greater than the sea; in 1988 that dropped by half, to a still impressive 4.5 times saltier. Salinity also depends on location within the lake. No matter what the spot or rate, if you've never been able to float, the high salinity here just might turn you into a creature of remarkable buoyancy.

The same high salinity makes the lake too salty to support many aquatic species, including fish, though brine shrimp and various types of algae do just fine. In addition to feeding the lake's large population of eared grebes, brine shrimp are commercially harvested here. The eggs are shipped overseas as prawn food, while the shrimp themselves become a prime ingredient in tropical fish food.

Great Salt Lake is all that remains of an enormous Ice Age body of water known as Lake Bonneville. From Buffalo Point on the northwest corner of Antelope Island, you can see the flat terraces—many perched 1,000 feet above the shoreline—that were eroded by waves from the ancient lake. At the height of the melt, Bonneville was 1,100 feet deep, it spread out into Idaho and Nevada, making islands of many of the mountain ranges visible today. Roughly 14,000 years ago, Lake Bonneville overtopped and catastrophically eroded its northern confinement, spilling a huge volume of water into the Snake River. In less than a year, a body of water that had covered nearly 20,000 square miles fell some 350 feet.

## What to See and Do

Start at the visitor center, located on the north shore past the marina. This is a fine place to get a good idea of **Antelope Island's** natural history. A number of short walks begin here, including the quarter-mile **Ladyfinger Point Trail,** which leads to the rocky **Egg Island Overlook** above a rookery used by migratory birds. From here you can view Egg Island as well as Bridger Bay. Also popular is the half-mile **Buffalo Point Trail,** a 300-foot climb to a wonderful overlook affording a broad view of the northern reaches of the island. This is also the best place to watch the sunset over the lake.

As for longer walks or rides, the 7.5-mile **White Rock Bay Loop** is well worth the time and effort; one of three spur paths off this trail climbs to **Beacon Knob,** soaring 800 feet above Great Salt Lake. Another option is the **Split Rock Bay Trail,** a 5-mile loop leading to a white sandy beach. Finally, the **Elephant Head spur** will take you to one of the most dramatic overlooks on the island, with vistas of the lake and mountains beyond.

Other, longer options allow you to explore the island's 35 miles of trails. Try the **Mountain View Trail,** an 11.4-mile trek winding from just beyond the marina south along the island's east side to the Fielding Garr Ranch. Be aware, however, that this trail is closed mid-May through mid-June for the pronghorn birthing season. Finally, you can access the island's highest peak (6,596 feet) via the 3.25-mile **Frary Peak Trail** to gain views of the entire island *(closed April-May for bighorn sheep lambing season).*

### Wildlife

Antelope Island is a wonderful place to see birds, many drawn here to feed on brine flies and brine shrimp. Walking along the shoreline you'll see California gulls, eared grebes, phalaropes, sanderlings, willet, black-necked stilts, and avocets. The surrounding grasslands, meanwhile, provide critical habitat for chukar, long-billed curlews, and even burrowing owls.

Antelope Island also contains an intriguing mix of mammals, from its namesake pronghorn antelope to mule deer, bighorn sheep, bobcats, badgers, and coyotes. You'll also find one of the largest publicly owned bison herds here, fluctuating between 500 and 750 animals. At the end of the 19th century, when America's once abundant bison herds had dwindled to a mere 800 animals, Utahans William Glassman and John Dooly laid one of the cornerstones in the effort to save them. They brought bison to the island in 1893; the animals you see today are not just genetically unique, but they belong to one of the oldest herds in the country.

An annual bison roundup takes place on Antelope Island sometime at the end of October. This is when animals are driven to corrals by a combination of volunteer horsemen and helicopters, then vaccinated and checked for general health. Because the island can support only about 700 bison, excess animals are sold at auction. ■

Balsamroot

# Deseret Peak Wilderness

■ 25,212 acres ■ Central Utah, south of Great Salt Lake ■ Best months April-May, Sept. ■ Hiking, horseback riding ■ Contact Salt Lake Ranger District, Wasatch-Cache National Forest, 6944 S. 3000 East, Salt Lake City, UT 84121; phone 801-733-2660. www.fs.fed.us/wcnf

AT SOME POINT DURING your forays into the Wasatch Front, you'll look across the great valley to the west and see the dusky flanks of the Stansbury Mountains, a classic Basin and Range uplift roughly 40 miles southwest of Salt Lake City. An engaging though somewhat demanding day hike can be made within the Wasatch-Cache National Forest along the **Mill Fork Trail,** in the heart of Deseret Peak Wilderness. This walk challenges you to climb more than 3,500 feet through a blend of aspen forest, Douglas-fir, chokecherry, bitterbrush, and a wonderful flush of wildflowers. The 8.4-mile round-trip hike leads to the summit of **Deseret Peak** and stunning views of the lonely, wind-tossed Basin and Range Country from a height of just over 11,000 feet. To the north you can see Great Salt Lake and Stansbury Island; on clear days Mount Nebo is visible to the southeast.

Taking the Mill Fork Trail to the top of Deseret Peak and continuing north and east into the Pocket Fork will turn this into a great loop hike, doable by hard-core mountaineers in a single day, or by mere mortals as a leisurely two- or three-day outing. To reach the trailhead, travel west on I-80 for 20 miles to the Tooele exit and Utah 36 and 138. Follow Utah 138 south and west into Grantsville. In the center of town, a sign for South Willow Canyon directs you left and about 12 miles along South Willow Canyon Road to the parking area. Another enjoyable area within the national forest lies to the north of this wilderness. It can be accessed by a trailhead adjacent to the O. P. Miller Campground, with paths leading along the eastern edge of the Stansbury Mountains. ■

# Uinta Mountains

■ Northeast Utah ■ Year-round ■ Camping, hiking, fishing, rock climbing, mountain biking, horseback riding, wildlife viewing, wildflower viewing, scenic drives ■ Use fee for Mirror Lake ■ Contact Kamas Ranger District, Wasatch-Cache National Forest, 50 E. Center St., Kamas, UT 84036; phone 435-783-4338. www.fs.fed.us/wcnf

LOVERS OF THE UINTA MOUNTAINS know this range for its medley of stony trails and collection of more than 2,000 quiet lakes as well as for its grand tumble of summits cradled by some of the most delightful wildflower

Riding the range above Tamarock Lake, Ashley National Forest

meadows imaginable. Indeed, with ten peaks above 13,000 feet, the Uintas are Utah's highest and most remote mountain range. Thanks to healthy levels of precipitation—more than 40 inches per year in some areas, mostly as snow—the range also provides the lion's share of the state's water supply. In addition, the Uintas are a wildlife lover's dream. Here you'll find native populations of moose, elk, black bear, marten, and mountain lion, along with reintroduced herds of bighorn sheep.

Geologists are fond of the Uintas for different reasons. It's important to understand that this range—an enormous, 150-mile-long anticline (an upward-arching fold), 30 to 40 miles wide—is part of the Rocky Mountains. At one time the Uintas were covered in thousands of feet of Paleozoic and Mesozoic sedimentary rock, all of which has since been eroded and washed down into the surrounding lowlands. What is truly unusual, however, is the range's east-west orientation, which goes against the trend of North American mountain ranges. Indeed, the Uintas are the only major east-west mountain range in the lower 48.

At 9,500 feet, the wooded shoreline of Mirror Lake curves among the Uintas's high peaks—a picturesque beauty rivaling far better known destinations. Without the overwhelming tourist traffic of other natural treasures, a stop here may reward you with glimpses of such area inhabitants as mule deer, weasels, pikas, mountain goats, and spotted cranes.

## What to See and Do
### Mirror Lake Scenic Byway

Utah 150, also known as the Mirror Lake Scenic Byway, which connects the town of Kamas, Utah (east of Park City), with Evanston, Wyoming, is a crown jewel in the two states' linked scenic byway system. Beginning in the west with a gentle climb through foothills covered with aspen and conifer, the byway rises ever higher into the clouds, passing hundreds of lakes before topping out on plateaus framed by 11,000- to 13,000-foot mountains. This outstanding high country forms the headwaters of four major rivers: the Provo, Bear, Weber, and Duschesne.

Those who intend to stop and use Forest Service facilities along Utah 150 (as opposed to merely driving through without stopping) will need to purchase a recreation pass, available at the Kamas and Bear River Ranger Stations (*50 E. Center St., Kamas, UT. 435-783-4338*), as well as at the highway entrance station just east of Kamas. All revenues from this modest fee are rechanneled to protect Mirror Lake area resources, and to subsidize the operation of recreational facilities and visitor services.

The **Mirror Lake** area, perched just outside the western boundary of the rugged **High Uintas Wilderness,** is notable for its sweeping views and for its incredible number of hiking trails that take off a mere stone's throw from Utah 150. (Though much of the backcountry is open to off-road vehicles, the higher portions of the **Lakes Roadless Area** and High Uintas Wilderness offer good opportunities to escape the drone of engines.)

Several miles east of Hayden Pass, the Mirror Lake Scenic Byway settles into a less abrupt landscape, marked by rolling high country and gentle runs of meadow filled with bistort, buttercup, marsh marigold, false hellebore, and elephant head.

### Hiking

As appealing as the Mirror Lake Scenic Byway is, these lands are first and foremost a walker's dream—combining high peaks and alpine lakes, clusters of spruce and fir, and flower-strewn meadows beyond counting. The relatively high elevation of most trailheads, combined with the abundant topography of plateau and basin, allows plenty of opportunities for meandering without significant

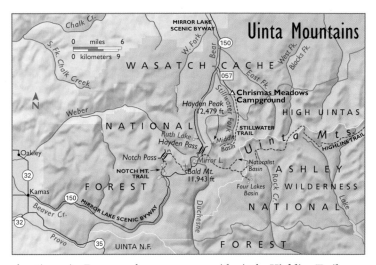

elevation gain. For example, approximately 25.5 miles east of Kamas, on the north side of the highway near Crystal Lake, the **Notch Mountain Trail** stays level for nearly 2 miles before making a modest climb on a series of switchbacks to scenic **Notch Pass.** Similarly, the 2-mile round-trip to beautiful **Ruth Lake,** located on the west side of Utah 150, some 35 miles east of Kamas, is the perfect ramble for walkers of all ages.

If you're willing to exert a little more effort for the reward of fantastic views, try the **Bald Mountain Trail,** 29 miles east of Kamas on the north side of Utah 150. This well-used path climbs 1,000 feet in 2 miles, ending on the sun-drenched, windblown summit of **Bald Mountain.** Whereas the terrain on most of these trails is fairly easy to negotiate, the paths themselves are often strewn with rocks; boots with good ankle support are a wise idea.

A variety of trailheads offer longer hikes into the High Uintas Wilderness. Among the best to consider is the **Highline Trail,** which accesses beautiful Naturalist Basin (6.5 miles one way) and Four Lakes Basin (7 miles one way) as part of a nearly 80-mile-long wilderness traverse. Equally engaging is the **Stillwater Trail** from Christmas Meadows to Middle Basin (6 miles one way). This trail is located in **Wasatch-Cache National Forest;** to reach it, turn south off Utah 150 onto Stillwater Road, about 46 miles east of Kamas, and follow the signs for the Christmas Meadows Campground.

## Red Cloud Loop Scenic Byway

This beautiful route (also known as Forest Road 018), traverses Ashley National Forest. Partly dirt, closed in winter, and not recommended in wet weather, this drive moves through majestic sandstone canyons, mixed conifer and aspen forests, and large meadow areas. Accessed from the town of Vernal (south of Flaming Gorge NRA, see pp. 158-160), there are great views of the high Uinta Mountains throughout the route. ∎

# Eastern Ashley National Forest

■ 1.4 million acres ■ Northeastern Utah and southwestern Wyoming ■ Year-round ■ Camping, hiking, boating, fishing, mountain biking, cross-country skiing, horseback riding, wildlife viewing ■ Contact the national forest, 355 N. Vernal Ave., Vernal, UT 84078; phone 435-789-1181. www.fs.fed.us/r4/ashley

THIS SPLENDID, HIGHLY DIVERSE section of the Ashley National Forest runs from the high Uintas to the red-rock deserts at the edge of Flaming Gorge (see pp. 158-160). More than 7,000 vertical feet separate the upper and lower regions of the forest, allowing for a wonderful mix of plants and animals and long seasons of hiking, camping, and wildlife-watching. Spring and late fall are often best spent in the tangle of sage, cottonwood, and red rock framing the gorge, while summer is perfect for exploring the peaks, coniferous woods and large meadows that are strewn east to west along the Uinta Divide.

## What to See and Do

If your time is limited, drive the 13-mile **Sheep Creek Loop,** which begins at Utah 44 roughly 5 miles south of Manila. The first section of the route meanders through beautiful **Sheep Creek Canyon,** where a number of good stream-access points are perfect for picnics. Eventually the road climbs to impressive views of the Uinta Fault.

Two-thirds of the way through the Sheep Creek Loop, Forest Road 221 heads west, passing near Browne Lake. (This road, easily

negotiated by cars, can become rough with washboard in summer, so allow plenty of time for getting in and out.) At **Browne Lake** hikers will delight in a network of trails heading south into the magnificent Uinta Mountains, including a 2-mile trek to the Ute Mountain Fire Lookout Tower. Equally inviting, the **Leidy Peak Trail** reaches the striking Tee Pee Lakes in 5 miles, continuing 8 more miles to the soaring views off Leidy Peak.

Roughly 17 miles farther on Forest Road 221, the lovely Spirit Lake Lodge *(435-880-3089; seasonal)* overlooks the shores of Spirit Lake amid pine and aspen forests. This area also offers easy access into the High Uintas Wilderness (see pp. 152-153), primarily on relatively quiet trails starting near the lodge and running past **Tamarack Lake** (1.5 miles), **Fish Lake** (5 miles), and **Island Lake** (10 miles).

This portion of Ashley National Forest is where you'll find the eastern end of the spectacular **Highline Trail.** It meanders nearly 80 miles along the high Uinta mountain summits from **East Park Reservoir** in the east all the way to 12,479-foot **Hayden Peak** (off Mirror Lake Scenic Byway/Utah 150) in the west. This half of the Highline Trail is much less used than the western half; it therefore offers more opportunities for peace and quiet. To reach the trailhead, head north out of Vernal on US 191 for approximately 20 miles, turning left onto Forest Road 018. In 2.5 miles Forest Road 018 veers left and becomes gravel; follow this for about

10 miles to Forest Road 043. Take this road toward Hacking Lake; the trailhead is 10 miles farther on Little Brush Creek Road, just north of East Park Reservoir.

Long before crossing the border of the High Uintas Wilderness, the Highline Trail rollercoasters in delightful (if strenuous) fashion through spruce-fir forests and wildflower-strewn meadows. It climbs 900 feet to Leidy Peak, drops most of that to amble along Chepeta Lake, then rises 1,700 feet again as it enters the wilderness.

## Mountain Biking

To put your mettle to the pedal, give the **Dowd Mountain Trail** a try. This 10-mile loop with roughly 800 feet of elevation change is best suited to intermediate riders; allow three to four hours to ride it. The trail begins along Utah 44, at the turnoff to Dowd Mountain on Forest Road 094 (about 14 miles south of Manila). From here a single-track trail runs roughly parallel to Dowd Mountain Overlook Road, offering nice views of the Uintas and ending at a breathtaking overlook of Flaming Gorge.

A large number of access roads and trails off US 191 south of the gorge are perfect for short treks through the meadows and aspen forests of the high plateaus. Pick up a map at the district office and ask for recommendations based on the conditions. In addition, Forest Road 539, off Utah 44 about 9 miles west of junction with US 191, leads to a signed network of challenging biking-hiking trails that make up sections of 18-mile-long **Elk Park Loop.** ■

Bull moose, Ashley National Forest

# Green River Days

FEW RIVERS IN THE intermountain West possess a more intriguing mix of natural and cultural history than the Green. For starters, the headwaters of the Green River lie in a phenomenal slice of western Wyoming High Country, around Fremont Peak in the Wind River Range. This glaciated region is a place of cold summer nights and lingering snowfields and ice-water streams. (Two other western rivers begin in the shadow of Fremont Peak: the Wind, which heads east toward the Missouri watershed, and the Gros Ventre, ultimately bound for the Columbia River.)

Scientist-explorer John Wesley Powell mistakenly identified this slice of high mountainscape as the real source of the Colorado River. "It runs," he said of the Green, "from land of snow to land of sun." True to Powell's description, the Green moves southward across western Wyoming through the lonely landscape of the Green River Plains, pushing into ever starker places—dry, dreamy waves of domes and pinnacles, ancient lake beds rich in fossils, cliffs, and dunes.

Then on it courses through the slack water of Flaming Gorge (see pp. 158-160), to be reborn in the wild tumbles of Colorado's Gates of Lodore. After running back through Utah in an outrageously dizzying series of twists and meanders, the Green finally joins the Colorado River in the sweet, stone bosom of Canyonlands National Park (see pp. 66-75). Along the way is the smell of sedge

Rafting the Green River near Rainbow Park, Dinosaur National Monument

and meadow grass and the sight of moose, bear, pronghorn, mule deer, and ghostly bands of desert bighorn—with enough geology en route to spin the head of even the most fervent earth scientist.

For all the history associated with the Green River, none stands out more in the American imagination than the doings of the mountain men. One, Jedediah Smith, roamed the tributaries of the Green. Flouting the stereotype, Smith neither drank nor smoked. Indeed, he was known among his peers for his religious nature—and for his survival of an unusually hair-raising experience: Mauled by a grizzly bear and left with his scalp hanging by an ear, Smith instructed a companion to reattach it as best as he could with needle and thread.

Another legendary pioneer, William Ashley, built two boats of buffalo hides and tossed them in the Green River at Flaming Gorge. He then bobbed and portaged all the way through what is now Dinosaur National Monument (see pp. 164-165). Ashley was largely responsible for hosting those famously boisterous trading-and-resupply parties known as the Rendezvous. Though trappers habitually worked alone or in small groups, once a year for 16 years (from roughly 1825 to 1840) they would gather around company wagon trains laden with goods for some of the biggest bouts of trading, drinking, lying, and fighting imaginable. Green-backs flowed like the Green River itself; according to some participants, it was not uncommon for reckless men to burn a thousand dollars a day on horses, whiskey, and women. Except for two sites—one in northern Utah and another on the Idaho side of the Tetons—all of the summer Rendezvous were held in Wyoming. Six of

those were along the upper Green River, west of present-day Pinedale, Wyoming. They included such mythic mountaineers as Jedediah Smith, Jim Bridger, William Fitzpatrick, Kit Carson, Joe Meek, and Jim Beckwourth.

The mountain men described anything of quality as being "up to Green River." Some historians think the phrase derives from knives made by Russell Green River Works. On the other hand, it's easy to imagine that the men meant the river itself—water that to this day captures the hearts and minds of nature lovers from around the world.

Many an early explorer stood on high perches and scanned the arid sprawls of the intermountain West for the telltale green of the cottonwood tree; wherever it appeared, water was close at hand. The Green River is no exception. Fom spring through fall, long, verdant ribbons of Fremont cottonwoods line its banks. Like many other plants here, cottonwood was important to native peoples for both ceremonial and medicinal purposes, helping to break fevers and reduce inflammation. Indeed, various parts of the cottonwood contain salicin and populin—both of which share properties with the active ingredients in aspirin.

Cottonwood seeds have highly specific requirements for germination. They remain viable for only about two weeks, and even then will sprout only on freshly soaked ground—a preference that corresponds to the normal spring flood cycle. With the installation of upstream dams, however, many places along the Green River no longer enjoy seasonal flooding. In the long term, sad to say, this will severely curtail the extent and growth of cottonwood groves. ■

# Flaming Gorge National Recreation Area

■ 207,363 acres ■ Northeast Utah and southeast Wyoming ■ Best seasons spring-fall ■ Camping, hiking, boating, rafting and kayaking, floating, sailing, canoeing, swimming, fishing, hunting, horseback riding, wildlife viewing ■ Adm. fee ■ Contact the recreation area, P.O. Box 279, Manila, UT 84046; phone 435-784-3445. www.fs.fed.us/r4/ashley

THIS REMARKABLE SLICE OF HIGH DESERT, red and flashing in the light of any given sunset, received its title a century and a half ago from that consum-

Red Canyon, Flaming Gorge National Recreation Area

mate explorer, Maj. John Wesley Powell. The Civil War veteran was capti-
vated by the area's Precambrian sedimentary rock formations—red shale
and siltstone mixed with red quartzite, thought to be a staggering 25,000
feet thick in places. After sighting the place in 1869, Powell wrote, "The
Green River enters the range by a flaring, brilliant red orange canyon
…composed of bright vermilion rocks….We name it Flaming Gorge."

Since 1964, the Green River has been contained in Flaming Gorge as a
reservoir and recreation area. Though 60 miles of the 91-mile-long Flaming Gorge Reservoir lie in Wyoming, the Utah portion of the recreation
area holds some wonderfully lonely country, the more dramatic scenery,
and the lion's share of visitor facilities. Moose, black bear, eagles, and elk
call the nearby forests home, and the red rock and limestone formations
reveal fossils of dinosaur bones, shark's teeth, and seashells.

## What to See and Do

Two highways, Utah 44 and US 191, officially the **Wildlife Through the Ages Scenic Byway,** offer access to the most appealing slices of Flaming Gorge. Utah 44 starts from US 191 south of the gorge, then winds 30 miles along the reservoir's southwest corner, passing through exquisite aspen and conifer woods to the village of Manila, Utah.

Along the way you'll pass the **Red Canyon Visitor Center** *(closed in winter)*—worthwhile not just for the maps and natural history information available, but also because of the excellent views it affords of both the gorge and the Uinta Mountains. This is also where **Canyon Rim Trail** begins, providing spectacular views of the gorge for roughly 2 miles. After that the trail breaks away from the canyon and heads into the woods, arriving in 5 miles at the Greendale Rest Area on Utah 44. This easy walk makes a fine one-way hike for those who have someone to shuttle a car to the rest area.

The main road into Flaming Gorge, traveling from either north or south, is US 191, also known as the **Uintas Scenic Byway.** From the south, it climbs sharply through beautiful runs of red rock into coniferous forests and some of the finest aspen woods in this part of Utah. Upon reaching Flaming Gorge, US 191 drops quickly to the dam; from here it snakes through the gorge for several more miles, finally veering off to the northeast and into Wyoming.

If you find yourself on this route, stop at the dam area for a wonderful downstream trek along the Green River on the **Little Hole National Recreation Trail.** This is a walking daydream—the Green River tumbles along in jade green pools and drops, framed by conifers and wild, rugged canyon walls. In 7 miles you reach **Little Hole,** a popular take-out point for kayakers, rafters, and experienced canoeists.

### Boating

Boating remains the most common way to see Flaming Gorge. Rentals of everything from ski boats to pontoons to canoes can be found at a variety of marinas, including Lucerne Valley Marina in Manila, Utah *(435-784-3483 or 888-820-9225),* Cedar Springs Marina in Dutch John, Utah *(435-889-3795),* and Buckboard Marina in Green River, Wyoming *(307-875-6927).* In addition, both Cedar Springs and Buckboard offer scenic tours of the canyon throughout the summer months.

If you're intrigued by the sights along the Little Hole National Recreation Trail, Hatch River Expeditions in Vernal *(435-789-4316 or 800-342-8243)* offers float trips of varying length and difficulty.

The reservoir's nooks and crannies can be good places to see a variety of waterbirds. This is especially true in the fall, when the area is rich with green-winged, blue-winged, and cinnamon teals, northern shovelers, redhead, lesser scaup, ring-necked ducks, buffleheads, and ruddy ducks. Keep an eye to the sky in summer and you're likely to see turkey vultures, ospreys, American kestrels, red-tailed hawks, and golden eagles. ■

Canoeing in Browns Park National Wildlife Refuge

# Browns Park National Wildlife Refuge

■ 13,455 acres  ■ Northwest Colorado, along Colo. 318  ■ Best seasons spring and fall  ■ Camping, fishing, boating, canoeing, biking, horseback riding, bird-watching, wildlife viewing, auto tour  ■ Contact the refuge, 1318 Hwy. 318, Maybell, CO 81640; phone 970-365-3613. www.r6.fws.gov/refuges/browns/

HUNG ON THE EDGE of a splendidly windswept no-man's land between the Wyoming Basin and the Colorado Plateau is beautiful Browns Park. This quiet, remarkably diverse slice of landscape offers wetlands of sedge and bulrush, grasslands, forests of pinyon and juniper, and riparian zones with long lines of green Fremont cottonwood.

The customary means of seeing the refuge is via an 11-mile self-guided auto tour along the north side of the Green River, which is also open to bicycles. Even better is a short float along the Green by raft or canoe, putting in at the boat ramp at Swinging Bridge Campground and taking out at the Crook Campground ramp *(supplies and fishing licenses available at Browns Park Store, Colo. 318, approximately 8 miles from Gates of Lodore; 970-365-3658).*

Although Browns Park is not a backpacking preserve, its unimproved roads serve as perfect routes for the casual ambler. Birders—especially those lucky enough to be here in the spring or fall—should explore the trail along **Beaver Creek,** near refuge headquarters, as well as **Vermillion Creek** and **Carr Bottom** in the southeast corner of the refuge.

The park's diversity extends to its wildlife. In winter hundreds of elk and mule deer drift out of the surrounding uplands to feed on the refuge bottoms, while eagles perch along the river. Spring and fall bring a huge array of both migrating and nesting birds, from white-faced ibises to pintail, as well as songbirds from warbling vireos to Bullock's orioles. And the drier, more rugged sage-and-pinyon-juniper zones host short-horned lizards and desert cottontails, sage grouse, peregrine falcons, and kangaroo rats. ■

*Following pages:* Green River, Browns Park National Wildlife Refuge

Rock art at McKee Springs, Dinosaur National Monument

# Dinosaur National Monument

■ 210,278 acres ■ Northwest Colorado ■ Year-round. Summers are hot and winters cold with moderate snowfall ■ Camping, hiking, backpacking, fishing, rock climbing, boating, biking, wildlife viewing, auto tour, rock art ■ Adm. fee; noncommercial river permit and fee required for private white-water trips ■ Contact the monument, 4545 E. Hwy. 40, Dinosaur, CO 81610; phone 970-374-3000. www.nps.gov/dino

MOST PEOPLE KNOW Dinosaur National Monument for its remarkable bone quarry 7 miles north of Jensen, Utah. At this amazing facility you can take close-up looks at a fantastic fossil quarry—a massive rock panel containing a rich toss of bones some 150 million years old. Interpretive programs are offered here, too, as well as windows through which you can watch technicians working on an array of fossils.

As a matter of fact, the **Dinosaur Quarry** occupies only a tiny corner of the national monument. Beyond it—in that portion of the reserve added when the national monument was enlarged in 1938—lies a stunning tapestry of river and canyon, accented by windswept plateaus and silent bottoms decked out in bee plant, balsamroot, penstemon, and prince's plume.

What's more, the entire region is an amateur geologist's dream. Dinosaur National Monument contains the most complete record of Earth history of any American national park—more so even than the Grand Canyon—though the intense folding and faulting of the rocks here have made it impossible to see all the strata in a single location. Here's another way to look at it: The archaeological resources of this park represent one of the most complete records of human occupation on the continent.

## What to See and Do

Within easy reach of the Dinosaur Quarry is the 22-mile **Tour of the Tilted Rocks** auto route. This long drive heads east across the Green River and along Cub Creek to a wonderful array of rock art. Hikers should plan an early morning or late evening trek along the self-guided **Desert Voices Nature Trail,** a 2-mile loop that begins across the road from the Split Mountain Campground parking lot.

When exploring this area, be aware that much of the vegetation is greatly changed from what it was before the advent of fire suppression and domestic grazing. For one thing, there's probably far more greasewood and sagebrush, which may have choked out many native grasses. Such changes in plant life have serious consequences for wildlife. Bighorn sheep, for example, are hesitant to pass through tall shrub communities to reach distant grazing areas for fear of predators they cannot see. This sometimes results in overcrowded communities of animals, leaving them more vulnerable to a variety of diseases.

Elsewhere, the feathery lavender plumes growing along many of the washes are tamarisk (see sidebar p. 52), an exotic ornamental that has overwhelmed much of the native vegetation. Tamarisk, also called saltcedar, not only absorbs far more water than most indigenous plants, it also produces salt crystals, which can destroy plants growing nearby. As the vegetative community becomes less diverse, so does the wildlife that depends on it.

A dramatic way to see Dinosaur is via **Harpers Corner Drive,** a 62-mile-long journey beginning at Monument Headquarters Visitor Center, 2 miles east of Dinosaur, Colorado. (Next to the visitor center is a short desert nature trail well worth the walk.) This is a spectacular roadway, ending at the mile-long Harpers Corner self-guided **nature trail;** the trail culminates in a staggering view of the area near **Echo Park,** 2,300 feet below, at the meeting point of the Green and Yampa Rivers.

Echo Park was once home to a colorful loner named Pat Lynch, who in the 1880s laid "claim on this bottom for my home and support." As Lynch told it, at one point he was held prisoner in Africa; he was also a naval veteran of the Civil War. Here he kept company with a strange assortment of spirits, as well as with a mountain lion that spoke to him in a voice "as fine as Jenny Lind," a reference to a popular singer of the day (hence the name of a nearby landform: Jenny Lind Rock).

Also worth a visit is the beautiful **Deerlodge Park and Campground,** located along the Yampa River, 53 miles east of Monument Headquarters. Those with high-clearance vehicles may also want to make the 71-mile drive along the **Yampa Bench Road,** connecting Harpers Corner Drive (which has a number of excellent hiking trails) to US 40. Finally, fine high-desert hiking and camping can be had at **Gates of Lodore,** near the southern part of Browns Park; for starters, try a trek along the **Gates of Lodore Nature Trail,** or check out the petroglyphs in **Irish Canyon.** ■

## Keeping One Wild River Untamed

WHEN THE BUREAU of Reclamation released its plan for the massive Colorado River Storage Project in 1950, conservationists around the country were alarmed to discover that two of the dam sites would be located in Dinosaur National Monument. One location—in Whirlpool Canyon downstream from Echo Park—would have backed up water the length of the Canyon of Lodore, as well as through much of Yampa Canyon. Besides devastating a precious wilderness resource, the plan would have paved the way for similar development in other national parks. The intense battle that followed proved a defining moment in the history of several conservation groups, including the Sierra Club.

Though conservationists prevailed here, the Flaming Gorge Dam built farther up Green River had profound

Hiking Harpers Corner above the Yampa River, Dinosaur National Monument

effects on Dinosaur National Monument. Intense spring flooding—critical for cleaning out heavy riparian thickets and cobbled spawning grounds—no longer occurs; the dam traps sediment, leaving the river less turbid. Today few of the backwater zones that once served as important feeding grounds for young fish still exist. Because dam-released water is colder than free-flowing river water, species such as the endangered Colorado squawfish now struggle to survive.

If the showdown over the Colorado River Storage Project reaffirmed the sanctity of wild areas within our national parks and monuments, it also served notice that the roots of healthy ecosystems rarely stop at borders. Today the Yampa is the last free-flowing major watercourse in the entire Colorado Plateau river system—a status that many are working long and hard to uphold. ■

Green River in the Ouray National Wildlife Refuge

# Ouray National Wildlife Refuge

■ 11,987 acres ■ Northeast Utah, near Vernal ■ Best seasons spring and fall
■ Hiking, fishing, mountain biking, horseback riding, bird-watching, wildlife viewing, auto tour ■ Travel permit required for portion of refuge on tribal lands
■ Contact the refuge, HC 69 Box 232, Randlet, UT 84063, phone 435-545-2522.
http://mountain-prairie.fws.gov/ouray; or Tribal Offices, P.O. Box 807, Fort
Duchesne, UT 84026, phone 435-722-0877 (Uintah and Ouray Reservation
travel permit).

ALTHOUGH OURAY NATIONAL WILDLIFE REFUGE hosts intriguing wildlife-
watching for much of the year (long-billed curlews and Lewis's woodpecker, for example, nest on site), it is above all a valuable stopover for
birds heading north in the spring and south in the fall. At these times
Ouray provides a haven for a fantastic display of wild wings, some of
them rather unusual: sandhill cranes to yellow-billed cuckoos, Caspian
terns to willow flycatchers.

Golden eagles are seen in all seasons; they perch on sandstone cobbles
or soar above the swath of dusky green desert that cradles the Green
River floodplain.

Ouray is one of several western refuges that uses controlled saturation
of the floodplain to mimic the spring high-water cycles common before
the advent of dams. The idea is to shallowly flood certain areas, creating
a warm, wet environment that encourages plants such as bulrush and a
host of insects and other organisms that feed visiting birds. Thanks to the
Yampa River, this portion of the Green is not completely devoid of natural flooding. The Yampa flows undammed from the northern Colorado

Rockies, joining the Green upstream in Dinosaur National Monument.

Besides wetlands and riparian corridors, Ouray offers over 1,000 acres of grassland, and more than twice that of high-desert scrubland peppered with sagebrush, greasewood, saltbush, and cactuses (including the rare Uinta Basin hookless cactus). There are fine cottonwood groves and sandstone crannies here, as well as clay bluffs and gravel terraces. Such diversity makes this a perfect home—or at least passageway—for a variety of nonavian species, including mountain lions, white-tailed prairie dogs, elk, mule deer, muskrat, raccoons, and even the occasional marmot, moose, or black bear. That clever, graceful fisherman, the northern river otter, is also spotted more and more often in the Green River and its surrounding marshes. Fishing by humans is permitted on the Green River.

The most accessible way to experience Ouray is along the enjoyable 12-mile self-guided **auto tour,** which can also be used by bicycles. Many unimproved roads in the refuge are open to vehicles, though some require high-clearance 4WD; these secondary roads also serve as excellent walking and mountain-biking routes. (Mountain biking and horseback riding permitted on auto tour and levee roads only.)

That said, the best way to appreciate this unique wildlife preserve may be to float through it—ideally, from the west end of Dinosaur National Monument (see pp. 164-165). Be forewarned though that take-out at Ouray Bridge (as well as any travel downstream past the bridge) requires a permit from the Uintah and Ouray Indian Reservation. Write or call for more information. ■

## Selenium

One of the biggest challenges facing managers at Ouray National Wildlife Refuge is high concentrations of the chemical element selenium in certain ponds and wetlands. Though selenium is critical to the health of both humans and animals, it can be extremely toxic at high levels. Too much selenium in livestock, for example, can lead to "blind staggers"—a condition noted by Marco Polo, whose horses fell ill in China while grazing on local forage.

In general, an excess of selenium can cause neurological problems, liver damage, and respiratory failure. High levels of the element are often found in soils derived from Cretaceous shale. They typically become a problem to waterfowl through irrigation drainage, as well as in agricultural areas where the soil is constantly flushed to avoid salt buildup. In the early 1980s, for instance, selenium-rich irrigation water flowing into Kesterson National Wildlife Refuge in California's San Joaquin Valley was suspected of killing thousands of ducks and geese.

Ouray's managers are screening wildlife from areas of high selenium. They are also using natural marsh plants and grasses as filters. Elsewhere, researchers are working to solve the problem through the use of microorganisms, as well as with a natural iron oxide known as "green rust"; this substance chemically converts toxic selenium to elemental selenium, which does not dissolve in water.

# Northern
# Colorado Rockies

View from Tundra Communities Trail, Rocky Mountain National Park

IT WOULD BE HARD TO NAME another natural region anywhere in the country that has kindled the hearts and spirits
of more Americans than the Colorado Rockies. In the
state's northern reaches alone stretch day after day of exciting itineraries for those who have the time—and the
sense of adventure—to explore. The northern Colorado
Rockies, defined in this book as the area north of I-70, are
especially wild: They encompass everything from the
dizzy heights of Trail Ridge Road—where it often seems

WYOM

Sierra Madre

MEDICINE
Continental
Divide
BOW-ROUTT

230 N. Platte 130

789

70

NATIONAL

SAVAGE RUN WILD.

230

HUSTON PARK
WILDERNESS

ENCAMPMENT
RIVER WILD.

Little Snake

13

CONTINENTAL DIVIDE
NATIONAL SCENIC TRAIL

ROUTT

Routt Divide Blowdown

STEAMBOAT LAKE S.P.

Elkhead Mountains

Hahns Peak

Gilpin Lake

Seedhouse

Slavonia
Trailhead

NATIONAL

400

miles          20

kilometers      30

0     20

0     30

129

MOUNT ZIRKEL
WILDERNESS

Buffalo Pass
10,300 ft

318

Maybell

40

Craig

Yampa

Elk

FOREST

60

Fish
Creek
Falls

Dumont
Lake

Yampa

40

Steamboat Springs

Rabbit Ears Pass
9,426 ft

27

131

40

N

13

16

SARVIS
CREEK
WILDERNESS

ARAPAHO
N.F.

Ripple Creek Pass
10,343 ft

17

ROUTT
NATIONAL
FOREST

Yampa

ROUTT
N.F.

134

WHITE

FLAT TOPS

COLO

64

Meeker

White

FLAT TOPS TRAIL SCENIC BYWAY

N. Fk. White

8

Trappers Lake

Stillwater
Res.

WILDERNESS

Colorado

RIVER

White

Flat Tops

The Flat Tops

NATIONAL FOREST

13

Sweetwater Cr.

Deep Cr.

Castle Peak
11,275 ft

131

COFFEE
POT
ROAD

Dotsero

Eagle

6

70

6

Rifle Cr.

Rifle

Minturn

70  6

Colorado

Glenwood
Springs

WHITE RIVER

NATIONAL

Roaring

Fork

FOREST

HOLY
CROSS
WILD.

330

Collbran

WHITE RIVER

NATIONAL

FOREST

GRAND MESA
NATIONAL
FOREST

GUNNISON
N.F.

133

MAROON BELLS-
SNOWMASS
WILDERNESS

82

Aspen

HUNTER-
FRYINGPAN
WILDERNESS

Fish Creek Falls, Routt National Forest

possible to look across the Great Plains all the way into tomorrow—to the jumble of lake-strewn cirque basins high above Steamboat Springs, and from the chains of high meadows scattered across The Flat Tops Wilderness to the hushed aspen groves of Roosevelt National Forest.

Some lucky souls devote a good chunk of their nonworking lives to scaling all 54 of Colorado's Fourteeners (peaks at least 14,000 feet high). Others make a point of exploring Colorado's more than three dozen wilderness areas. Residents and visitors alike are drawn to the water: While some are inspired to toss a kayak or raft into the Colorado or Yampa Rivers, others are driven by the desire to wet a line in the multitude of streams that drain the high country. Whatever your passion, you would probably need several lifetimes to exhaust it in this region.

The star attraction of the Colorado Rockies—those nearly endless huddles of high peaks and alpine parks that keep travelers rubbernecking from Denver to Grand Junction—spring from a complex and concealed geology. Scientists often dub the Rockies a "young" mountain range because its peaks are still forming: Even as you read this sentence, the entire region continues to be uplifted. Actually, this area was once covered by seas, sand dunes, swamps, and marshes—a shifting array of landscapes that included a previous mountain range, long since eroded, now referred to as the ancestral Rockies. Although the current peaks are indeed young, the rocks that underlie them are much older—up to 1.7 billion years. They include gneiss and schist that were metamorphosed by heat and pressure when they sat far below the Earth's crust; only later were they uplifted to high elevations, exposing the modern Rocky Mountains.

The patient hands of erosion and weathering joined forces with the impulsive processes of uplift to sculpt the Rockies into the wild wonderland we see today: The Colorado River cut down into ancient rock, leaving magnificent canyons in its wake; the freezing water splintered stone; massive sheets of glacial ice thousands of feet thick ground down from the high country. Indeed, the immediacy of such processes is visible in

Trappers Lake, White River National Forest

virtually every bend of the trail: You feel as if you've stumbled across a land fresh out of creation.

As you hike the Colorado Rockies, note the dramatic difference in plant life—and often, therefore, in animal life as well—that stems from different exposures to the sun; in being next to a mountain stream rather than 100 yards away; in growing on limestone-rich soil, not granite. Similarly, certain wildlife are highly specialized when it comes to nesting and feeding locations. The tiny kinglet, for example, tends to feast on the very tips of branches, while olive-sided flycatchers focus their efforts mostly on the crowns of pines.

This dynamic process of exploiting microclimates, or niches, whereby plants and animals find places most favorable for their growth, is one of the great joys of studying nature in the mountains. By learning the identity of individual species and noting the habitats where you most often find them, you'll soon be able to predict the plant and animal life likely to show up in any wilderness spot.

The locales profiled in this chapter have been selected for their scenic beauty as well as for their displays of geology, vegetation, and wildlife emblematic of the region. Rocky Mountain National Park, for example, offers unmatched opportunities to witness the powerful effect of glaciation on granite and the subtle ways in which a forest changes character with elevation. At lower altitudes, lodgepole pines and aspen trees (and, on the east side of the park, ponderosa pine) dominate woodland tracts. Farther up stand Engelmann spruce and subalpine fir.

The exquisite meadow complexes of Golden Gate Canyon State Park—not to mention Arapaho-Roosevelt and White River National Forests—are bedecked in breathtaking blankets of wildflowers from mid-July through mid-August. Elsewhere, elk, bear, and mountain lions find safe haven in the deep woods of Routt National Forest, while such classic migrating birds as avocets and willets, snipes and grebes, gadwalls and scaup happily splash down in the chilly waters of Arapaho National Wildlife Refuge. ■

# The Flat Tops

■ 235,000 acres ■ Northwestern Colorado ■ Best seasons summer and winter ■ Camping, hiking, backpacking, rafting, fishing, hunting, biking, wildlife viewing, caving, scenic drives ■ Contact White River National Forest, 900 Grand Ave., P.O. Box 948, Glenwood Springs, CO 81602; phone 970-945-2521. www.fs.fed.us/r2/whiteriver/contact_us.html

THE FLAT TOPS REGION, found within the northern portion of the White River National Forest, is wonderfully diverse. It is named The Flat Tops because the region was covered by a thick sequence of horizontal, resistant lava flows that eroded into flat-topped mesas, rather than the jagged

Trappers Lake, The Flat Tops, White River National Forest

sharp peaks present in the surrounding Colorado mountain ranges. The Flat Tops encompass the sunbaked gulch and ridge country surrounding Three Forks Creek as well as the soaring mountains framing Trappers Lake, the plunging canyons of Deep Creek, and the mix of scattered meadows and pocket lakes that delight the intrepid hiker.

The many miles of road threading this region lead vehicles to stellar attractions. The Flat Tops Trail Scenic Byway over Ripple Creek Pass, the twisted tangle of Forest Road 600 on its way to Coffee Pot Spring, and the beautiful reach of the South Fork are all routes well worth your attention.

But to really *see* this area, to tuck it forever in your memory, go by foot. Hundreds of miles of trail crisscross the area weaving through open meadows, spruce-fir forests, and dramatic erosional features.

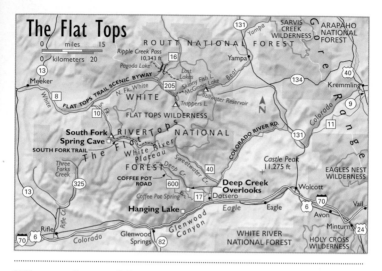

The Flat Tops

....................................................................................

# What to See and Do

## Flat Tops Trail Scenic Byway

The centerpiece of the northern half of White River National Forest is the lands in and around 235,000-acre **Flat Tops Wilderness.** The 82-mile-long Flat Tops Trail Scenic Byway, connecting Meeker and Yampa, offers wonderful access to this region, traversing the center of a landscape that was the nation's second federal timberland reserve. The **South Fork Trail** offers a gentle access into the wilderness—highlighting valley views rather than mountaintops—gained by way of the **South Fork White River.** To reach the trailhead, take the byway east from Meeker, turning right onto County Road 8. Follow this for 18 miles until County Road 10; turn right and continue 12 miles to the South Fork Campground, where the trail begins.

The South Fork is a walker's dream. Here, clear pools alternate with polished flumes of white-water while tufts of geraniums, monkeyflowers, and columbines flourish barely out of reach of the spray. Beyond the riparian zone itself the valley opens into a wide reach of grasses and mature aspen, ending abruptly on either side at the feet of some rather sheer runs of conifer and rock and sky. Near the South Fork trailhead a path breaks to the right and climbs to **Spring Cave,** a good destination for spelunkers.

Farther east on Forest Road 8, Forest Road 205 branches to the southeast, passing the 4.5-mile round-trip trail to beautiful **Skinny Fish** and **McGinnis Lakes,** which lie beneath a dramatic volcanic escarpment, the **Chinese Wall.** At the end of Forest Road 205 glitters **Trappers Lake,** an enormous blue-water jewel framed by dramatic cliffs. Beyond its camping, fishing, and boating opportunities, the lake's many trail combinations could keep you busy on outings of several hours to several days.

As you reach a point on the Flat Tops Trail Scenic Byway

Elk, Rocky Mountain National Park

## Bugle Boys

Elk tend to venture into open meadows around first light, then again at dusk. They spend most of their time in the timber, making them especially difficult to see. Because elk have a strong sense of both smell and hearing, choose your viewing location downwind from the animals, and remain as quiet as possible.

These are magnificent animals, with the large males standing 5 feet at the shoulder and weighing more than 700 pounds. Elk like to spend their summers in high pastures such as the ones near Colorado's Ripple Creek Pass. In late fall they descend to the more mild, easier grazing conditions offered in the lower valleys, often congregating in mixed-sex herds that are several hundred animals strong.

During the autumn rut, when males four to five years and older vie for breeding rights, the haunting sound of their bugling rings through the forest. These calls draw the larger bulls together, at which point a spirited battle often breaks out. Some fights last but a few minutes. Others go on for well over an hour, with the sharp antler tines occasionally inflicting serious wounds. Single calves are born in May or June, usually on the winter range but sometimes en route to the high country.

Although there's truth to the old adage that bulls tend to be somewhat less cautious in the fall—and therefore, in theory at least, easier to see—this is also when they are being pursued by hunters. This chase drives them deeper into the more remote pockets of the forest.

Fly-fishing, White River National Forest

roughly 3 to 4 miles west of **Ripple Creek Pass,** note the steep hillside on the south side of the highway. In 1898, this was the site of a fierce 80,000-acre fire, which consumed the vast majority of the spruce-fir forest that once grew here. (Fires are less common in spruce-fir forests, known for their relatively moist conditions.) As you gain views through the switchbacks, observe the dynamic patterns of regrowth that have occurred.

Before the fire, this part of the White River Valley was primarily Engelmann spruce and subalpine fir; now the forest is mainly such

pioneer trees as aspen and lodgepole pine. These trees—unlike spruce, and especially fir—are able to sprout quickly in areas exposed to full sun. As a result, the drier, south-facing hills along this portion of the highway may be dominated by lodgepole, rather than spruce and fir, for decades to come.

From the scenic overlook just west of Ripple Creek Pass, The Flat Tops spread out to the south—open swaths of grass framed by dark clusters of subalpine fir and Engelmann spruce. Such woods are often called snow forests because of their fondness for the

high country. The trails to **Lost** and **Pagoda Lakes,** south and north of Ripple Creek Pass, now and then pass through dark, nearly primeval woods, the understory thick with shade-loving moss and currents as well as huckleberry, pipsissewa, and arnica. Such woods are often scattered with blowdowns, making off-trail travel difficult. Though fir and spruce stand tall in this area, they get shorter the higher you climb. Finally they grow nearly prostrate, hugging the ground in the face of the icy winds and blowing snow.

Besides the fabulous blend of forest and meadow, these upper reaches are home to one of the largest elk herds in the country (see sidebar p. 179). The Flat Tops herd contains some 20,000 animals—a far cry from conditions at the end of the 1800s, when overhunting nearly exterminated the population.

## More Scenic Drives

Many other dramatic entry points into The Flat Tops are scattered through the northern half of White River National Forest. Of special note are **Coffee Pot Road** (County Road 17 and Forest Road 600) and **Sweetwater Creek,** located north of Dotsero. Sixteen miles up Coffee

Pot Road, a pair of short, easy trails lead to overlooks of **Deep Creek.** Seen some 2,300 feet below, it flies headlong through a magnificent twist of canyon, much of it lined with dark huddles of Douglas-fir. You can often spot grazing elk in the high sweeps of meadow across the canyon; beyond the Colorado River Valley, far to the east, rise Castle Peak and the Gore Range.

Adjacent to the small parking area for the Deep Creek Overlooks grows the oldest living thing in this national forest: an ancient limber pine, thought to have sprouted around the year 1300.

The entire region receives heavy use during July and August. Consider visiting after Labor Day, but keep a close eye on changes in the weather.

### Hanging Lake

Just off I-70 you can savor a small jewel of the northern White River National Forest by making the short, steep climb to Hanging Lake (*trailhead off rest area at Hanging Lake exit off I-70 E, on left before bridge*). No dogs are allowed, and be sure to bring drinking water.

With a climb of just over 1,000 feet in slightly more than a mile, this isn't exactly a walk in the park. Still, the destination is so exquisite—a small lake framed by conifers, cottonwoods, and limestone cliffs, with a small but broad and lovely waterfall dropping into the north end—that whatever discomfort you experience will soon be forgotten. Indeed, were you to set about dreaming up the perfect place to while away the day, it would likely look very much like Hanging Lake.

A geologic fault caused the lake bed to drop away from the valley floor above, leaving a basin to be filled by **Bridal Veil Falls.** Water pounding the limestone dissolved its carbonates, which in turn were deposited on the shore. Keep to the boardwalk, as the fragile shoreline breaks easily. Even swimming is prohibited here; body oils in the water would affect the carbonates.

Two-tenths of a mile north on a well-marked trail, an underground stream exits through a hole in the cliff to form a beautiful waterfall. This feature has long been known to locals as **Spouting Rock.** ■

### Roll Over, Aldo!

Although scholars often trace the origins of wilderness preservation to the work of Aldo Leopold in New Mexico's Gila National Forest in the late 1920s, the concept actually took root a decade earlier, in 1919, at Trappers Lake. That year Forest Service landscape architect Arthur H. Carhart was sent out to survey the lakeshore for the development of summer cabin sites.

When Carhart beheld the lake's magnificent shoreline, however, he quickly concluded that no such development should occur. The best way to "use" this resource, Carhart determined, would be to keep it in pristine condition for wilderness recreation. Thanks to this visionary, Trappers Lake was set aside as a preserve, free of permanent development—the first such preservation action on Forest Service lands.

Camping at sunset, Routt National Forest

# Routt National Forest

■ 1.2 million acres ■ Northwestern Colorado, near Yampa ■ Year-round
■ Camping, hiking, backpacking, biking, fishing, mountain biking, downhill skiing,
cross-country skiing, snowshoeing, horseback riding, wildlife viewing ■ Contact
Medicine Bow-Routt National Forests, 2468 Jackson St., Laramie, WY 82070;
phone 970-879-1870. www.fs.fed.us/mrnf/mbrwelcome.htm

ENCOMPASSING MORE THAN A MILLION ACRES, Routt National Forest (named
after Colorado's first governor) is a mountain-lover's paradise. The forest
ranges in elevation from around 7,000 feet in the valleys to more than
13,000 feet along the Continental Divide. It contains the headwaters of
the North Platte River, which flows east to the Missouri, as well as the
Yampa, which remains one of the last un-dammed major waterways in
the entire Colorado River watershed. US 40 is the principal access route
to many of the Routt's major recreation areas, and in itself offers some
rather stunning vistas, including a grand crossing of the Continental
Divide at Rabbit Ears Pass.

A wide variety of wildlife resides among the long, sweeping meadows
and rugged uplands of the forest. Elk, deer, black bears, moose, mountain
lions, pronghorn, and the occasional bighorn sheep may be spotted,
going about their lives. For anglers, the sparkling streams and placid lakes
of the highlands provide excellent fishing.

## What to See and Do

Even if you're simply passing through the area, at least explore the trail from Dumont Lake Campground to the "ears" of **Rabbit Ears Pass,** the shaped remains of volcanic plugs forming the western end of the Rabbit Ears Range. Three miles east of Steamboat Springs, at the end of Fish Creek Road (Forest Road 320), a short walk leads to where **Fish Creek Falls** drops almost 300 feet in a glorious spray. This popular path serves as a beautiful first look at one of the hundreds of enchanting riparian corridors of the Routt. Continue on the increasingly less populated path as it ascends to **Fish Creek Canyon,** topping out in about 6 miles with glorious views along the Continental Divide. Several lakes and subalpine meadows along the way provide perfect settings for backcountry camping.

### Mount Zirkel Wilderness

The lands east and north of Steamboat Springs boast a variety of high

Riding along Dumont Lake, Routt National Forest

country destinations in and around 160,000-acre Mount Zirkel Wilderness—one of the original preserves set aside as part of the 1964 Wilderness Act. Ice flows from the last glacial epoch some 18,000 years ago scoured the area's peaks and basins, excavating hundreds of bowls that filled with water to become lakes. Though the mountains here are generally less rugged than those in other Colorado ranges, the Mount Zirkel area is rich with beauty, both in the sweeping meadows that drape the high country and in the spry,

timber-lined creeks that fast-step east and west off the divide.

Access roads to numerous trailheads and three developed campgrounds may be found along the west side of this Continental Divide region, from County Road 129 running north from Steamboat Springs to Hahns Peak. An example, the **Slavonia Trail** *(trailhead just east of Seedhouse Campground)* travels in 4 miles to **Gilpin Lake** and the heart of this scenic area.

Also outstanding, the Flat Tops region (see pp. 176-182) extends into Routt National Forest and can be accessed via a network of trails. One, the lovely **East Creek Trail,** begins at Stillwater Reservoir southwest of the town of Yampa.

Heavy snows in the high country of Mount Zirkel Wilderness—more, in fact, than anywhere else in Colorado—create a unique phenomenon known as ribbon forests. In such places spruce-fir trees line up in a curious pattern of narrow strips, like so many snow fences, each one separated by swaths of meadow. Beyond the knowledge that this growth pattern is a function of heavy snow loads, ribbon forests are little understood. One of the best places to see them is just south of Buffalo Pass, via Forest Road 60, northeast of Steamboat Springs.

## Environmental Education

While in Steamboat Springs, take time to visit the extraordinary nonprofit organization **Yampatika** *(10th and Lincoln. 870-879-8140).* Dedicated to the interpretation of the Yampa Valley and surrounding regions, it works closely with Routt National Forest. Summer offerings range from guided walks at Fish Creek Falls to flotillas on Steamboat Lake, tree identification tours, campfire programs, moonlight hikes, and walks among the flowers at **Yampa River Botanic Park** *(1000 Pamela Ln. 970-870-0173).* The extensive collection of labeled native plants here allows budding naturalists to learn how to identify the lion's share of species present throughout northern Colorado. ■

## Uprooting the Routt

On a cool morning in late October 1997, fierce winds in excess of 120 miles per hour screamed out of the east across the Continental Divide. In a remarkably short time, a slice of Routt National Forest roughly 30 miles long and 5 miles wide—some four million trees—had been toppled, either torn out by the roots or snapped off at the trunk. A great many of these trees were subalpine fir and Engelmann spruce, both of which sport relatively shallow root systems. Most winds in this region prevail from the west, so the trees were particularly vulnerable to a hard eastern blow.

As the Forest Service reopens trails in the affected area, hikers can get an intriguing glimpse into how such lands sprout life anew. Spruce and fir seedlings will grow relatively easily in the shade and loosened soil of log and root debris. Branches of subalpine fir, pushed onto the ground but still connected to live roots, may begin again as new trees. Sun-loving lodgepole pine may take over open areas, to be replaced one day by shade-tolerant spruce and fir. Cavity-nesting birds and woodpeckers will increase in number, while elk and pine squirrels will probably go elsewhere.

A good place to see the blowdown is along a stretch of the Continental Divide Trail northeast of the Slavonia Trailhead *(end of FR 400, N of Steamboat Springs).* Exercise caution if you decide to visit this area. Some of the standing trees, destabilized during the storm, may be prone to falling. Likewise, piles of toppled trees will be settling for years to come.

Arapaho National Wildlife Refuge

# Arapaho National Wildlife Refuge

■ 24,804 acres  ■ Northern Colorado, near Walden  ■ Best months May-Oct.; peak waterfowl migrations in late May and late Sept. or early Oct.  ■ Hiking, bird-watching, wildlife viewing, auto tour  ■ Contact the refuge, 953 Cty. Rd. 32, Walden, CO 80480; phone 970-723-8202. www.r6.fws.gov/refuges/arapaho/

FORMER RANCHES ARE NOW HOME to a different breed altogether in the middle of North Park, the high mountain basin northwest of Rocky Mountain National Park. Developed by the Fish and Wildlife Service into an important refuge for migratory waterfowl and geese, visitors to the Arapaho National Wildlife Refuge are likely to see ducks, yellow warblers, grebes, snipes, Wilson's phalaropes, avocets, and willet. A half-mile **interpretive boardwalk trail** wanders along the Illinois River through willows and wet meadows, offering close-up encounters with gadwalls, lesser scaup, and mallard.

The refuge is managed for wildlife, so human activities are limited. There is no picnicking or camping, and the several unpaved county roads that cross the refuge may be closed to protect the habitat. However, the self-guided **auto tour,** supported by a well-done brochure, covers about 6 miles of unpaved road through uplands and grassy meadows and past several ponds. In addition to bird life, you'll notice cows, used here as a management tool to mimic bison grazing patterns. These areas also serve as winter range for elk and deer.

Arapaho is also an outstanding place to see moose, reintroduced to the mountains southeast of here by the state in the late 1970s. The new arrivals have thrived. Though they often prefer the mountains in summer, moose have shown up in the river here in the middle of August. ■

# Rocky Mountain National Park

■ 265,383 acres  ■ North-central Colorado, near Estes Park and Granby  ■ Best months Sept.–early Oct.; Trail Ridge Rd. open late May–mid-Oct.  ■ Camping, hiking, backpacking, fishing, biking, mountain climbing, rock climbing, horseback riding, cross-country skiing, bird-watching, wildlife viewing, wildflower viewing, scenic drives  ■ Adm. fee. Fishing permit required  ■ Contact the park, 1000 Hwy. 36, Estes Park, CO 80517; phone 970-586-1206. www.nps.gov/romo

IF IT WEREN'T SO ACCURATE, the name Rocky Mountain National Park might seem presumptuous. After all, the Rocky Mountains extend from northern Canada all the way to Mexico, forming one of the largest, most

Emerald Lake, Rocky Mountain National Park

spectacular natural landscapes in the world. Can one park capture all of that? The answer is yes, as proved by this perfect sampling of the region's most stunning natural wonders.

Especially outstanding are the park's alpine areas, draped across the Continental Divide. Here the evidence of glaciation is both stunning and obvious: U-shaped valleys, cirques, and moraines create the impression that the glaciers broke camp only yesterday. More than 30 percent of the park is at or above timberline, accessible in part via Trail Ridge Road, one of the nation's great scenic highways, which climbs to over 12,000 feet with a dozen miles traversing alpine tundra.

One of the road's most impressive features is its abundance of exposed rock, which relates the region's geologic story. At Rock Cut, for example, are veins of pink pegmatite that solidified 1.5 billion years ago from liquid magma, which worked its way upward through the surrounding dark gneiss and schist. At Many Parks Curve you can see a huge exfoliation dome on the side of McGregor Mountain: Erosion released pressure on a covered dome of granite, allowing it to expand and crack into smooth, curved rock sheets that look like the skin of an onion. A number of mountains on the park's east side offer close-up views of granite—interlocking crystals of gray quartz, white feldspar, and black mica that formed when huge magma bodies froze 1.5 billion years ago.

After being uplifted millions of years ago, the rocks started eroding. The most effective erosional forces were glaciers, which scraped their way through in several periods, from 750,000 to 12,000 years ago. Though the highest points in the park were above the glaciers, snowfields in areas protected from wind or sun year-round grew into rivers of ice that scoured the valley bottoms. Rocky Mountain National Park's high country features many cirques, or basins with steep walls that once served as headwalls for these glaciers. When cirques back up on one another, they create spiky ridges called arêtes or pyramid-shaped peaks called horns. Because winds blew snow from the west, snowfields generally formed on the east side of the mountains; this led to the dramatic sculpting of pinnacled valleys on the east side of the park, leaving the west side more gentle and rounded.

## Low Life in High Places

The stunning array of midsummer flowers is a big attraction of alpine tundra—a beautiful reminder of the plants' need to bloom and reproduce within the span of an extremely short growing season. The biggest challenge to plant life on the tundra is the fierce, bitter cold. Even in summer the average temperature here is only 50° F; the year-round average is below freezing. In addition, these highlands are buffeted by fantastic winds.

Tundra plants have adapted to both conditions by staying low to the ground, nearer the sun-warmed surface and less exposed to big blows. Some plants—such as moss campion, with its glorious pink blossoms—grow in dense mats.

What you see on the surface, however, is just that: a cover story. A plant such as claytonia may poke but a few inches above the ground; its root system, meanwhile, plunges 2 feet or more down into the ground, yielding stability and nutrients. The taproot of the big-rooted spring beauty often extends down more than 6 feet; the roots store the sugars generated by summer photosynthesis over the winter, releasing them as energy to spur growth at the first sign of spring.

Other plants excel at tundra life by shunning the flower-and-seed reproduction process. They may grow new shoots from root structures, or send tiny runners over the ground. Like the alpine bistort, they may even produce ready-to-sprout bulbs that begin their new lives as soon as they fall from the stem.

Herds of elk (see sidebar p. 179) frequently browse the park's high meadows in summer, attracting large crowds of people. Since they were reintroduced here from Yellowstone National Park in 1913, elk have done very well. Today more than 3,000 live in the park, and although the herds are not as large as those in Yellowstone, they are impressive nonetheless. You may also see bighorn sheep and mule deer browsing the tundra; marmots and pikas often poke their heads in and out of rocky areas.

Lower elevations can be spectacular in their own right. On the east side of the park, the classic mountain valleys offer meandering streams, majestic conifers, and dramatic vistas. In late spring an explosion of wildflowers such as pasqueflowers and wild irises add color, and fall's aspen gold seems far richer than anything mined from the ground. Autumn is also when elk visit the lower meadows, while bighorn gravitate to the mineral licks at Sheep Lakes.

The flip side to this natural splendor is the nearly overwhelming crowds that dominate the park in midsummer. The few unreserved campsites usually fill before noon, traffic clogs Estes Park, and popular trailhead parking lots can be filled by 7 a.m. Spring and fall offer fewer crowds but more uncertain weather, with Trail Ridge Road closed from mid-October to late May. If you must visit in midsummer, have a plan (ideally with lodging or camping reservations), get going early in the morning, and expect to share this outstanding park with at least a few fellow fans.

Rocky Mountain National Park

## What to See and Do

The Beaver Meadows Visitor Center, located at the main Estes Park entrance, is a great place to get oriented. Books, maps, and summary materials, as well as friendly rangers, can help you plan your visit. Or start your park experience with a scientific overview of the park's natural and cultural history at the **Moraine Park Museum** *(Bear Lake Rd.)*. Housed in an attractive old log building about a mile and a half from the visitor center, the museum's several interactive exhibits appeal to youngsters.

Outside, a nature trail identifies numerous common plants, from tansy aster to bitterbrush to serviceberry, and offers vistas of the gorgeous **Moraine Park** valley. It may be more enjoyable to learn in the museum and then walk the trail on your own, as the trail's brochure *(fee)* repeats much of the information from inside.

Starting at the museum is an especially good idea if you arrive on a summer afternoon, when the region's extreme lightning storms are likely. Indeed, the high peaks of central Colorado get more lightning strikes than anywhere in the country except central Florida, and the tundra and meadows provide little shelter. This is one reason trailheads fill up so early—hikers have been struck by lightning, most of which occurs in the afternoon.

If you find yourself in a lightning storm, get down off the summits and ridges and stay away from prominent trees. If you are caught in an open field, crouch low in a depression—tucking your head and arms in—until the storm passes.

### Trail Ridge Road

A crucial first step to any visit to Rocky Mountain National Park is a drive over Trail Ridge Road (US 34). Rising from the park's Beaver Meadows entrance in the east, it twists and turns with such abandon that drivers are continually stunned by the shifting views: meadows and moraines, forests and snowcapped peaks. Eventually it rises above tree line to follow a ridge—**Trail Ridge,** in fact, hence the road's name—for a good dozen miles.

Particularly dramatic along this route are the drop-offs on either side of the pavement. Unlike most mountain roads, which were constructed through passes to provide the fastest, easiest approach to the other side, this one was built for the opportunity to appreciate the dazzling surroundings. Cirques and valleys abound in every direction, while several pull-offs provide opportunities to get out and admire the scenery and wildlife along the Continental Divide.

A few of the turnouts are especially notable. At **Forest Canyon,** a very short (one-eighth of a mile) trail leads to an overlook of a gigantic glacial valley. The bottom is forested, while the far side is pockmarked with cirques. The glacier that excavated this wonderland formed in a valley along a major fault line, which accounts for its straight, simple structure.

At **Rock Cut,** not only do you drive along an impressive run of metamorphic rock (take note of the veins of pegmatite, a younger

*Following pages: Never Summer Mountains*

igneous rock), but you can also hike the **Tundra Communities Trail.** Less than a mile long, it's one of your best chances to properly enjoy the tundra, learning about features such as solifluction terraces, formed when freeze-thaw cycles cause water-saturated soil to flow downhill. Also note the patterned ground, where "streams" (networks of broken rock that were thrust up during similar freeze-thaw cycles) are visible.

Many visitors turn back at Fall River Pass. However, Trail Ridge Road's less crowded west side is wonderful and should not be missed. From the Continental Divide 4 miles west, the road descends rapidly into the Colorado River valley. At this point near its headwaters the river is about three hops wide, meandering along the bottom of a U-shaped glacial valley.

Signage alerts you to one great place to enjoy it all—a stroll along the easy half-mile trail through **Never Summer Ranch.** Here, forests anchor the sides of the valley, high peaks guard the headwaters, deer graze in meadows, and raptors fly overhead—the sort of "ranch" experience that otherwise exists only in Robert Redford movies. It's also a perfect place to watch normally wary wildlife such as elk (see sidebar p. 179) or moose at dusk.

Farther downstream, the half-mile wheelchair-accessible **Coyote Valley Trail** emerges from tall spruce to follow the river upstream, with wonderful views of paintbrush-dotted meadows. Interpretive signs discuss the riparian ecosystem and the valley's history. Elk may also be seen here.

## Old Fall River Road

Another nearby scenic drive follows Old Fall River Road (*guidebook available at visitor centers*) up a back canyon, to the Alpine Visitor Center (*closed for renovation in 2001*) at the summit, Fall River Pass. This one-way, uphill dirt road is not suitable for larger vehicles. Compared with Trail Ridge Road, it offers fewer switchbacks and vistas, but this route allows you to more fully appreciate the rise through the montane, subalpine, and alpine tundra ecosystems.

## Mountain Hikes

Some popular mountaintop day hikes include **Flattop Mountain, Longs Peak,** and **Twin Sisters Peaks.** The strenuous day hike to Flattop (accessed from the Bear Lake trailhead) gains almost 3,000 feet in 4.5 miles, with stunning views from the Continental Divide.

The shorter (3.7 miles) hike up the Twin Sisters Peaks, accessed from Colo. 7 east of the park, is more suitable for the average walker, but still requires an elevation gain of 2,300 feet.

Longs Peak, also reached from Colo. 7, is the park's highest mountain—a landmark visible for a good 100 miles. Despite the strenuous nature of the trek (8 miles, gaining almost 5,000 feet), the trail is often very crowded. This mountain was named for Maj. Stephen H. Long, who explored the area on a military survey in 1820. Its first recorded climb was made by Maj. John Wesley Powell during his geographic and topographic study of the Colorado River in 1869.

Yellow-bellied marmot

## Whistle While You Watch

Most walks on talus slopes near timberline have a certain lyrical quality to them—an almost steady pattern of whistles and teeth-chattering trills, each announcing your approach. The whistling watchmen are marmots and pikas, ever on the lookout for intruders.

The pika is especially fleet of foot, scurrying about the rocks with great energy. Also known as a haymaker, this tiny member of the rabbit family spends its long summer days gathering plants for winter. Before storing this stash (which may grow to four bushels), the pika drapes the plants on rocks to dry—a tactic that obviates mold damage. Walk the high country often enough, and time and again you'll come upon these minuscule haystacks of grasses and stems, laid out in the sun. Just as we might race to get laundry off the line before it rains, so do pikas scamper about the boulders when a storm threatens, carrying their collections to shelter.

The much larger yellow-bellied marmot seems to have it easier here in the highlands. Sometimes called the "rockchuck" because of its preference for the rockier areas of western North America, it leads a simple life: Eat, sleep, sun. During the tough winter months, rather than cache food stores as the pika does, the "whistle pig" (as it is also known) snoozes the season away. With the first snows of September, the marmot retreats to an underground den; there it burns up its fat stores while hibernating all winter long, sometimes losing more than half its body weight in the bargain.

Next time you take a break at tree line, settle onto a warm boulder field and watch quietly for these two animals. The marmot, you may note, seems to have a favorite rock from which it belts out its high whistle. Similarly, the pika often calls its distinctive squeak from a rock splattered with red-orange lichen, a plant that flourishes under its steady nitrate bath of pika urine.

Calypso Cascades, Rocky Mountain National Park

## Lake Hikes

Rocky Mountain National Park holds a total of 146 lakes, many of which can be reached via the park's 347 miles of trails. Shorter trails abound on **Bear Lake Road** above Moraine Park.

**Bear Lake** itself is a small, scenic gem surrounded by thick spruce-fir forest, broken here and there to reveal close-up views of rocky peaks. A wide, smooth, accessible half-mile nature trail *(guide available at visitor centers and parking lot booth)* circles the lake. The views of barren mountain peaks are more dramatic from the far side of Bear Lake, especially from the aspen grove at stop no. 10. Stop no. 18 is an opportune place to pause and reflect on the power of avalanches: One of them brought a collection of enormous boulders to rest here beside the trail.

**Dream** and **Emerald Lakes** are accessed from the same trailhead, by way of a partially paved path through lodgepole pine, Douglas-fir, and occasional stands of aspen. After half a mile you'll reach tiny **Nymph Lake,** covered with lily pads. Notice the variety of trees in this subalpine forest: Engelmann spruce, blue spruce, limber pine, and lodgepole pine.

The trail climbs steadily for a quarter mile, offering views back down the valley you drove up; from this vantage point you can see how glacial moraines enclose the valley. After an open, rocky stretch the path enters aspen and pine forest before curving into gorgeous Dream Lake Basin.

Farther back down the valley on Bear Lake Road, **Sprague Lake,** surrounded by a half-mile wheel-chair-accessible path, is worth a look. Compared with places such as Bear Lake, Sprague Lake is more open, with thinner forests and therefore better views of the surrounding mountains. Here, too, the best views open up as you get halfway around the lake, where you can get a good look at the glacial cirques on Flattop Mountain and Hallett Peak.

This trail also provides entry to a great, wheelchair-accessible backcountry campsite. Away from the lake in a mixed pine forest next to an aspen stand, this wonderful find features a tent site, table, fire ring, and bear boxes.

From the trailhead at Glacier Gorge Junction, one-eighth of a mile before Bear Lake, a view of Glacier Creek thundering over the **Alberta Falls** may be had by hiking about a mile round-trip. Other popular, single-day destinations include **Bierstadt Lake, Cub Lake, Fern Lake,** and **Lawn Lake,** all on the east side of the park.

## Fishing

In 1975, after years of stocking non-native fish, the Park Service began restoring such indigenous species as the Colorado River cutthroat and the greenback cutthroat trout. The latter, currently an endangered species, is catch-and-release only. You must have a Colorado fishing license *(available at park offices),* and use artificial flies and lures—children under 12 can use worms. The many beautiful lakes and rivers are tempting, but check at a visitor center before fishing; some are closed, some are fishless, and some are exclusively catch-and-release. ■

# Of Quaking and Cloning

THE MOST PREVALENT tree in North America is anything but ordinary. Of the many far-flung corners of the continent in which the aspen grows, nowhere does it seem more glorious—nowhere does it possess more power to revive the spirit of the weary traveler—than in the highlands of Utah and Colorado.

True, these are not the complex, highly diverse hardwood forests of the East and Middle West. Yet be it in summer, when larkspur and columbine gather at their feet, or in autumn, when their leaves flash gold in the long, clean light, walking through a mature aspen forest remains one of America's transcendent outdoor experiences.

Aspens typically grow 40 to 100 feet tall, with a trunk diameter of 23 inches or more. The full common name of this tree, quaking aspen, refers to the fact that its heart-shaped leaves tremble at the slightest hint of a breeze. The sound of this distinct flutter is a comforting whisper; along with the characteristic tang of tannin, it often betrays the tree's identity.

A naturalist would tell you that the quaking occurs because the aspen's long leafstalks, or petioles, are flattened contrary to the plane of its leaves. Other, more fanciful explanations abound: According to the voyageurs of Canada, aspen furnished the wood for the cross, and the tree has not stopped quaking since.

Besides boasting a broad geographical distribution—from California to Alaska, from Minnesota to Maine to Mexico—aspen is the only tree that grows in every mountain ecozone except the tundra. Indeed, the tree's most significant deterrents are heat and drought, not cold. Aspen grows best in middle- to upper-mountain zones, where winters are fairly cold but summers are warm, and moisture—either rain or snow—comes in annual quantities of at least 25 inches.

Aspen, a pioneer species, quickly overtakes areas disturbed by fire, blowdown, or avalanche. Key to this rapid advance is the aspen's ability to regenerate through clonal growth—in other words, by sprouting new trees (so-called suckers) from a parent root system. This is why the aspen forest you see sprawling across a mountainside is usually a collection of clone groups. To find where one clone group ends and another begins, examine leaf development: The leaves of a single clone group have the same shape and size, and they all change color at the same time in the fall; they even turn an identical shade of gold or orange.

When it comes to survival, aspens have some interesting tricks up their trunks. The bole and branches store prodigious amounts of water, enabling the leaves to draw on this moisture in times of drought. Should the leaves be killed by a late freeze—or should the canopy be devastated by insects—aspen is one of the few trees with enough chloroplasts in its bark (hence its sometimes greenish tint) to carry on a lower but still productive level of respiration.

In many areas but not all, aspen is a temporary resident. It will be replaced one day by more shade-tolerant species such as Engelmann and Colorado blue spruce, Douglas-fir and subalpine fir—members of the so-called climax community. On the other hand, an aspen woods containing little understory but grass or shrubs—no

Aspen grove

conifers and no young aspen trees—could be a place where suckers are being heavily browsed by cattle or wildlife, a condition that will eventually deplete the vigor of the rootstock.

The list of species supported by this tree reads like *Who's Who in the Wildlife World*. The buds and bark are an important food for everything from moose to bears, rabbits to elk, deer to grouse. And don't forget the beaver: It finds the inner bark of aspen more appealing than any other food, including willow, cottonwood, or alder.

Birds, too, are at home in aspens. Woodpeckers excavate nests in the trunks, creating cozy homes later used by swallows, nuthatches, or bluebirds. ■

# Arapaho and Roosevelt National Forests

■ 1.5 million acres  ■ Year-round  ■ Camping, hiking, backpacking, rock climbing, boating, white-water rafting and kayaking, canoeing, fishing, hunting, biking, mountain biking, horseback riding, downhill skiing, cross-country skiing, snowshoeing, bird-watching, wildlife viewing, scenic drives  ■ Fee for toll road and some parking areas  ■ Contact the national forests, 1311 S. College Ave., Fort Collins, CO 80524; phone 970-498-2770. www.fs.fed.us/arnf

CRADLING THE MAGNIFICENT UPLANDS of Rocky Mountain National Park, Arapaho and Roosevelt National Forests (now administratively linked, though frequently referred to as separate entities) boast qualities similar to those of the more famous park—as well as similar problems.

The attributes have much to do with the high peaks of the Continental Divide, which generally separate these two forests along a north-south axis. With its endless runs of craggy, snowy peaks, enormous forests, and icy streams, the divide seems bigger here than anywhere else in the country. In these areas, the land falls away with such abandon that it feels as if all America is sprawling out beneath you.

These national forests contain a string of beautiful wilderness areas—including Rawah, Neota, Cache la Poudre, and Commanche Peak to the north; Never Summer Wilderness to the west; Indian Peaks to the south; Byers Peak and Vasquez Peak farther to the southwest; and Mount Evans to the south of I-70. Though their status protects them from man-made development, the more accessible areas can leave many visitors with a clear sense of the notion that the Colorado wilderness is being loved to death. In these so-called urban-interface forests, closely linked to the populations of Denver, Boulder, and Fort Collins, many trailhead parking lots fill early, most campgrounds ask for reservations, and certain wilderness areas require camping permits.

## What to See and Do

### Cache la Poudre-North Park Scenic Byway

This enjoyable drive offers numerous accesses to wilderness areas and hiking trails. It runs 101 miles east-west across the northern portion of the forests, along the **Cache la Poudre River Valley** from Fort Collins to Walden. The name refers to French trappers of the 1820s who allegedly stashed their gun-powder along this river; the name means "hide the powder."

The road climbs out of juniper and cottonwood country into gorgeous stands of aspen mixed with ponderosa and, at higher elevations, lodgepole and spruce. Bitterbrush and mountain mahogany provide winter nourishment for deer. At some points along the river, the cliffs rise 3,000 feet high.

Fly-fishing on Big Thompson River

The popularity of the Cache la Poudre River, Colorado's first national wild and scenic river, grows stronger each year. The river's volume stays fairly high through the summer, as water is diverted from a variety of other river basins.

**Cache la Poudre Wilderness** flanks the south side of the river, and the **Mount McConnell Trail** *(trailhead near Mountain Park Campground)* provides interpreted access. This 2-mile-long, moderately steep loop (with an optional 2-mile loop leading to the summit) climbs through clusters of ponderosa and Douglas-fir huddled on the gneiss and schist. The second mile of the trail, with more south-facing slopes, features prickly pear, yucca, and juniper.

Below the hamlet of Gould, the road leaves the dense forests to join hayfields against a background of craggy peaks. Note the quality of the willows in **Michigan River.** Together with state and federal agencies, ranchers here in North Park created the Owl Mountain Partnership to collaborate on ecosystem management. In addition to creating wetlands, erecting fences to reduce conflicts between wildlife and livestock, and collecting information on vegetation and wildlife, the partnership has planted hundreds of willows to restore the health of riparian areas.

## Peak to Peak Scenic Byway

This pretty 55-mile route runs south from Estes Park to Black

Hawk on Colo. 7, 72, and 119, serving as a logical entryway to and through Rocky Mountain National Park (see pp. 188-199). Rising steadily out of the Big Thompson Valley, it offers access to several destinations, including **Twin Sisters Peaks, Longs Peak,** and the **Wild Basin** area. Along the way, a pleasant, well-groomed but unspectacular gravel trail circles grassy-sided **Lily Lake,** with views of Twin Sisters and Longs Peaks. The road south of here, a popular biking route, dips and rolls through foothills of aspen and ponderosa pine.

Above the village of Ward, **Brainard Lake Recreational Area** is a enviable spot for picnicking and hiking that offers easy access to the **Indian Peaks Wilderness.** Although you must pay a parking fee and walk a bit from the car to the trailhead, you're starting at 10,300 feet, as your vehicle gained most of the elevation for you.

One trail, the 2-mile loop around **Long Lake,** is so popular with families and dogs that some of the meadows have boardwalks to lessen impacts. Tree line is not far away, and the more ambitious, somewhat less populated, jaunt to **Lake Isabelle** gets you even closer.

### Mount Evans Scenic Byway

Farther south still, this 28-mile high-altitude drive takes you up **Mount Evans,** which serves as a launching point for several hikes. The road leaves I-70 at Idaho Springs, where you can buy an interpretive tape or booklet for the byway at the small Idaho Springs Visitor Center *(101 Chicago Creek. 303-567-3000).* From here the route rises through montane, subalpine, and alpine ecosystems. **Echo Lake** offers fishing and camping, as well as a trailhead for hikes into **Mount Evans Wilderness.** These include the **Chicago Lakes Trail,** a 9-mile round-trip into a glacial valley. Another trail goes to **Resthouse Meadows,** a 13-mile round-trip hike to a gorgeous chain of lakes. Echo Lake also marks the entrance to the Mount Evans toll road.

On summer afternoons **Mount Goliath Natural Area** (also called Mount Evans Information Center) offers a variety of programs. Among its interesting trails is a quarter-mile wheelchair-accessible tour of an alpine garden with plants from a variety of elevations. Another loop trail visits a grove of bristlecone pines. Keep a lookout, too, for krummholz and "banner tree" Engelmann spruce—stunted, often nearly prostrate trees, severely pruned by the bitter prevailing winds in this harsh country just below tree line.

About 3 miles south of Echo Lake Lodge, the **M. Walter Pesman Trail** climbs almost 2 miles up the back of **Mount Goliath** through a research natural area, a designation that highlights non-wilderness areas with unique environmental qualities. The loop trail intersects Mount Evans Scenic Byway up top.

In spring the hillside is a riot of wildflowers, including wallflower, rosy paintbrush, and harebell, as well as the occasional bristlecone pine. Thanks to the remarkable density of this tree's wood, water cannot penetrate and cause rot. This means that some of the dead bristlecones you see standing here have been that way for more than a hundred years; the fallen trees may have died 600 years ago. An excellent wildflower guide to this trail is for sale at the visitor center.

This is one of the nation's first roads designed primarily as a scenic drive, created in 1912 by Frederick Law Olmsted, Jr., son of the landscape architect who planned New York's Central Park. Both Olmsteds were leading conservationists: Olmsted Sr. drafted a management plan for the Yosemite wilderness, while Olmsted Jr. plotted scenic roads in Maine's Acadia National Park and helped set up the National Park Service in 1916. At the time, Coloradans were lobbying to include Mount Evans in the nascent National Park System. Driving this road, it's easy to see why: The route slowly circles to showcase outstanding vistas in all directions.

Viewing scopes at the summit overlook (where you'll see ruins of a Denver University observatory) are good for spotting area wildlife, including marmots, pikas, bighorn sheep, and mountain goats.

## Arapaho National Recreation Area

West of Rocky Mountain National Park, the Colorado River has been dammed in order to send water east through tunnels under the Continental Divide to irrigate lands to the east of the Front Range. This area—known informally as Colorado's Great Lakes, and managed by the Forest Service as Arapaho National Recreation Area—hosts a frenzy of weekend motorized recreation. However, the national forest lands surrounding this dramatically scenic spot contain some prime hiking trails, most of which are included in the **Continental Divide National Scenic Trail** system (see sidebar at left).

Motors are prohibited on **Monarch Lake,** at the southeast end of Lake Granby, so portage your canoe or kayak the 300 feet from the parking lot. The islands at the south end of **Shadow Mountain Lake** (also closed to motors) are worth exploring. If you're on foot, take the 4-mile **Monarch Lake Trail** around that body of water, or use this as a jumping-off point to the Indian Peaks Wilderness, popular for wintering bald eagles. ∎

### Conquer the Divide

A magnificent, 3,100-mile footpath from the Mexican border at Antelope Wells, New Mexico, to the Canadian border at Montana's Glacier National Park, the Continental Divide National Scenic Trail is the country's ruggedest long-distance walkway. Though the trail leads through a living museum of habitat diversity, including desert and basin country in New Mexico and Wyoming, it is best known for traversing some of the finest uplands in the West, including portions of Rocky Mountain National Park and Mount Zirkel Wilderness.

As of 2001, roughly 70 percent of the trail had been completed, much of it thanks to the efforts of a dedicated group of backers and volunteers from 46 states. For more information on the CDNST, contact the Continental Divide Trail Alliance (888-909-2382; www.cdtrail.org).

Grand Lake, Arapaho National Recreation Area

Rock climbing, Eldorado Canyon State Park

# Eldorado Canyon State Park

■ 1,442 acres ■ Colo. 170 near Boulder, west of Eldorado Springs ■ Year-round ■ Hiking, rock climbing, fishing, biking, mountain biking, horseback riding, bird-watching, wildlife viewing ■ Adm. fee ■ Contact the park, P.O. Box B, Eldorado Springs, CO 80025; phone 303-494-3943. parks. state.co.us/eldorado

SOUTH OF BOULDER, a tiny creek wends its way through 1.7 billion years of Rocky Mountain geology. Eldorado Canyon State Park covers a stretch of narrow canyon at the edge of this uplift, where rock layers have been tilted nearly vertical and rivers cut through stone in a race for the lowlands.

The park entrance lies next to Eldorado's most recent geological phenomenon: the **Lyons formation.** This hard, red sandstone originally accumulated as windblown sand dunes that were compacted into stone some 240 million years ago. As you drive upstream, notice the line of high, reddish cliffs. These are part of the famed **Fountain formation,** which is the rock visible in the Flatiron Mountains, the Red Rocks amphitheater, Garden of the Gods, and other favorite slices of the Front Range. This stone resulted from the erosion of the ancestral Rockies, an ancient mountain range in the same location as today's Rocky Mountains. The Fountain formation was distributed as sand and pebbles in the nearby lowlands, then later compacted into sandstone. When this particular sandstone erodes, it tends to leave rough, jagged edges—a mainstay of the region's dramatic scenery.

At **Supremacy Rock,** where the bridge crosses South Boulder Creek, the cliffs change to a smoother, grayish rock formed from sandstone that was squeezed and pulled like taffy deep below the Earth's surface, eventually metamorphosing into quartzite. Finally, at the western edge of the park you can see what remains of the molten magma that pushed through cracks in the Earth's crust some 1.7 billion years ago, the magma slowly cooled, solidifying into granite, composed of interlocking quartz, feldspar, and biotite crystals.

Eldorado Canyon is a popular picnicking destination. On summer Sundays it fills to capacity, with cars turned away at the gate. Families eat lunch, play volleyball, and wade in the shallow creek around a tiny visitor center, which features an interesting exhibit on the history of this former private resort. The cliffs of the park provide challenges for rock climbers —as well as plenty of entertainment for those who watch them.

The handful of hiking trails, suited to a variety of abilities, are far less crowded than the number of cars might suggest. From South Boulder Creek, the 0.7-mile **Fowler Trail** is relatively flat, wheelchair accessible, and cuts along the side of the canyon, penetrating a huge slab of the Fountain formation at a place called the Bastille. It also provides views of the creek and the dramatic cliffs. By contrast, the **Rattlesnake Gulch Trail** climbs more than 800 feet in 1.4 miles, leading to the ruins of an old hotel. Though the ruins themselves are unremarkable, the high vantage point provides views of the canyon and eastern plains that are anything but.

Eldorado Canyon State Park contains inviting weaves of vegetation, from south-facing slopes peppered with ponderosa pine and juniper to moister north-facing slopes covered with quiet huddles of Douglas-fir. Fine grasslands are also here, many composed of an interesting mix of both shortgrass and tallgrass prairie species, including little bluestem, needle-and-thread, junegrass, and smooth brome.

As for wildlife, look for red fox, coyote, mule deer, raccoon, and mountain lion. Finally, more than 80 species of resident and migratory birds have been spotted at Eldorado Canyon, from turkeys to great horned owls and from prairie falcons to red-tailed hawks—and even some golden eagles. ■

Panorama Point, Golden Gate Canyon State Park

# Golden Gate Canyon State Park

■ 14,350 acres ■ 16 miles northwest of Golden ■ Best season summer
■ Camping, hiking, rock climbing, fishing, mountain biking, horseback riding, cross-country skiing, snowshoeing, bird-watching, wildlife viewing, wildflower viewing ■ Adm. fee ■ Contact the park, 3873 Hwy. 46, Golden, CO 80403; phone 303-582-3707. parks.state.co.us/golden_gate

NESTLED IN THE FOOTHILLS between Golden and Rollinsville, where it ranges from 7,600 feet to nearly 10,400 feet in elevation, Golden Gate Canyon State Park offers visitors a backcountry experience less than an hour from downtown Denver. This is almost entirely a montane forest ecosystem, featuring beautiful stands of ponderosa and aspen, as well as some lodgepole pine and Douglas-fir. Initially settled in the 1800s by homesteaders and nearly denuded for lumber to supply the mining industries of Central City and Black Hawk, it sat largely forgotten for about 60 years, home to a handful of ranchers, farmers, and loggers. In 1960 the state of Colorado purchased the first land and established the park, which has since grown through the acquisition of adjacent lands. Now totaling more than 14,000 acres, this is the second largest state park in Colorado (after Colorado State Forest State Park).

The term "canyon" in the name of this preserve is somewhat deceiving. Though indeed centered around a couple of valleys—one winding 13 miles down to Golden—the park includes numerous uplands, meadows, forests, and small peaks. These are not pristine lands, yet they are largely undeveloped and have regenerated since being so heavily logged more than a century ago. The park provides habitat for elk and deer as well as the occasional black bear, mountain lion, and bobcat. Subalpine forests cover the high areas in the park's northwest corner, including **Panorama Point**—part of a granite body that extends north of Boulder—which provides yawning views of the Continental Divide. **Tremont Mountain,** at 10,388 feet the park's highest point, lies just to the south.

The small, modern **visitor center** has a good bookstore and friendly staff who can help you plan your visit, while a couple of interpretive exhibits keep the kids busy. The center offers a good deal of cultural history, particularly profiles of the ranchers who once lived here.

## What to See and Do

Hundreds of picnic sites dot the valleys and the steep, beautiful **Mountain Base Road.** There are three developed campgrounds (one reserved for groups) and four backcountry shelters (three-sided structures similar to those on the Appalachian Trail), as well as a couple dozen backcountry tent sites. The highlight of the park is its 35 miles of trails—some reserved for hikers, others strung together in loops that provide a day's ride by bike or horseback.

About a mile northwest of the park's visitor center, the **Frazer Meadow Trail** (also known as the Horseshoe Trail) rises almost 2 miles through a riparian valley. On the warmer south-facing slopes, ponderosa roots reach down as far as 35 feet to hit moisture; the extensive root systems extend as far as 100 feet from the trunk, which accounts for their wide spacing. The last half mile of the trail passes through a thin aspen grove—the forest reclaiming what was once pasturage—much of it thick with wildflowers. This area is the site of the historic homestead of John Frazer, who lived here more than a century ago.

The trail ends in a T at the 5.2-mile **Mule Deer Trail,** which wanders through a peaceful glade that

could have been designed by a mountain biker looking for a slow, peaceful ride. This is **Frazer Meadow,** a slight basin that has collected deep, fine soils. Its grasses yield wildflowers such as yarrow, black-eyed Susan, lupine, wild iris, and cinquefoil. The mixture of grass, aspen, and nearby conifer woods creates a rich environment for wildlife. Mice, pocket gophers, meadow voles, and cottontails feast on meadow plants, attracting predators such as weasels and coyotes. This meadow is also a great place to see elk (see sidebar p. 179).

The eastern part of the park harbors an interesting network of paths. The **Burro** (4.5 miles), **Buffalo** (1.2 miles), and **Mountain Lion** (6.7 miles) **Trails** give hikers the choice of visiting an old homestead in **Forgotten Valley** or climbing more than 9,000 feet to the top of **Windy Peak** (map available at park office).

Snow is light at these lower elevations, so hiking is often possible year-round. Because you needn't walk far to enter natural settings, these trails are popular with families. Again, trailhead parking fills up on summer Sundays, and reservations (303-470-1144 or 800-678-2267) are recommended for weekend camping. ∎

# Two Ponds National Wildlife Refuge

■ 62.7 acres ■ Denver suburb of Arvada ■ Best seasons spring and fall
■ Hiking, bird watching, nature programs ■ Contact Rocky Mountain Arsenal
National Wildlife Refuge, B613, Commerce City, CO 80022; phone 303-289-
0232, ext. 100. www.r6.fws.gov/refuges/twoponds

TUCKED RIGHT IN THE TOWN of Arvada, Two Ponds National Wildlife
Refuge protects a tiny slice of vital wetland habitat for various songbirds
and waterfowl. It also provides a wonderful opportunity to educate the
local population—including many inner-city kids—about the value of
protected lands.

At barely 63 acres, Two Ponds is the nation's smallest urban refuge.
Nine acres of wetlands (the rest are prairie uplands, including a tiny portion of native shortgrass prairie that was never farmed) support 85
species of birds, 10 of which nest here. Despite the name, there are actually three ponds, accessed by two quarter-mile trails, located in the West
80th Avenue portion of the refuge. Hours are limited, but additional
trails are open from the back parking lot of the medical center (9210 W.
80th Ave., at Kipling).

When it was privately-owned farmland, this land supported a variety
of crops, including hay, apples, Japanese maples, asparagus, and bullfrogs
(sold to downtown Denver restaurants). The ponds are fed by natural
spring waters that were once used to irrigate the entire area; now they
support cattails, willows, and cottonwoods. These plants in turn provide
habitat for a variety of birds, including nesting night-herons and great
blue herons. Curiously, these latter two species may sometimes be found
occupying the same cottonwood tree, with the night heron tending to
favor the lower branches. This ability to get along may have something
to do with the fact that the great blue fishes by day, while the night heron,
true to its name, is largely nocturnal.

The cottonwoods host many birds, including the hardy Swainson's
hawk; many use the refuge as a stop over every fall on their three-month
journey from farther north in the western United States to Argentina.
Kestrels can also be seen in the bigger cottonwoods; because many nearby
trees have been cut down for development, these birds are increasingly
unable to find suitable habitat in the area. Currently only about ten pairs
of kestrels remain in greater Denver.

Plans call for increased development at the refuge, including boardwalks into the wetland areas, bridges over some of the old irrigation canals,
and additional trails with interpretive signs. Even in its current state, however, this preserve provides the silence of the cattails, occasionally breached
by busloads of school kids or by a suburban bird-watcher seeking a little
relief from the world of traffic, television, and shopping malls. ■

Cottonwood trees, Two Ponds National Wildlife Refuge

Butterfly catch-and-release at Rocky Mountain Arsenal National Wildlife Refuge

# Rocky Mountain Arsenal National Wildlife Refuge

■ 17,000 acres ■ North-central Colorado, 10 miles from downtown Denver ■ Best seasons spring and fall; open Saturdays, call for hours ■ Hiking, fishing, biking, bird-watching, wildlife viewing, trolley tours ■ Entrance by shuttle bus only, available at West Gate. Reservations required for all nature programs and trolley tours ■ Contact the refuge, Building 111, Commerce City, CO 80022; phone 303-289-0232. www.pmrma-www.army.mil

THAT A FORMER MUNITIONS facility and pesticide factory could evolve from a federal EPA Superfund Site into a treasured, nearly 27-square-mile slice of wildlife habitat within a stone's throw of downtown Denver seems nothing short of miraculous.

Over decades of industrial use, as native shortgrass prairie habitat in the area was lost first to agriculture and later to sprawl, the arsenal served as a kind of de facto refuge. Here thrived various small mammals, mule and white-tailed deer, white- and black-tailed jackrabbits, coyotes, and a profusion of birds, including ferruginous hawks and bald eagles. When the true potential of the place became apparent, citizen groups pushed hard to transform it into a sanctuary. In 1992, they succeeded.

Because this is still an active Superfund Site, and because protection of wildlife is a higher priority than outdoor recreation, visitor use is tightly controlled. The refuge is open Saturdays only, as well as for special events. Access is by shuttle bus from the main gate, which takes you to a **visitor center** with helpful displays and short but highly rewarding hiking-birding loop trails to **Lake Mary** (1 mile) and **Lake Ladora** (1.1 miles).

Spring birders should keep an eye peeled for migrating songbirds, while summer walkers are likely to see lark buntings, meadowlarks, white pelicans, and great blue herons. A cavalcade of ducks shows up in fall, while late autumn brings bald eagles to the cottonwoods along First Creek. ■

# Roxborough State Park

■ 3,324 acres  ■ Colo. 121, just south of Littleton  ■ Best seasons spring and
fall  ■ Hiking, cross-country skiing, snowshoeing, bird-watching, wildlife viewing
■ Adm. fee  ■ Contact the park, 4751 Roxborough Dr., Littleton, CO 80125;
phone 303-973-3959. parks.state.co.us/roxborough

PICTURE SLABS OF RED ROCK about to soar through the air: streamlined,
aerodynamic, poised at a 45-degree angle for takeoff from the surrounding oak scrub. These are the dramatic features of Roxborough State Park.
As at other spots along the Front Range, erosion here has exposed sweeping diagonals of brilliant red rock from the Fountain formation. Although
this preserve also encompasses ridges of the Lyons and Dakota formations
as well as a peak of ancient granite, it is the iron-filled Fountain red rocks
that make it such an exquisite place. These rocks seem lifelike, as if they
are stretching upward after their long confinement, or perhaps bowing
down to the high country just beyond.

The **Fountain Valley Trail** provides an easy, 2-plus-mile amble through
meadows filled with scrub oak and aspen, and creek bottoms lined with
cottonwood. From its start at the visitor center (where you can also pick up
a trail guide), head off on the loop trail's right-hand side first, as it affords
great views of the longest continuous exposure of Fountain rock in Colorado. From here you can see the formation continuing far to the north.

At the trail's halfway point stand several structures built by Henry
Persse, the man who popularized this region in the late 1800s. From there
the trail heads back up through the Fountain Valley, offering dramatic
views along the way. Regular visitors wax rhapsodic about how the rocks

change color with lighting and
moisture; they are particularly
dramatic after a rain, which
brightens the lichen to an almost
silvery glow. The trail's **Lyons
Overlook spur** also has fine valley
views, as well as glimpses of striking erosional patterns fashioned
by water and weather.

Roxborough State Park contains seven distinct plant communities, as well as a host of wildlife
including mule deer, coyotes, and
golden eagles, plus bobcats, bears,
and elk. To help preserve the natural landscape, pets, bikes, rock
climbing, and camping are not
allowed. Visitors must stay on the
10 miles of developed trails, and
the park closes at dusk. ■

Circa 1901 homestead, Roxborough SP

# Southern
# Colorado Rockies

Yankee Boy Basin, San Juan Mountains

THE SOUTHERN HALF OF Colorado's Rockies, here defined
as the area south of I-70, is a mix of plains and peaks.
The high country of the White River Plateau, the West
Elk Mountains, and above all the mighty San Juan Mountains offer vast forests and open vistas, quickly stepping
streams, a variety of outdoor activities, and geology by
the ton. Beginning about 40 million years ago and continuing for the next 30 million years, the area witnessed an
outrageous cacophony of spewing volcanoes and lava

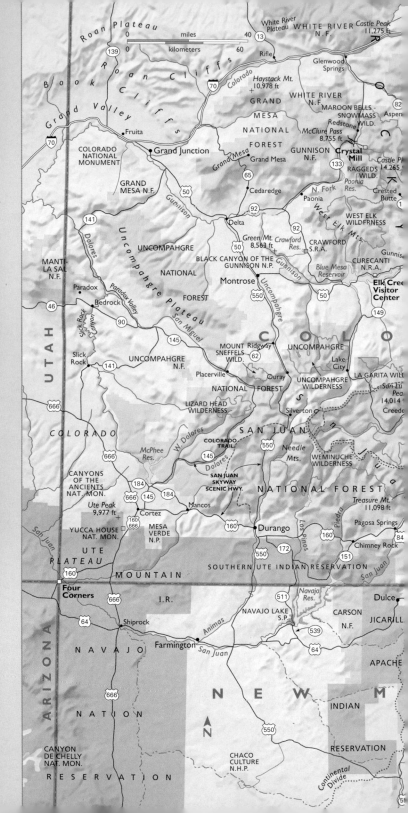

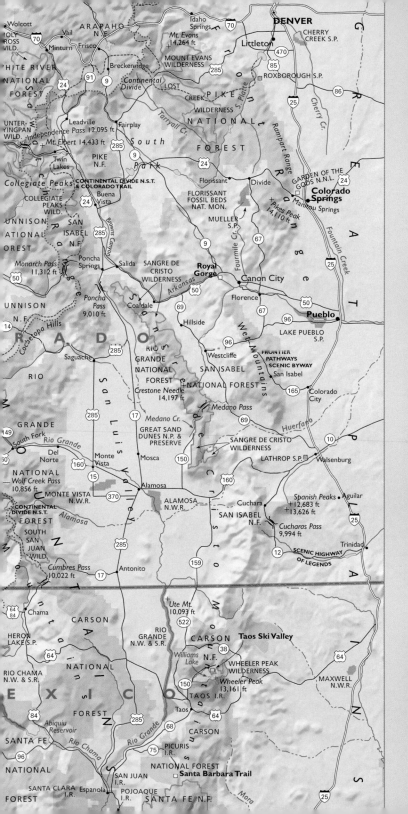

flows, not to mention cinder and ash falling by the millions of tons. One mound of lava and debris thrown up near the present-day town of Silverton in the early phase of these eruptions measures more than 3,000 feet thick and 40 miles across.

Today Silverton sits at the southern edge of a volcanic caldera (though most of it has been filled in by later lava flows). Surrounding this ancient crater, precious metals were deposited by hot water in quartz veins. This was one of nature's mother lodes, allowing the harvest of millions of dollars' worth of silver and gold in the late 1800s.

To the east, the rocks tell a different story. From the peaks of the southern Front Range (the first series of mountains rising from the Denver Basin), views to the east reveal a virtual ocean of relatively flat grasslands known as the Great Plains. The soil just beneath the grass of the Great Plains is a mix of sand, gravels, and clays carried eastward by streams and rivers—watercourses that were once flat and lazy, but became rejuvenated as the Rocky Mountains began to rise. The actual amount of debris carried out of the Rocky Mountains is staggeringly huge—big enough to form a slightly tilted plain that runs east all the way into western Kansas and Nebraska.

Although the southern Colorado Rockies share many ecological traits with the northern portion, a number of the valleys display the unmistakable signs of decreased moisture and increased temperatures. Speaking very generally, and assuming a constant elevation, there's a 3.5-degree rise in average temperature for approximately every 300 miles traveled as you move south toward the border with Mexico. Even this topographical truism, however, is influenced by a tremendous number of variables, among them regional rain-shadow effects and the prevailing track of storm systems. The San Juan Mountains, for instance, are first in line to

Molting mountain goat near Mount Evans

Hikers in autumn, White River National Forest

receive major precipitation from storms heading northeast out of the warm Pacific Ocean. Many years see such systems only infrequently, but when they do arrive, they roll in with force, generating phenomenal amounts of snow. In 1978–79, Colorado's Wolf Creek Pass received the state's record seasonal snowfall: a whopping 70 feet.

This region is more than simply beautiful. Here is truly a land of unexpected pleasures. From the red spires and cliffs of Garden of the Gods to the great sweeps of alpine tundra in the upper San Juan Mountains; from hints of the ancient world in the rocks of Florissant Fossil Beds National Monument to the dancing dunes of Great Sand Dunes National Park and Preserve, this land is unforgettable. In short, the southern portion of the Rocky Mountains offers myriad outdoor activities amid jaw-dropping scenery. All year round—from car, kayak, or on foot—you will be rewarded by your travels. ■

Climbing Montezuma's Tower, Garden of the Gods

# Garden of the Gods

■ 1,367 acres  ■ Colorado Springs at 30th St. & Gateway Rd.  ■ Best months June-Jan.  ■ Hiking, rock climbing, mountain biking, horseback riding, wildlife viewing, theater  ■ Contact the park, 1805 N. 30th St., Colorado Springs, CO 80904; phone 719-634-6666. www.gardenofgods.com

THIS ENCLAVE OF PINYON and juniper interspersed with slender red-rock outcroppings has been preserved since 1909 within the city limits of Colorado Springs. Fancifully named Garden of the Gods, the popular site is managed for crowds. Purists may object to some of these policies— pets, bikes, and horses are allowed; there are picnic areas with fire grates; climbers are welcome, although they must register at the visitor center— but the 1.7 million people who visit each year are grateful. Here you can drive up close to the rocks, and walk even closer (although there are prohibitions against leaving the trail). Unlike many other, more rustic protected areas, this park is equipped with such modern attractions as a café, a seasonal climbing wall, and a historical ranch staffed by inter- preters in period clothing. No matter what the rules and regulations (or lack thereof), the park centers on and celebrates the remarkable geology of this national natural landmark.

   Start at the **visitor center,** where a 12-minute film gives a worthy in- troduction to Rocky Mountain geology. From here you can see the power of erosion up close on a guided walk, or explore one of the dozens of nature trails—some wide, paved, short, and crowded, others dusty, long, and lonely—that wander through the juniper, ponderosa pine, and scrub oak. Or you can simply stare out at the awesome views of sheer red cliffs backed by magnificent Pikes Peak (see pp. 226-27). ■

# Mueller State Park

■ 5,121 acres ■ East-central Colorado, west of Colorado Springs ■ Year-round ■ Camping, hiking, fishing, hunting, mountain biking, horseback riding, cross-country skiing, snowshoeing, bird-watching, wildlife viewing, wildflower viewing ■ Adm. fee ■ Contact the park, P.O. Box 39, Divide, CO 80814; phone 719-687-2366. parks.state.co.us/mueller/

THE NICE THING ABOUT Mueller State Park is its superabundance of trails; two dozen of them wander for 55 miles through aspen and montane forests past meadows, old homesteads, and tiny ponds. You could visit this foothill preserve a dozen times and find new areas to explore on each trip. These pathways—open to various combinations of foot, horse, and bicycle travel—provide a wonderful respite from the crowds atop Pikes Peak, or even an enjoyable tune-up for a more challenging high-country adventure.

Some of this area was logged during the boom days of the gold rush, centered just south of here, at Cripple Creek and Victor. Aspen trees, which have a remarkable ability to recolonize disturbed areas, today show off their ivory trunks and fluttering leaves in dozens of lovely groves. Viewing aspen is a favorite pastime here, especially in autumn, when the weather turns cool and the leaves golden, and the woods ring with the sound of bugling elk. Other large mammals frequenting the park include black bear, mountain lion, mule deer, and bobcat. The park's official name—Mueller State Park and Wildlife Area—demonstrates its concern for protecting critical habitat in the face of sprawling development in and around Colorado Springs.

The **Grouse Mountain Overlook Trail,** an easy half mile walk from the end of the campground road, wends through parklike uplands rich with Douglas-fir, blue spruce, ponderosa, aspen, and limber pine. A tiny boulder field showcases the pink Pikes Peak granite, much of it covered with lichen. The walk ends with a peaceful vista of meadows, forests, valleys, hills, and distant mountains—an especially nice view at sunset.

Two trails begin behind the visitor center. The 0.8-mile **Wapiti Self-Guided Nature Trail** wanders through various habitats, each of which is profiled in a helpful brochure. For a longer adventure, the **Rock Pond Trail** descends approximately 2 miles through ponderosa and aspen groves—with occasional views to distant ridges—to a tiny, nutrient-rich pond framed by smooth rock outcroppings. This trail, along with a few others, continues into **Dome Rock State Wildlife Area** *(719-227-5200),* a lambing ground for bighorn sheep. (Massive, granite **Dome Rock** itself is most easily accessed through Fourmile Creek Canyon, which has a separate entrance area off County Road 61, south of Mueller.)

Be sure to get a park map at the entrance gate, and take it with you wherever you go, marking your trail numbers as you choose them. The intersections here are marked only by numbers, not names or destinations, and it would be easy to get lost. As at many busy areas managed in part for wildlife, hikers are restricted to maintained trails. ■

# Florissant Fossil Beds National Monument

■ 5,998 acres  ■ East-central Colorado, west of Colorado Springs  ■ Year-round  ■ Hiking, horseback riding, cross-country skiing, bird-watching, wildlife viewing, wildflower viewing  ■ Adm. fee  ■ Contact the monument, P.O. Box 185, Florissant, CO 80816; phone 719-748-3253. www.nps.gov/flfo

AFTER SPENDING A FEW DAYS in this part of the world, you may begin to equate awesome with large scale—the magnificent mountains, the sprawling vistas, even the wildlife here seem to possess physical stature. But a visit to Florissant will show you an equally impressive sight: the hairs on the legs of an ancient butterfly. Its fossils—well preserved, fascinating, utterly different from anything else in the state—make this national monument a compelling stop. One caveat, though: You may have to warn kids who lump "fossil" with "dinosaur" that these fossils were deposited some 30 million years after the big guys went extinct.

You can see all of Florissant's unique features on two easy, flat trails, which start from behind the visitor center (*off Cty. Rd. 1, 2 miles S of Florissant*). The half-mile **Walk Through Time** and the mile-long **Petrified Forest Loop** each come with an interpretive brochure, but you'll probably learn more on one of the hourly ranger-guided hikes offered summer afternoons. Several other trails meander through gentle terrain of meadows and forests—a good way to get used to the elevation.

The fossils here date back 35 million years, to a warm, wet time when the trees of this region included sequoia, hickory, beech, maple, and oak. Then a volcano erupted near the current town of Guffey, 18 miles to the southwest, flooding the valley with lahars, or mudflows of ash and melted snow. Some of these lahars blocked the drainage for the valley, creating a lake. Today, two consequences of that lake—one large and fairly easy to grasp, the other tiny and mind-boggling—are visible.

The large effect is a series of petrified trees. Some of the valley's biggest trees withstood the volcano's eruption but were buried under the ash, which then consolidated into a silica-rich rock called tuff. When water from the lake later seeped into the tuff, it dissolved the silica and penetrated the wood of the buried trees, replacing up to two-thirds of their cell walls with silica molecules. The structure of the trees was so well preserved that modern scientists can study the growth rings of these ancient trees as well as their cellular composition—which is how they know that sequoias grew in a wet environment here. One 19th-century settler reported petrified trees so thoroughly strewn across this valley as to make it nearly impassable. Many have been carted off since then, but 80 or 90 still remain, some barely covered with soil.

The tiny effect resulted from continued (but smaller) eruptions of the volcano. These produced ash that settled to the bottom of the lake in layers from 1 to 5 inches thick. The ash also gathered on the shores of the lake,

Petrified leaf, Florissant Fossil Beds National Monument

where occasional rainstorms washed it into the water in thin layers. These layers in turn preserved debris that had fallen into the lake: leaves and sticks, seeds, cones, flowers, grains of pollen. They also included animal parts such as bones, teeth, shells, feathers, and even the occasional whole bird. More extraordinary still are the 1,400-plus different species of arachnids and insects—from winged ants to tsetse flies—petrified in fossil form.

Scientists are particularly happy to have a fossil record of soft-bodied creatures such as insects, normally too fragile to survive this long. At Florissant they were preserved because the volcano erupted again, big time. A new lahar—a slower moving volcanic mud, mixed with surface gravel—produced a caprock called breccia that preserved the crumbly, flaky layers of shale formed from the hardened ash. In some places the breccia has eroded to the point of exposing many of the underlying shales; on the valley floor, though, both the breccia and the shales have eroded, leaving only the lower tuff.

Tuff is rough stuff—particularly difficult for tree roots to penetrate. You can see the general outline of the ancient lake by noting those places where, 35 million years later, trees still do not grow. ■

# Pikes Peak

■ 1.1 million acres ■ East-central Colorado ■ Best seasons late spring–early fall ■ Camping, hiking, rock climbing, boating, fishing, mountain biking, cross-country skiing, snowshoeing, bird-watching, wildlife viewing, wildflower viewing, scenic drives, cog railway ■ Fee for Pikes Peak Toll Rd. ■ Contact Pike and San Isabel National Forests, 1920 Valley Dr., Pueblo, CO 81008; phone 719-545-8737. www.fs.fed.us/r2/psicc

LAID OVER CENTRAL COLORADO'S high country in a blanket of conifers, Pike and San Isabel National Forests (now administratively linked, though frequently referred to as separate entities) offer a frenzy of high and low peaks covering an area so vast you get dizzy figuring out where to begin.

A logical place is Pike National Forest's 14,110-foot namesake peak, perhaps the most famous—and maybe the busiest—mountain in America. Named for explorer Zebulon Pike, who first saw it in 1806 (but failed to reach the summit), it gained notoriety in 1869 when gold prospectors heading for nearby strikes adopted the slogan, "Pikes Peak or Bust." Katharine Lee Bates wrote "America the Beautiful" after a visit to its summit; the city of Colorado Springs mushroomed at its base.

Geologically, most of this mountain is a batholith—a large body of igneous rock. The Pikes Peak batholith, which formed as a molten mass about a billion years ago and then slowly cooled, stretches for hundreds of square miles. This gigantic mass of pink-tinted granite took shape far beneath the Earth's surface where it lay for 700 million years before being uplifted to form the ancestral Rockies. Over the next 200 million years the land was covered with seas, swamps, and beaches, and those mountains eroded away. Later, the batholith was again pushed upward by the Laramide orogeny, which began some 63 million years ago. The fault line for this upthrust runs roughly parallel to I-25.

Today's visitors can drive to the very top of Pikes Peak on a 19-mile **tollway** with mileposts and elevation signs charting their progress through foothill, montane, subalpine, and alpine ecosystems. Driving lets you take the trip at your own pace and stay at the summit as long as you like. Alternative—and more enjoyable—means of getting to the peak include the **cog railway** from Manitou Springs and the 14-mile climb up the **Barr Trail** *(trailhead off Ruxton Ave., West Manitou Springs, near cog railway parking lot)*. The hike requires some planning; you must leave early and then, of course, figure out how to get down. Biking down the road is a much lauded way to experience the mountain, but you'll probably want to do it with an outfitter because individual bikes and horses are discouraged.

Though crowded, Pikes Peak's summit is an inspiring place. Eastward stretches the vast expanse of the Great Plains; north, south, and west—but still beneath you—mountain peaks form a bold-looking wilderness. Slanting sunlight alternates with rain falling from clouds drifting below over a patchwork of road cuts and big valleys and small towns. ■

Switchback on the road to Pikes Peak

Mount Evans Wilderness, Pike National Forest

# South Park

■ 540,299 acres ■ East-central Colorado, southeast of Fairplay ■ Best seasons spring-fall ■ Camping, hiking, backpacking, orienteering, mountain climbing, rock climbing, mountain biking, horseback riding, cross-country skiing, bird-watching, wildlife viewing ■ Contact Pike and San Isabel National Forests, 1920 Valley Dr., Pueblo, CO 81008; phone 719-545-8737. www.fs.fed.us/r2/psicc

PIKE NATIONAL FOREST contains far more than its namesake peak. Within its borders, Mount Evans and the Park and Mosquito Ranges form a 50-by-35-mile ring around a high-desert area of the national forest designated South Park. Like North Park in Arapaho National Wildlife Refuge, and Middle Park, near Granby, South Park is an old sedimentary basin, now eroded flat by the South Platte River and its upper basin tributaries. (Calling these places "parks," by the way, alludes to the French *parc,* meaning "game preserve"; early trappers were overwhelmed by the size of buffalo and pronghorn herds here.) Though most of the area is now private ranch land, filled with more cows than elk, driving through South Park remains one of the great road trips of the Rockies.

**Hoosier Pass,** north of Fairplay on Colo. 9, is one of the most celebrated botanical sites in the state. The elevation and soil of the pass, combined with its unusual east-west orientation, have created an environment that has encouraged some extremely rare plants to flourish here. One, braya, a 2-inch-tall plant with white blossoms, grows nowhere else in the world. You'll also be surrounded by a virtual garden of other, more common plants, including needle grass, harebell, false dandelion, death camus, false buckwheat, and cinquefoil. Tundra is remarkably fragile. A tin or aluminum can discarded here can kill the plants beneath it in less than a month; growing those plants back again may take 25 years. Major disturbances in some tundra locations can require a thousand years to heal.

Other intriguing areas include the **Rampart Range,** a heavily used region between Colorado Springs and Denver that includes the Devils Head promontory, as well as the headwaters of the South Platte, which is being considered for possible designation as a Wild and Scenic River. **Lost Creek Wilderness** *(719-836-2031)* is here, too, with its striking rock formations, unique plants, and a creek that continually disappears into the earth and then reappears again. Various county roads north of US 24 have trailheads that lead into this wilderness area.

## What to See and Do

The easternmost portions of the **Colorado Trail** (see pp. 256-57) run through Pike National Forest, from just south of Denver through Lost Creek Wilderness, and up to the Continental Divide above Fairplay. **Kenosha Pass,** where the route crosses US 285, provides a splendid opportunity to sample a few delights of this trail. Pick up the path by parking in front of the Kenosha Pass Campground on the north side of the road, then cross the highway. The first mile of this foot, horse, and bike path offers easy grades through lovely clusters of aspen, lodgepole pine, and spruce. The terrain then opens up for a stunning view of the bare peaks overlooking South Park, especially dramatic in early summer, when snow still covers the high peaks, or in fall, when the aspen leaves turn gold.

Northeast of Kenosha Pass, the **Guanella Pass Scenic Byway** offers access to **Mount Evans Wilderness.** This interesting drive's southern end offers picnic areas and campgrounds, as well as (poorly signed) trailheads for a variety of lengthy treks into the wilderness. The road then climbs through stands of lodgepole pine, aspen, and spruce, with occasional views of pine-covered hillsides to the south. The top of the pass is a good place to get out of the car and walk.

Some 5 miles to the southwest, out in the proverbial nowhere, the 2-mile hike to Square Top Lakes on the **South Park Trail** is a beautiful walk, whether you ever actually make it to the lakes or not. This is alpine tundra at its best—a place of bitter winter winds, dazzling summer wildflowers, and the effect of the sun's rays sometimes stronger than in the lower valleys.

Along the way you'll pass alpine avens, buttercup, Parry clover, tufted hairgrass, and bunchgrass, along with lovely clusters of marsh marigold. In addition to plant life, this trail offers stunning views of the timbered flanks of Geneva and Arrowhead Mountains to the southwest.

After hiking just under a half mile, bear left at a fork. Here you will enter a fine huddle of low willows, which provide forage, stabilize the soil, and offer important protection for various birds. Look among the branches for white-crowned sparrows, many in migration to this alpine rooftop to or from their wintering grounds in Mexico. Not only do the willows make it difficult for predators to reach the sparrows, but their leaves trap heat—a requirement for incubating the eggs.

**Lower Square Top Lake** is reached in 1.5 miles. This lake, like its nearby neighbors, typically stays frozen until early July; the stark, rock-strewn shores of such water pockets mean there is little in the way of organic material to be washed into the water—and, therefore, little life. These waters shimmer in the sun for eight to ten weeks, then freeze over and are lost again beneath a blanket of snow. ■

Near Independence Pass, San Isabel National Forest

# San Isabel National Forest

■ 1.2 million acres ■ South-central Colorado ■ Best seasons summer and winter ■ Camping, hiking, backpacking, mountain climbing, boating, rafting, fishing, mountain biking, horseback riding, downhill skiing, cross-country skiing, snowshoeing, wildlife viewing, scenic drives ■ Contact the national forest, 1920 Valley Dr., Pueblo, CO 81008; phone 719-545-8737. www.fs.fed.us/r2/psicc

THIS FOREST IS A PATCHWORK quilt of wooded pockets that spreads across the south-central part of the state, south and west of Colorado's Pike National Forest. The entire forest has the potential to provide visitors with a tranquil and uplifting experience; the following covers the most noteworthy of these spots, from south to north. Included are the headwaters of the Arkansas River and, west of Trinidad, the **Spanish Peaks,** traversed by the **Scenic Highway of Legends** (Colo. 12). Among the more interesting natural features in this area is a series of dikes extending in all directions from the Spanish Peaks—the result of molten rock forcing its way into fractures in the since eroded sedimentary rocks above. About 400 dikes populate this area, some extending to 14 miles; not all of them, however, are exposed.

From Cucharas Pass on Colo. 12, take the gravel road toward Aguilar at least as far as the **Farley Wildflower Trail,** a quarter-mile jaunt through a meadow with a view of the upper Cucharas Valley. This is near Cucharas Recreation Area, where you can fish, picnic, and camp. North of the pass, the road follows the Cucharas River through a fine valley filled with lush sweeps of grass.

Some 50 miles north, the aptly named Wet Mountains, west of Pueblo, are traversed by the **Frontier Pathways Scenic Byway** (Colo. 165). From Colorado City, off I-25, this road climbs through scrub oak, ponderosa, and spruce forests, occasionally opening to fleeting views to the east. There isn't much in the way of public access here except at **Lake Isabel**—a small, scenic spot with a pleasant, low-key resort. In any other state, these watery gems and forested mountains would be hailed as paradise; lacking the dramatic heights of other Colorado ranges, however, they are viewed as just another typical earthly delight.

To the west, San Isabel National Forest covers the eastern side of the narrow Sangre de Cristo Mountains (see pp. 272-77), offering access points near Westcliffe, Hillside, and Coaldale. The popular **Rainbow Trail** begins at Silver Creek and runs south 100 miles along the base of the Sangres to Muddy Creek. It welcomes not only horseback riders, cyclists, and hikers, but motorcycle riders as well.

The largest section of San Isabel National Forest covers dramatic high-country peaks on both sides of the upper Arkansas River Valley from Salida to Leadville. The Continental Divide west of here is Four-teener country (see pp. 238-39), including 14,433-foot **Mount Elbert,** the highest peak in the state, and the **Collegiate Peaks,** a busy wilderness area where the mountains are named after such colleges as Princeton, Yale, and Harvard, the highest of the bunch at 14,420 feet.

Lower down, the forest provides several good recreation opportunities, including camping, hiking, biking, fishing, and rafting on the **Arkansas River** (see sidebar opposite). The **Colorado Trail** (see pp. 256-57) runs north-south through the foothills of the Collegiate Peaks, with several access points just west of US 24, before climbing to the Continental Divide near Monarch Pass. Don't be put off by the trail's access at US 50, the first few miles of which pass through ponderosa forests ravaged by mountain pine beetle.

Twenty miles south of Leadville is **Twin Lakes Reservoir**—two large, interconnected, beautiful bodies of water surrounded by peaks ripping through tree line. The Bureau of Reclamation visitor center here is mostly concerned with the hydroelectric power plant at the lakes (which have grown some 400 surface acres from their natural size), but it also offers handouts on area trails. Well worth your time is the drive on Colo. 82 over **Independence Pass;** at 12,095 feet, the highest highway crossing in the state. This road, originally established to connect communities in the Sawatch region with gold camps west of the divide, was kept open during late 19th-century winters by shovel brigades—teams of men who hand-dug trenches 15 to 20 feet deep through the windblown drifts—enabling cargo-laden sleighs to get through the pass. Summer posed a different challenge—and solution—as specially trained dogs were sent ahead of downhill bound wagons and stagecoaches to warn oncoming traffic to get out of the way. From the top of Independence Pass you'll have striking vistas to the west; a short, paved trail leads to a beautiful overlook.

West of Leadville, on the west end of **Turquoise Lake,** an unmarked trailhead provides access to the Colorado Trail and Holy Cross Wilderness. To the north, **Galena Lake** is a good destination for those seeking an all-day hike. ■

# Rafting the Arkansas

The Arkansas River—the second longest tributary of the Mississippi watershed—has a fascinating geologic history.

During the Laramide orogeny, the period of Rocky Mountain building that occurred some 70 million years ago, a large region of central and southern Colorado rose in a sprawling hump known as the Sawatch Uplift. Some 50 million years later the North American plate began to pull apart. This action began forming the Rio Grande Rift—a process that is still ongoing—as well as the Arkansas Valley. Faulting and more uplift eventually caused a boundary between rift and valley, so that water flowing into the valley from the Sawatch Range to the west and the Mosquito Range to the east created the Arkansas River.

These waters in turn carved a narrow canyon through layers of igneous, metamorphic, and sedimentary rock. They then plowed onto the plains beyond Canon City, at which point they glided eastward to the Mississippi.

The upper Arkansas valley is unique in its outstanding variety of white-water resources. More than 100 miles of river feature rapids ranging from Class II to Class V, fitting the skill levels of boaters from kids to white-water cowboys. The high mountain flows—augmented by upstream diversions from the other side of the Continental Divide—ensure rapids that last to mid-August, creating one of the longest river-running seasons in the country on the nation's most popular rafting river. People mainly take half- or full-day floats; the river tends to be short on good overnight trips.

Rapids on the upper Arkansas River

Which section of the river you float depends both on your abilities and on seasonal water levels. Above Buena Vista, Pine Creek, and the Numbers are challenging Class IV and Class V rapids. Below Buena Vista the river enters Browns Canyon, where it crashes over igneous and metamorphic rock in literally hair-raising fashion. Below the canyon the river slows and widens, offering leisurely views of the Collegiate Peaks to the west. At Salida the rapids become somewhat tamer, allowing floaters to spot bighorn sheep along the banks. The river cuts to its deepest point at Royal Gorge, just west of Canon City; within this 8-mile-long canyon, the walls soar more than 1,000 feet above the water and the river again builds into Class V rapids.

You can also view the Arkansas rumbling through the Royal Gorge from the top down, on the world's highest suspension bridge. Complete with merry-go-round and hot dog stands, the city park is woefully out of place. Still, the bridge here offers dramatic views of sheer cliffs made of gneiss, schist, and granite.

# White River National Forest: South

■ Central Colorado ■ Best seasons summer and winter ■ Camping, hiking, backpacking, rafting, fishing, biking, downhill skiing, wildlife viewing, scenic drives ■ Contact the national forest, 900 Grand Ave., Glenwood Springs CO 81602; phone 970-945-2521. www.fs.fed.us/r2/whiteriver/contact_us.html

ONE WORD—WILDERNESS—SUMS UP the White River National Forest south of I-70. This region contains some of the most stirring mountain-scapes in all of Colorado, protected by various wilderness districts of the

Maroon Lake, White River National Forest

national forest: scenic Maroon Bells-Snowmass, watery Holy Cross, and high-altitude Hunter-Fryingpan. Every single one of them sees an extra-ordinary amount of summer use, however, so if possible plan your trip for weekdays in the fall, when the traffic is lower.

In truth it would be hard to find a time of year or a road in this region that doesn't offer magnificent scenery: Colo. 82 from Aspen over Inde-pendence Pass to Twin Lakes; Colo. 24 along the east side of Holy Cross Wilderness and south to Leadville; and a network of vehicle-friendly and not-so-friendly dirt roads fanning across many of the old mining districts that first made Colorado a household name. Follow the suggestions in these pages, the lead of new friends you'll make in your travels, or strike out on a trail that catches your fancy—you can't lose.

## What to See and Do

### Maroon Bells–Snowmass Wilderness

If Colorado has to this point been but a dream destination, you've probably envisioned a scene from Maroon Bells-Snowmass Wilderness—in particular, the twin peaks of the Bells, both Fourteeners. Few places have been more frequently photographed—and few serve as a stronger symbol of nature's beauty—than this 181,000-acre gem southwest of Aspen. One of the five original wilderness areas set aside under the Wilderness Act of 1964, it has been enlarged considerably; what began as protection for only the central Elk Mountains now includes legendary benchmarks such as the Conundrum Valley and Castle Peak.

As in all of Colorado's high country, this region owes much of its appeal to the handiwork of glaciers, which carved out long, lovely valleys where streams tumble and aspen quake. Popular entryways and destinations for hikes into Maroon Bells-Snowmass Wilderness include **Maroon-Snowmass Trail** and the **West Maroon Creek Trail,** as well as **Buckskin Pass,** all off Maroon Creek Road. Additional trailheads are located south of Aspen at Ashcroft, and west of Aspen near Colo. 133 at Marble.

To relieve congestion at the trailheads, take advantage of access options such as the shuttle buses from Ruby Park in Aspen that deposit hikers at trailheads along Maroon Creek Road. From 8:30 a.m. to 5:00 p.m., travel on this road beyond T-Lazy-Seven Ranch is restricted to buses. Overnight backpackers on foot can enter Maroon Creek Road at any time, but they must secure an overnight parking pass at the Forest Service Entrance Station. If the lot is full, you'll have return to Ruby Park and take the bus instead.

Similarly, places such as **Cathedral, Snowmass,** and **American Lakes,** likewise located in Maroon Bells-Snowmass Wilderness, get so much summertime use that you shouldn't even consider visiting them until after Labor Day. This is the place to practice your leave-no-trace skills—camping well away from lakeshores and streams, not cutting switchbacks, carrying out all your (and sometimes other peoples') trash.

### Holy Cross Wilderness

Holy Cross takes its name from the peak of the same name, made famous by 19th-century landscape photographer William Jackson. Jackson shot a perpendicular set of couloirs resembling a cross on the east face of the mountain, then enhanced them in his darkroom to look even more dramatic. Thousands of the faithful came to pay their respects and were disappointed when the cross appeared less remarkable than expected.

This is a wilderness rich with water—quiet lakes, tiny ponds, and streams that go from loud torrents to quiet whispers in the course of a single summer. The 10-mile round-trip hike to **Lonesome Lake,** from the end of Forest Road 703 on the east side of Homestake

Crystal Mill at Crystal River, White River National Forest

Reservoir, is a wonderful day trip. Equally unforgettable is the 11-mile round-trip hike to **Notch Mountain,** which begins at the **Half Moon trailhead,** located off Colo. 24 at the end of Forest Road 707 *(S of jct. of I-70 and Colo. 24).*

### Hunter-Fryingpan Wilderness

Much less used than other wilderness areas in the southern reaches of White River National Forest, the Hunter-Fryingpan is a perfect destination for those with a penchant for high-altitude walking (8,500 to 12,500 feet). The 8-mile round-trip **Midway Pass Trail** offers fabulous panoramas of the Elk Mountains;

it begins on Colo. 82 (Independence Pass Highway) at the **Lost Man trailhead.** The same trailhead accesses beautiful South Pass, as well as Lost Man Lake.

### West Elk Loop Scenic Byway

The West Elk Loop Scenic Byway— a 205-mile loop from Paonia Reservoir and back again—could keep you busy exploring for days. This route passes great runs of aspen and sprawling views. It is also a good way to launch an extended foray into the lovely, 176,000-acre **West Elk Wilderness,** a wonderland of high meadows and eroded volcanic spires and pinnacles. ◼

# The Fourteeners

THE HUMAN URGE to climb the highest peak—either because it's there, or for a host of older and more complex reasons—seems to flower anew in every generation. What we really get from the climbing adventure, claimed mountaineer George Mallory, "is just sheer joy. And joy is, after all, the end of life."

If Mallory was right, it is logical that Colorado, home to a staggering 54 Fourteeners—peaks above 14,000 feet—has become the climber's equivalent of the Elysian fields.

Although Fourteeners are scattered throughout the state, the highest concentrations are in the San Juan Mountains of southwest Colorado, which hold 13, and in the Sawatch Range of north-central Colorado, which boasts 15. In the Sawatch Range looms the state's highest peak, 14,433-foot Mount Elbert—the second highest mountain in the lower 48 (California's

View from the summit of Mount Evans, 14,264 feet

Mount Whitney is a mere 61 feet higher). Another hundred or so peaks above 13,800 feet are found within Colorado's borders.

Climbing Fourteeners is not an activity to be taken lightly. Though several peaks, including Elbert, can be hiked in a day, you must be in good shape and dress appropriately.

In 1990, some 75,000 people climbed the state's Fourteeners. Today, visitation has nearly tripled that amount. Given the extremely fragile nature of alpine environments, such enthusiasm has not been without serious cost. Habitat leading to and around many of these summits has been severely degraded over the past few years, mostly through braiding trails and other physical scars that increase erosion.

At these elevations, where an inch of soil may take a thousand years to accumulate, erosion is especially serious. Luckily, conservation groups such as the Colorado Fourteener Initiative (*303-27-7525, ext. 115; www.colorado fourteeners.org*) are taking steps to help preserve this spectacular area. ∎

Gunnison River in Black Canyon, with Painted Wall rising to right

# Black Canyon of the Gunnison National Park

■ 130,388 acres  ■ Southwest Colorado, near Montrose  ■ Best months May, June, and Sept.  ■ Camping, hiking, backpacking, orienteering, rock climbing, kayaking, fishing, biking, horseback riding, cross-country skiing, bird-watching, wildlife viewing, auto tour  ■ Adm. fee; kayaking permit required  ■ Contact the park, 102 Elk Creek, Gunnison, CO 81230; phone 970-641-2337. www.nps.gov/blca

THE LANDS OF THE GUNNISON RIVER watershed are a mix of high, windswept plateaus, eroded pinnacles, hidden draws, and long, soaring reaches of high country—all of it tumbling down to the extraordinarily wild and forbidding Black Canyon of the Gunnison. At its deepest the canyon plunges 2,660 feet from rim to river, and—some 2 to 3 miles away—

narrows to just under a quarter mile from rim to rim. This canyon has the greatest depth-to-width ratio of any in the United States.

The Gunnison River has had a steep gradient for a long time, thanks in part to an uplift that wrenched apart the terrain in this section of Colorado some 60 million years ago; this allowed the river to cut through the erosion-resistant Precambrian gneiss and schist that make up the canyon walls. Long after the initial cutting of the canyon began, the Gunnison River swelled with sand and rocky debris during the melting of glacial ice, further scouring the canyon. The area's dark gneiss, swirled with lines of pink granite and some muscovite, is especially beautiful.

The ancestral Gunnison River did not always flow along the line it traces today. Two distinct volcanic regions—the San Juans in the south and the West Elk Mountains in the north—poured out massive volcanic fields during their respective eruptions, pushing the river well north, then south again. Various spots such as Exclamation Point along the north rim offer spectacular views of the islands of towering rock in the river's main channel. These are remnants of larger blocks of rock—loosened along vertical fractures—that fell off the canyon walls into the river below.

## What to See and Do

The beautiful 7-mile-long **South Rim Drive** connects Tomichi Point to High Point, with ten wondrous scenic overlooks along the way. One, **Gunnison Point,** is also the location of a well-done **visitor center** where exhibits interpret the geology and natural history of the canyon. All these stops offer expansive vistas, but highest on the list of most impressive views and greatest variety of scenery are **Chasm View** and, 2 miles farther along, **Sunset View,** both located along the last third of the drive.

Those inclined to a do a bit of walking—the best way to enjoy this park—can begin with the 2-mile round-trip **Rim Rock Nature Trail,** a self-guided interpretive path winding along the rim of the canyon from the visitor center to the campground. Here you will encounter a variety of vegetation, from Gambel oak and sagebrush to Utah juniper and pinyon pine.

Similar in length and concept is the 2-mile round-trip **Cedar Point Nature Trail.** The path offers dramatic views of the magnificent **Painted Wall,** which at 2,250 feet is the tallest cliff in Colorado. This trail also has signs identifying many plants common to the region. Indeed, the Black Canyon is remarkably diverse in foliage. Atop or slightly below the rim are clusters of pinyon and juniper, serviceberry, Gambel oak, aspen, Douglas-fir, and adaptable mountain mahogany.

### North Rim

The north rim of the Black Canyon of the Gunnison is reached via Colo. 92 and an 11-mile trip on Black Canyon Road from Crawford (the last few miles are unpaved). Advanced and expert level climbers may be seen clinging to the sheer vertical walls plunging from this edge of the canyon. A place of wind and coyotes, the north rim has a somewhat wilder, more remote feeling to it than the south rim. Even the peregrine falcons, ravens, and red-tailed hawks that wheel from one side of the canyon to the other seem more at home here.

The astonishing steepness of the Black Canyon is readily apparent from the half dozen overlooks that punctuate this rim, any of which has the power to take your breath away. In addition to the easy and altogether pleasant 0.4-mile **Chasm View Nature Trail,** accessible from the north rim's campground, this side of the canyon offers good options for longer hikes. The 7-mile round-trip **North Vista Trail,** for example, leaves from the North Rim Ranger Station and leads in 1.5 miles to the fabulous and fittingly named **Exclamation Point,** where you'll find staggering views into the depths of the Black Canyon.

For a more strenuous and even more glorious walk, climb another 2 miles from Exclamation Point to the summit of **Green Mountain.** Here the views extend beyond the canyon to Grand Mesa (see pp. 118-123) to the north, the San Juan Mountains (see pp. 245-255) to the south, and the West Elk Mountains to the east.

The interpretive programs at Black Canyon are above average. The geology programs in particular are worth going out of your way to attend—check out "Scrap-Booking with the Earth," "Once Upon a Time," "Tales of the Sausage Rock," "Time in the Canyon," or "Muscle, Hammer, and Chisel." In addition, **Canyon Caravan,** the excellent ranger-led auto tour along the South Rim, gives visitors a thorough overview of canyon geology.

### Boating

Much of the Gunnison River through the national park consists of extreme white-water—Class V and VI—and can be negotiated only by expert kayakers willing to make a number of strenuous portages. *(Those who qualify will need a Park Service permit.)* That said, a number of outfitters in the area offer exciting raft trips below the most severe water, typically ending at the junction of the North Fork of the Gunnison. ■

### A Sage Shrub

The mountain mahogany (genus *Cercocarpus*) is ingeniously well adapted to dry conditions and relatively poor soils. Like most other arid-land shrubs, mountain mahogany sprouts smaller leaves than shrubs in wet areas, a quality that helps limit the moisture it loses. The plant further reduces exposure to the drying effects of the sun by curling under the edges of its leaves.

Its roots have special nodules that serve as homes for certain single-cell bacteria; these bacteria convert nitrogen into nitrate compounds, which then fertilize the plant. The genus name "Cercocarpus" comes from the Greek words for "tail" and "fruit"—a reference to this shrub's wispy, twisted seeds.

Gunnison River running through Black Canyon

# Curecanti National Recreation Area

■ 41,043 acres ■ Southwest Colorado, west of Gunnison ■ Best months May-Oct. ■ Camping, hiking, backpacking, orienteering, rock climbing, boating, rafting, kayaking, canoeing, swimming, fishing, biking, horseback riding, cross-country skiing, snowshoeing, bird-watching, wildlife viewing, wildflower viewing ■ Contact the recreation area, 102 Elk Creek, Gunnison, CO 81230; phone 970-641-2337. www.nps.gov/cure

CURECANTI'S MAIN ATTRACTIONS are its three large reservoirs, created by damming the Gunnison River. The majority of users tend to be boaters, windsurfers, and those in search of fish—one of the reservoirs, Blue Mesa Lake, is among the largest Kokanee salmon fisheries in the country. In summer the park offers educational programs, some at the Elk Creek Visitor Center, on the shores of Blue Mesa Lake. A descent into the canyon via 232 stairs and a three-quarter-mile walking path leads to the dock for Morrow Point Lake's Pine Creek Boat Dock, whence a ranger-led boat tours the reservoir. The third reservoir, Crystal Lake, features the Gunnison Diversion Tunnel, a national historic civil engineering landmark.

## What to See and Do

For nature lovers, the best thing about Curecanti is the trails that let the casual hiker rub elbows with beautiful forests, riparian areas, and sweeping vistas. The flat, easy, 1.5-mile round-trip **Neversink Trail** *(off US 50, 5 miles W of Gunnison on north shore of Gunnison River),* wanders past cottonwoods and willows with views of a fabulous great blue heron rookery. The 5-mile round-trip **Crystal Creek Trail,** located along Colo. 92 approximately 24 miles northwest of its junction with US 50, winds through aspen and conifer groves, ending with sweeping views of the Cimarron Valley.

Well worth your time is the 2-mile trek (one way) to the **Dillon Pinnacles.** The trail begins 21 miles west of Gunnison at a picnic area along US 50 near the shore of the Blue Mesa Reservoir and winds through a long sweep of sage. It ends at the base of a stunning set of volcanic pinnacles—oddly shaped towers and spires eroding in the face of wind, rain, and ice.

These points, capped in places by erosion-resistant tuff, are grand reminders of the fiery loads of ash and rock spewed out by the West Elk and San Juan Mountains. At one time, geologists estimate, the blanket of molten rock from these two volcanic centers may have had a volume of 150 cubic miles. During the summer this walk can be a hot one; bring water *(no drinking water available on any trails)* and trek early in the morning or late in the afternoon.

Recent archaeological work has uncovered dinosaur fossils as well as dwellings 6,000 years old. ■

Aspen below Twilight Mountain, Weminuche Wilderness

# San Juan Mountains

■ 10,000 square miles ■ Southwestern Colorado ■ Best months Jan.-Feb., July-Aug. ■ Camping, hiking, backpacking, mountain climbing, boating, fishing, mountain biking, horseback riding, cross-country skiing, snowshoeing, wildflower viewing, scenic drives ■ Contact San Juan National Forest, 15 Burnett Ct., Durango, CO 81301; phone 970-247-4874. www.fs.fed.us/r2/sanjuan

TRY TO CONDENSE the most satisfying vacation of your life into a single sentence and you'll know what it's like to sum up the San Juans, the largest mountain range in the American Rockies. Plain and simple, you would be hard pressed to find a more awe-inspiring collection of peaks, wilderness areas, hikes, drives—and even towns—than you'll discover in this southwestern corner of Colorado. A day in the San Juans may begin

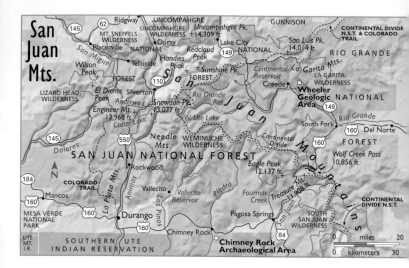

at dawn with the climb of a Fourteener (see pp. 238-39), continue with a soak in natural hot springs, and end with a plate of crawfish étouffée at a Cajun restaurant. Though this area is increasingly popular, it's still possible to spend long days roaming the wilds without ever feeling crowded.

Like other ranges in the region, these peaks came about through the geologic minuet of mountain-building—an endless dance of uplift and erosion. Between periods of rising landscapes, which began some 1.8 billion years ago with profound shifts in the continental plates, the San Juans rested; they took on sediment from ancient seas and slowly changed shape as landmasses folded into each other and slipped along lines of weakness called faults.

Then, about 35 million years ago, the sparks really started flying. The San Juans spewed flames, lava, rock, and dust over hundreds of miles, burying parts of the landscape in a mile-thick blanket of volcanic debris. During this violent era massive volcanic explosions repeatedly devastated the region, each releasing a thousand times the raw energy of the 1980 Mount St. Helens event. After a brief pause of some 7 million years, the peaks near Silverton erupted, leaving a collection of calderas—basin-shaped depressions around the centers of collapsed volcanoes. Another period of uplift interrupted the fireworks for a time. Then a final cataclysm buried the eastern slopes in black basalt.

More recently came the forces of erosion, which continue to this day. Though Colorado did not lie in the path of the four major periods of glaciation, ice caps have covered most of the San Juans several times in the past two million years. Some 18,000 years ago, for example, an especially large ice cap—the Animas Glacier—extended from north of Silverton as far south as Durango. This colossal cooler carved the Needle Mountains, scooped out basins to form such alpine lakes as Molas and Crater, and sculpted the Animas Valley into the U-shaped profile it bears today. Shallow glacial lakes took shape in rocky debris called moraines and later filled with sediment, eventually becoming the meadows that now serve as wild pasturage for grazing elk.

The San Juans remain a wild range; here you'll find six federal preserves, totaling nearly one-third of Colorado's three million acres of federally designated wilderness. **Lizard Head Wilderness** (41,193 acres) flanks the western edge of the San Juans near Telluride, and takes its name from Lizard Head, a tower of crumbling rock considered among the state's most dangerous and difficult climbs. This area contains three Fourteeners—Mount Wilson, Wilson Peak, and El Diente Peak.

The **Mount Sneffels Wilderness** (16,565 acres), near Ouray, is best known for Yankee Boy Basin's spectacular midsummer wildflower display of such blossoms as columbine and mountain bluebells. The neighboring **Uncompahgre Wilderness** (102,721 acres) holds three of the state's highest peaks and, for climbers, a technically challenging collection of rock castles. North of Creede, San Luis Peak dominates the 128,158-acre **La Garita Wilderness**—a land of rushing streams, alpine wildflowers, and sprawling forests teeming with elk and mule deer. La Garita means "the lookout," a name that hikers along the 27 miles of the Colorado Trail (see pp. 256-57) that traverses this landscape are quick to appreciate. La Garita includes the largest volcanic outpouring on Earth, thought to have happened some 28 million years ago. This reserve is administered by both the Gunnison and Rio Grande National Forests.

Straddling the Continental Divide near Pagosa Springs, and managed by San Juan and Rio Grande National Forests, the 158,790 acres of lovely **South San Juan Wilderness** make up the least known, least used backpacking area in the region. Here you'll find 180 miles of trails crossing glacial valleys and jagged pinnacles.

To many outdoor enthusiasts, the San Juans are synonymous with 487,912-acre **Weminuche Wilderness,** a grand sweep of wild land located roughly north of US 160 between Durango and Pagosa Springs. Several of the state's 54 Fourteeners are located here, attracting climbers from around the world.

........................................................................................................................

## What to See and Do

One of the best ways to experience the San Juan Mountains is to hike its vast network of trails. From various access points, including Wolf Creek Pass (east of Pagosa Springs) and the Molas Pass Area (south of Silverton), you can traipse along the backbone of the range via 86 miles of the **Continental Divide Trail** (see p. 206).

You'll meander at tree line for much of the way, skirting the headwaters of the San Juan, Piedra, Los Pinos, Rio Grande, and Animas Rivers. The trail also affords tremendous views of the individual mountain clusters that make up the San Juans, including the Needles and La Garita. Dramatic talus slopes, dark huddles of spruce and

*Following pages:* Hiking above Yankee Boy Basin, San Juan Mountains

fir, and finally, in the montane zone, the soft, dappled light of aspen groves round out the route.

To sightsee by car, the **San Juan Skyway** (see pp. 258-263) is a wonderful way to experience this alpine wonderland. Another good route, designed primarily for 4WD vehicles, is the 65-mile **Alpine Loop Byway.** This figure-eight drive circles two volcanic calderas and passes some abandoned tramways and mill sites, vestiges of the late 1800s mining boom that attracted thousands of immigrant prospectors to these slopes. The byway also climbs Cinnamon Pass to views of three Fourteeners: Handies (14,048 feet), Redcloud (14,034 feet), and Sunshine (14,001 feet).

Be forewarned: Although this trip crosses one of the least populated regions in the lower 48, on sunny weekends in midsummer it's quite possible to find yourself in a tundra traffic jam. The loop is accessed in Ouray from US 550, in Silverton from Colo. 110, and in Lake City from Colo. 149. Each of these towns has jeeps to rent and outfitter-guides for hire. An excellent guidebook to the Alpine Loop is *Alpine Explorer,* available from the San Juan Mountains Association *(970-385-1210).*

## Weminuche Wilderness

Colorado's largest and perhaps most spectacular natural landscape lies in this wilderness at the heart of the San Juan Mountains. Within its soaring sweep of high country (average elevation 10,000 feet), elk graze in summer and ptarmigans stand camouflaged against the rocks of the tundra.

Here, too, red squirrels chatter in the coniferous forests, and pikas whistle from above tree line.

High use on certain trails has led the Forest Service to prohibit camping, campfires, and the grazing of recreational livestock at such favorite locations as Archuleta Lake and West Ute Lake (on the Rio Grande National Forest side of the wilderness) and Chicago Basin and Fourmile Falls/Lake (on the San Juan side). Dogs must be leashed or under voice control at all times. As part of planning your trip, check the current site-specific regulations with the Forest Service. No matter what the season, be sure to prepare for inclement weather—rain, hail, snow, and biting winds can and do occur all year.

### Crater Lake

If you're in the mood for a dose of the alpine, head to this sparkling gem nestled in the trees below 13,075-foot North Twilight Peak, just off US 550 near Molas Pass. The 5.3-mile (one way) **Crater Lake Trail** climbs 1,650 feet through wildflower meadows, revealing views of the area's most beautiful lakes and summits. Beginning at Andrews Lake on US 550 near Milepost 63, the path switchbacks for roughly 500 feet, then levels off after 1.2 miles. After hiking for 2 miles you cross into Weminuche Wilderness area, where stunning views open up of pyramid-shaped Engineer Mountain to the southwest and Snowdon Peak to the east.

The trail passes through a number of drainages rich with riparian zones (minimize your

Rafting the Animas River

## Rapid River Running

Tumbling from a rocky birthplace in the slopes above Silverton, the Animas River makes a headlong dash through a long, glaciated valley, undeterred by dams, diversions, or other man-made water projects. Indeed, among 24 contenders, this is the only completely free-flowing navigable river on the Colorado Plateau, offering a wealth of recreation opportunities for water enthusiasts of every interest and ability. The original name of the river was Rio de los Animas Perdidas—"River of Lost Souls"—so named by early Spanish explorers after members of their party died while crossing it.

The 28-mile stretch of river known as the Upper Animas drops 85 to 150 feet per mile, plunging through the Animas Gorge and ending at the 1870s settlement of Rockwood. As a commonsense sign of respect for this Class V section, the few raft companies offering trips here require passengers to take swimming tests in the river prior to departure.

After this turbulent beginning, the river leaves the high country to flow in easy meanders through the valley that bears its name. (Remember to respect private property rights along the waterway.) Those new to river running can learn paddling techniques along a 10-mile stretch here, beginning about 8 miles north of Durango.

In Durango itself, the "downtown section" begins at the 32nd Street launch site, attracting both paddling competitors and those new to boating. Whitewater Park, just south of town, is a racecourse for white-water canoeists and kayakers. Smelter Rapid, rated a low Class II, marks roughly the halfway point. Managed by hundreds of volunteers, this is one of the few full-length, world-class white-water slalom courses in the country. Animas River Days, a white-water festival, is held here each summer. South of the city limits, the Animas flows through the Southern Ute Reservation, where permits are required.

Despite being an obviously priceless resource to boaters, fly fishermen, and nature lovers alike, the Animas faces an uncertain future. The threat since 1968 has been (and still is) the Animas River Project, a water diversion and storage plan that would have an enormous impact on the region. Both locally and nationally, the project remains a hotly debated issue.

Balloons over San Juan National Forest

impact by staying on the path, regardless of how muddy it might be). Wildflowers thriving in these cold, saturated soils include the fleshy leafed king's crown, its rose-colored partner queen's crown, and fine huddles of elephant heads. True to their name, these clustered blooms resemble small red pachyderms trumpeting from thigh-high stems. The final 3 miles of the trail lead to Crater Lake, popular for fly-fishing and spin casting for cutthroat and rainbow trout.

**Highland Mary Trail**
Seven shimmering high-altitude lakes await you at the end of this hike, which climbs 1,650 feet and crosses numerous creeks and marshes in 3.5 miles. You can reach the Highland Mary Trail by following Colo. 110 east out of Silverton 5 miles to the old town of Howardsville. Turn right onto Forest Road 589, then continue 4 miles up Cunningham Gulch to the trailhead located at the remains of the Highland Mary Mill.

After an earnest climb of 500 feet in the first half mile, you'll reach the **Cunningham Gulch Trail;** the left fork quickly leads to the rcgister for the Highland Mary Trail. In July and August, Colorado blue columbines abound in these meadows, attracting hummingbirds and sphinx moths to flutter about the blooms. Be aware, however, that after years of enthusiastic picking, it is now illegal to

gather this columbine—Colorado's state flower—from the wild.

## Fourmile Falls

Resembling a 300-foot wedding veil hung from a black precipice, this grand destination is for hikers of all ages. Walking up the canyon alongside Fourmile Creek, the easy **Fourmile Falls Trail** gains 750 feet in 3 miles, through a mix of flower-filled meadows, stands of aspen, marshes, and the occasional dark, quiet forest of fir and spruce.

To reach the trailhead from Pagosa Springs, head north onto County Road 400 off US 160. Continue 8.4 miles, then bear right onto Forest Road 645 (Fourmile Road) and follow it

to the end. The trail starts at the parking lot.

In just over half a mile the trail crosses into Weminuche Wilderness, and 12,137-foot Eagle Peak begins to dominate the horizon. Meanwhile, the fine meadow complex at your feet supports the beautiful chiming bells, named for the shape of its downward-hanging flower clusters. This adaptable wildflower is found in a wide variety of wind, moisture, and heat conditions; it may stand only knee high in this meadow, for example, while in a nearby marsh it could reach 5 feet.

The path's final 300 feet climb to the base of the falls. The dramatic dark backdrop to the falls is called breccia, a rock composed of ash and debris blasted from the volcanoes that erupted in the region millions of years ago.

## Dolores River

Flowing through ponderosa pine parklands to sunbaked slickrock canyons while offering exccllent fishing, white water for every ability, and 250 million years of geologic history, the Dolores River is considered by many to be one of the most sublime destinations in the West.

From its source in the San Juan Mountains near Telluride, Colorado, the Dolores runs south to its namesake town. From there it follows a curving path north to the Colorado River near Moab, Utah. At one time the Dolores flowed north to south, feeding into the San Juan River. When subterranean forces began uplifting Ute Peak and Mesa Verde some 10 million years ago, however, the river ultimately reversed its course.

Although most of the water from this river is diverted for irrigation, the Dolores remains one of the few southwestern rivers to host at least three different multiday trips. In early spring, when the waters from McPhee Dam are released, boaters flock to the river's

Mountain meadow of asters, orange sneezeweed, paintbrush, and larkspur

two most popular canyons, Dolores and Slick Rock.

Well-known for harboring the region's most challenging rapid, Snaggletooth, **Dolores Canyon** begins sliding south with a gentle 19-mile section cradled by stands of ponderosa pines. Indeed, the rocks of these soaring canyon walls display a geologic time span greater than that seen at Canyonlands, Bryce, or Zion National Parks. This quiet start to the canyon, from Bradfield Bridge to Dove Creek Pump Station, is accessed north of Cortez, Colorado, via US 666 and County Road R16. When water flows are less than 1,000 cubic feet per second, white-water boaters bound for Snaggletooth must instead portage their rafts around this rapid and the 9 miles of churning water below it.

After leaving the tumult of Dolores Canyon, the river enters sculpted sandstone near the tiny town of Slick Rock, Colorado. Aptly named **Slick Rock Canyon** is a twisted run through multicolored rock. Most boaters allow three days to travel this 48-mile section, then take out at the small village of Bedrock.

Access to Slick Rock Canyon is from Dove Creek on US 666, some 18 miles north on Colo. 141. Bedrock sits in the Paradox Valley, near the Utah state line, on Colo. 90. The following will help you plan a visit: For information about water releases and boating requirements, call 970-385-1354; for current water flow information, call 800-276-4828; for estimated release dates, check out www.doloreswater.com. ■

## Chimney Rock Archaeological Area

Driving through the green sweep of ranchland between Pagosa Springs and Durango, you can hardly miss it: A 7,900-foot-high sandstone spire silhouetted against the sky, centerpiece of religious practices that governed the area's Ancestral Puebloans about a thousand years ago. A tour led by the San Juan Mountains Association (970-385-1210 Oct.-May 14 or 970-883-5359 May 15-Sept.) is a great way to view the unique prehistoric sites that straddle the mesa in Chimney Rock Archaeological Area.

The tour visits a great kiva, an excavated village, and several unexcavated pit houses, as a guide describes the challenges Ancestral Puebloans faced in building their kivas and dwellings 1,000 feet above the fertile river valley. You'll also learn about archaeoastronomy, and how the people who lived here conducted complex calculations based on their observations of the night sky.

A highlight is the Great House at the edge of the mesa, offering views of the San Juan Mountains to the east and the Piedra River Valley below, as well as Chimney Rock and its smaller neighbor, Companion Rock. This pair may have lured early religious leaders to the area, where they created the highest, most northeastern of all Ancestral Puebloan sites. The dwelling was situated so that its inhabitants could watch the moon rise between the two pinnacles every 18 years.

# The Colorado Trail

SPANNING A MAGNIFICENT stretch of alpine slopes and montane forests, the Colorado Trail connects Denver to Durango in nearly 500 miles. Along the way the trail passes through seven national forests, six wilderness areas, eight mountain ranges, and five major river systems. Only those on foot, horseback, or bike are allowed on this trail. Mountain bikes are prohibited from the trail's wilderness sections, but cyclists can simply detour around these segments on 4WD roads and some paved highways. Resupply towns range from 4 to 34 miles off the beaten path.

Beginning in Waterton Canyon to the south of Denver, the route climbs over Kenosha Pass, skirts Breckenridge and Copper Mountain, winds through the Collegiate Peaks, then vaults Marshall Pass to continue west past Lake City. From there it continues over Molas Pass near Silverton and meanders into the La Plata Mountains before finally descending to Durango.

Like so many worthwhile public works, the Colorado Trail owes its

Sawatch Range, Collegiate Peaks Wilderness, San Isabel National Forest

existence to a large group of dedicated volunteers—in this case, the Colorado Trail Foundation *(710 10th St., Golden, CO 80401; 303-384-3729, ext. 113)*. In 1973 the foundation began planning the creation of 180 miles of new trail that would connect already-existing routes in the national forests. Limited construction began in 1977 and continued for the next decade, guided by the infectious enthusiasm and focus of conservationist Gudy Gaskill. To take the Colorado Trail from dream to completion, Gaskill and others sought more funding and more volunteers—both nationally and internationally—thereby galvanizing public support. The Colorado Trail was officially completed in 1987.

An ideal half-day sampling of the Colorado Trail—rich in lakes, wildflower meadows, and mountain vistas—begins roughly 600 feet north of the sign for Molas Pass Summit *(5.5 miles S of Silverton on US 550, and 64 miles N of Durango)*. The trail wanders through gentle terrain toward Little Molas Lake, then veers west through a wooded area before hitting an old road marked by blazed posts. This 5-mile segment ends where it meets US 550 again southwest of Silverton. ■

# San Juan Skyway

■ 236 miles ■ Southwest Colorado ■ Best months June-Oct. ■ Camping, hiking, backpacking, white-water rafting and kayaking, fishing, mountain biking ■ Contact Grand Mesa-Uncompahgre-Gunnison National Forests, 2250 Hwy. 50, Delta, CO 81416, phone 970-874-6600; or San Juan National Forest, 15 Burnett Ct., Durango, CO 81301, phone 970-247-4874. www.fs.fed.us/r2/sanjuan/

REPEATEDLY PRAISED as "the most beautiful drive in America," the San Juan Skyway has a lot more going for it than great looks. The 236-mile loop

Telluride at twilight

embraces an astonishing array of southwestern Colorado attractions that will have you braking for photo opportunities, soaking in hot springs, riding a gondola 2,000 feet up the side of a mountain, panning for gold, and exploring the remnants of an ancient civilization.

The drive passes through the towns of Durango, Silverton, Ouray, Ridgway, Telluride, Dolores, Cortez, and Mancos, each offering a blend of camping, accommodations, and restaurants to suit a variety of whims and budgets. Detailed mile-by-mile guides to the skyway's geology and natural history may well enhance your experience, some are available for purchase and the Forest Service has a free brochure *(970-247-4874)*.

Start by heading north on US 550 out of Durango, where the pull of rafting, hiking, and biking can keep visitors busy for days. One of the region's oldest and most relaxing diversions, **Trimble Hot Springs,** simmers along the skyway near Milepost 30. For centuries native people soaked in these hot sulfur waters; they were followed by settlers and later still by thousands of local residents and vacationers.

Back on the skyway, the route begins its 4,000-foot climb to **Coal Bank Pass.** Some travelers detour to the **Alpine Slide** at Durango Mountain Resort at Purgatory (near Mile 48), while others veer off onto **Lime Creek Road** (Mile 51) to immerse themselves in a wash of aspen—especially gorgeous in autumn. (This popular high-clearance 2WD road rejoins US 550 some 15 miles later.)

Farther north on the skyway, at Mile 63, you can breathe deep at 10,910-foot **Molas Pass,** where the air has been rated as among the cleanest in the country. Top-of-the-world views here include Colorado's largest wilderness, the Weminuche (see p. 250), as well as a good glimpse of the Colorado Trail—a nearly 500-mile footpath connecting Durango to Denver (see pp. 256-57). Nearby, **Little Molas Lake** is accessed from the gravel road on the highway's west (left) side, half a mile north of the pass.

Continue on to **Silverton,** once a rip-roaring mining town that hosted some 40 saloons and dozens of brothels. Wander the streets still lined with buildings from the Old West or, for an authentic sampling of mountain mining life, take the one-hour tour of **Old Hundred Gold Mine**

## To Launch an Avalanche

Situated in a storm track for weather systems coming out of the warm Pacific Ocean, the San Juan Mountains receive some of the highest snowfalls in the West. They also claim an extraordinary number of avalanches. Two snow tunnels divert dangerous slides over a section of US 550 south of Ouray—one of the nation's most avalanche-prone roadways.

When snow shows up in earnest here, Colorado's Lead Avalanche Forecasters hit the road, driving to various sites immediately behind the snowplows. These pros monitor conditions for a variety of slide indicators: snow accumulations of an inch or more per hour, rapid temperature changes, shifting winds.

They also note the shape of snowflakes on slopes of 30 to 40 degrees: Are they icy needles or pellet-like formations? Either one is known to create more unstable conditions than the classic star-shaped flakes.

These winter warriors oversee a total of 206 avalanche paths. To release large buildups—potentially deadly slides that could entomb snowplows or passenger cars on US 550—teams often launch explosives from gas cannon attached to the tops of trucks, shaking loose many small slides. Another tool, the howitzer, allows accurate targeting of distant avalanche "start zones." And in the most remote areas of all, crews drop explosives from hovering helicopters.

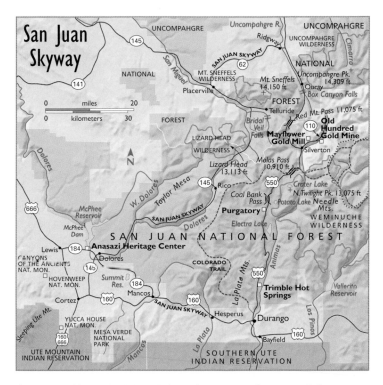

San Juan Skyway

(970-387-5444 or 800-872-3009), 5 minutes east of town on Colo. 110. Here you'll don a hard hat and yellow slicker, then ride the mine's "man-trip" train 1,600 feet into the mineral-rich heart of Galena Mountain. Former miners conduct these thoroughly engaging tours. The road heading back to Silverton passes the 1920s **Mayflower Gold Mill,** a national historic landmark, where you can see how gold was processed.

The 23 miles from Silverton to Ouray is a rubbernecking journey for passengers, but a white-knuckle affair for timid drivers. After winding along iron-stained Red Mountain, the skyway crests at 11,075-foot **Red Mountain Pass,** the highest paved pass in the San Juan Mountains, then descends into the awesome **Uncompahgre Gorge.** A good place to stop and catch your breath is the pullout at Mile 90, where **Bear Creek Falls** plummets 227 feet into the canyon below. Use extra caution here when crossing the highway.

Diversions in the village of **Ouray** include a soak in the town's historic hot springs pool *(fee)* as well as a walk to **Box Canyon Falls** (Mile 92), which pounds its way down a cavelike canyon. Columbines carpet the mountain slopes of Yankee Boy Basin, which can be accessed by way of a rugged 4WD route that begins on the road to Box Canyon. Ouray's namesake was a principal Ute chief of the mid-19th century. Uncompahgre, the name of the river flowing through town, is the Ute word for "warm stream."

Durango & Silverton Narrow Gauge Railroad

## Got Steam?

Southwestern Colorado's 113 miles of steel rails may reawaken your childhood dream of becoming an engineer. On either the Durango & Silverton Narrow Gauge Railroad *(970-247-2733 or 888-872-4607)* or the Cumbres & Toltec Scenic Railroad *(719-376-5483 or 888-286-2737)*, you'll travel through the heart of dark spruce forests and trundle past jagged peaks draped in snow. The gentle side-to-side sway and long whistle calls transport you back to the time when silver barons and settlers boarded the same train cars, bound for a new life at the end of the line.

The cry "Silver by the ton!" provided the original incentive for the Denver & Rio Grande Railroad to lay tracks to Silverton, in southwestern Colorado. At the time, the region was largely isolated, dependent on pack animals and teamsters to haul supplies in and carry ore out over the Continental Divide. The D&RG laid track to the west of its original north-south charter to El Paso, Texas, completing the line to Silverton in 1882. Today the Durango & Silverton Narrow

Gauge Railroad's 45-mile route to Silverton again climbs thousands of feet past the same mineral-veined rock once coveted by miners, entering the river gorge along a grade blasted wide by laborers in the winter of 1881-82 to accommodate the railroad tracks.

From late spring through the turning of the aspen trees in autumn, several trains leave Durango each day from the 1882 train depot on Main Street (built for the Denver & Rio Grande line). In winter, the Cascade Canyon train travels past the slopes of the Animas Valley and then halts at the Cascade Wye, stopping short of avalanche country.

The longest and highest narrow-gauge steam railway in the United States, the Cumbres & Toltec Railroad begins its 64-mile trek at the southeast edge of the San Juan Mountains in Antonito, Colorado. The route passes through aspen groves and dramatic rock formations before cresting at 10,015-foot Cumbres Pass and descending into Chama, New Mexico. Another extension of the Denver & Rio Grande, it originally served the region's mining and logging camps.

From Ouray the skyway opens wide, following US 550 north through the broad green valleys of Ridgway. At the junction of US 550 and Colo. 62, the Skyway turns west (left), slowly ascending through ranch-lands backed by saw-edged **Mount Sneffels Wilderness.** At 14,150 feet, Mount Sneffels dominates the view at the scenic pullout at Mile 14. According to Navajo legend, it was from these rugged peaks that "The People," the Dineh, emerged from another world inside the Earth. White men named the mountain range after a passage in Jules Verne's *Journey to the Center of the Earth,* that depicted Iceland's volcanic Mount Sneffels as the center of the Earth.

The skyway turns southeast on Colo. 145 in Placerville, continuing 14 miles to the 3-mile spur to **Telluride.** This scenic former mining town, founded in the late 1800s, has been transformed into a chic international resort, its historic downtown filled with restaurants and gift shops. Without question, though, its real attraction is the surrounding string of rugged peaks. For the best view of Telluride's stunning setting ride the free gondola, which begins at San Juan Avenue and climbs 2,000 feet to Mountain Village.

Another memorable experience is to stand in the mist of **Bridal Veil Falls**—at 365 feet, Colorado's largest free-falling waterfall. You can hike here via an unnamed trail. To reach the trail follow Colorado Ave. west to the old Idarado Mine site; the parking area for the trailhead is about 100 yards from the mine site. Or take your 2WD vehicle to a photo-perfect view of the falls by following Colorado Avenue just beyond its entry into Box Canyon. Four-wheelers can continue on up the road for a closer look.

From Telluride the Skyway continues on Colo. 145 as it climbs past the entrance to the ski area, topping out at the base of Lizard Head peak before descending into Dolores Canyon (see p. 255). Interpretive signs at the large pullout on **Lizard Head Pass**(Mile 59) orient you to the peaks within beautiful **Lizard Head Wilderness.**

In the 1970s, the Dolores River was dammed to create the McPhee Reservoir, flooding an area rich in Native American history. Just 3 miles south of the town of Dolores, Colo. 184 leads to the **Anasazi Heritage Center** *(970-882-4811),* a treasury of artifacts excavated from the area. The center's museum and ancient dwelling site feature hands-on displays, as well as life-size dioramas of Ancestral Puebloan homes.

Back on US 145, follow the skyway 6 miles to Cortez, turning east (left) at the junction with US 160. To the west is high-desert country, featuring the scrub vegetation of the upper Sonoran life zone. To the south, 9,244-foot Sleeping Ute Mountain forms the blue-gray profile of a man lying on his back. Ten miles ahead lies the entrance to Mesa Verde National Park (see pp. 62-65). From here US 160 travels through the small agricultural town of Mancos, past the glacier-sculpted La Plata Mountains, and finally back into Durango, where late Victorian architecture graces the town's various historic districts. From the 1882 train depot on Main Street the **Durango & Silverton Narrow Gauge Railroad** operates several trips along the old ore route to Silverton (see sidebar opposite). ■

# Rio Grande National Forest

■ 1.9 million acres ■ Southern Colorado and northern New Mexico ■ Best seasons summer and fall ■ Camping, hiking, backpacking, climbing, boating, fishing, mountain biking, horseback riding, wildlife viewing, scenic drives ■ Contact the national forest, 1803 W. Hwy. 160, Monte Vista, CO 81144; phone 719-852-5941. www.fs.fed.us/r2/riogrande

FROM ITS BEGINNINGS AS snowmelt streams from the peaks near Silverton, the Rio Grande flows east through the San Juan Mountains, snaking its way through rocky canyons before spreading out in full force in the wide San Luis Valley and heading south to New Mexico. Rio Grande National Forest cradles the river through Colorado, a mixed landscape of meadows and peaks, volcanic formations and forests.

This tour of Rio Grande country begins 15 miles from the San Juan River bridge in Pagosa Springs, just shy of the border with San Juan National Forest on US 160. An easy stroll here is the paved, mile-long trail to 105-foot-high **Treasure Falls,** a perfect leg-stretcher before driving up Wolf Creek Pass. **Treasure Mountain,** home to the stream that forms this waterfall, is an eroded remnant of the most massive volcanic eruption known to man, which occurred some 28 million to 30 million years ago. It spewed forth some 1,200 cubic miles of debris, including the black rock backing the waterfall.

## What to See and Do

Drive the twisting climb to **Wolf Creek Pass** (10,856 feet) and stop for a few moments at the interpretive kiosk on the summit; here you'll get the lay of the land, as well as a chance to ponder what remains of last winter's snow. Nearby is a road leading to perhaps the easiest stretch of the **Continental Divide National Scenic Trail** (see p. 206) to access. To reach it, drive east less than half a mile to a steep gravel road *(appropriate for 2WD vehicles after snows are cleared in early summer)* on the north side of US 160, which runs in 2.5 miles to **Lobo Overlook.** Like whitecaps in a rough, unsettled ocean, peaks and ridges fill the views from this fenced area.

From the west side of the radio tower near the overlook, the first half-mile of this portion of the Continental Divide National Scenic Trail ambles along an alpine meadow before dipping into a cluster of spruce and fir. You may notice a tarlike substance coating the ends of lower branches on some of the spruce. This is brown felt blight. Although spruce can reproduce where snowpack holds branches against the ground through the spring, this blight sets in especially if the snow lingers too long. Eventually it can seriously damage or even kill the tree.

From Wolf Creek Pass, US 160 descends eastward 16 miles to the town of South Fork. From there,

Upper Rio Grande, Weminuche Wilderness, Rio Grande National Forest

Fly-fishing on the Upper Rio Grande

Forest Road 360 leads south 1.5 miles to the **Big Tree Trail.** This 0.3-mile trail will deliver you to the Rio Grande's biggest tree— some 250 to 300 feet tall—and, at 500 years, very likely its oldest.

Return to South Fork and go west onto Colo. 149 to begin the 75-mile **Silver Thread Scenic Byway** *(800-571-0881).* This route begins as a 2WD road through Creede and Lake City, then becomes a four-wheel affair as it climbs Cinnamon and Engineer Passes; from there it shifts back to a two-wheel road, dropping into the Animas River Valley north of Durango.

### Wheeler Geologic Area

The City of Gnomes, Dante's Lost Souls, and Phantom Ships are just a few of the epithets given to the potpourri of pinnacles lacing the Wheeler Geologic Area, to the northeast of Creede in **La Garita Wilderness.**

The variable-size particles in each of these pale purple and white-banded volcanic tuff formations were never tightly cemented together, making them particularly susceptible to the erosive power of wind, ice, and rain. Because of their fragility, it's important not to climb on or around them. To further protect them, the area is restricted for day-use only.

A 1909 NATIONAL GEOGRAPHIC article introduced this area to the public, comparing it favorably to the Garden of the Gods near Colorado Springs (see p. 222). Although named after George Wheeler, an army captain who surveyed the region between 1873 and 1884, he and his team never made it to these wild-looking formations.

To reach the Wheeler area, turn north on Pool Table Road (Forest Road 600), which branches off Colo. 149 some 7.3 miles southeast of Creede. Drive 9.7 miles on this gravel road to the signed trailhead for the **East Bellows Trail** near the site of Hansons Mill (4WD vehicles can continue on Forest Road 600 14 miles to reach the entrance of the geologic area). Beginning in a forest of Engelmann spruce and subalpine fir, this trail heads north 7 miles to the entrance to Wheeler and a sweep of intriguing rock formations.

For some, the area still feels haunted by the events that befell explorer John Frémont and his party some 5 miles to the east in the winter of 1848. Snowbound for weeks, the men resorted to cooking and eating their mules; all 100 of the animals had died of starvation. Kit Carson finally rode in to rescue the few men who were still alive. The 4- to 6-foot tree stumps that are visible here may be remnants of the trees used as fuel to cook the mules. Little wonder that Frémont came to describe the peaks of this region as "the highest, most rugged and impractical of all the Rocky Mountain Ranges."

## Rio Grande River

The nation's third longest waterway begins as a mere trickle on a windswept slope of the San Juan Mountains. Flowing 1,910 miles to the Gulf of Mexico, the Rio Grande is a delight for anglers, kayakers, and rafters. Though almost two-thirds of the Rio Grande serves as the border between the United States and Mexico, rafters focus on the river far upstream, beginning

at the Rio Grande Reservoir.

The region surrounding this 2,000-acre impoundment, located about 27 miles west of Creede and 10 miles up Forest Road 520, continues to draw fishermen, as it has for decades. Large brown trout are known to lurk in sparkling clear pools above the reservoir, and the three campgrounds positioned along the main body of water serve as good bases from which to reach a number of prime fishing streams. The 22-mile stretch of the Rio Grande from Creede to South Fork is popular with canoeists and rafters seeking a relaxing float with mountain views. River outfitters based in both towns offer trips on the Rio Grande's water ranging from the mild to the wild. ∎

### Feeling Boxed In?

Fed by scores of feeder streams once it crosses into New Mexico, the Rio Grande can swell to 100 feet wide. Highly charged, it soon enters the turbulent, sheer-walled canyons of the Taos Box, formed in a rift valley between the Sangre de Cristo Mountains and the much bigger mountains to the west, the San Juans. This wild and dangerous water is home to such well-named rapids as Boat Reamer, Corkscrew, and Dead Texan Hole. The Upper Box contains an 11-mile stretch of rapids rated Class V and VI (Class VI is unrunnable even by experts), while the Lower Box has 12 miles of Class III to IV. For more information, call the BLM Taos Field Office at 505-758-8851 (505-758-8158 or 888-882-6188 for recording).

# Alamosa National Wildlife Refuge

■ 11,169 acres ■ South-central Colorado ■ Best seasons spring and fall
■ Hiking, bird-watching, auto tours ■ Contact the refuge, 9383 El Rancho
Ln., Alamosa, CO 81101; phone 719-589-4021. www.r6.fws.gov/alamosanwr

ALTHOUGH THE SAN LUIS VALLEY qualifies as a desert environment—
receiving on average only 7 inches of rain a year—the snowpack in the
surrounding mountains contributes considerably to its groundwater.
Throughout much of the 19th century, the valley floor was flush with
wetlands, providing habitat for native wildlife, and migratory birds. In
the past 130 years, however, humans have harnessed much of that water
in canals, wells, and various irrigation schemes, drying up many of the
wetlands. The Alamosa National Wildlife Refuge attempts to maintain
some of what is left.

The Rio Grande River flows along the refuge's southern boundary,
and although the refuge has become drier in recent years, managers here
help re-create past habitat and conditions through the use of canals and
dikes. These wetlands feature a bounty of ducks all year, from mallard,
gadwalls, pintail, and teal (green-winged, blue-winged, and cinnamon)
to American wigeon and northern shovelers. In spring look for Wilson's
phalaropes and northern harriers, and in winter for ferruginous hawks
and bald eagles. You can also see American avocets, white-faced ibises,
chorus frogs, and black-necked
stilts. In the uplands watch for
sage thrashers, Brewer's sparrows, and horned lizards.

Alamosa National Wildlife Refuge

Like most wildlife refuges,
much of Alamosa is closed to
the public to maintain quality
habitat, yet a 3-mile **auto tour**
and the **River Road Walk** offer
chances for exploration. This
easy trek among willows, birds,
and butterflies basically parallels the river for 2 miles; both
bikes and leashed dogs are allowed. Stop at refuge headquarters for a map
to these self-guided trails, then drive several miles southeast to the **Bluff
Overlook,** which provides fine views of the ponds and wetlands and their
host of teal, mallard, gadwalls, pintail, and Canada geese.

Twenty miles east of the Alamosa and managed jointly with it, the
**Monte Vista National Wildlife Refuge** has some of the highest waterfowl
nesting densities in the country. At 14,189 acres, it provides a resting spot
for thousands of migrating sandhill cranes in spring and fall. September
and October are also peak months for the 35,000-plus ducks that stop by.
The wetlands at Monte Vista, viewed via a short **auto tour,** are mostly
man-made, created out of former agricultural areas. ■

Sunset, Great Sand Dunes National Park and Preserve

# Great Sand Dunes National Park and Preserve

■ 38,625 acres ■ South-central Colorado, near Fort Garland ■ Best seasons spring-fall. Medano Creek may flow spring through early summer only ■ Camping, hiking, backpacking, mountain biking (on Medano Pass Primitive Road only), horseback riding, sand skiing and snowboarding, wildlife viewing ■ Adm. fee ■ Contact the park, 11500 Hwy. 150, Mosca, CO 81146; phone 719-378-2312. www.nps.gov/grsa

SOMEWHERE THERE MAY BE a more unlikely spot for a 39-square-mile patch of fine-grained sand, arranged in dunes so high that most Midwesterners would call them mountains. Finding these great sand dunes here, in the remote San Luis Valley, backed up against the snowy Sangre de Cristo range (see pp. 272-77), seems a profound geologic oddity. These dunes—and the fragile ecosystem that maintains them—are a wonder to walk through.

The San Luis Valley is part of the Rio Grande Rift, and for centuries that river meandered across a relatively flat bottom. Sediments from the surrounding mountains flowed downhill quickly, then were deposited in the meanders as sand. As the Rio Grande changed course, it released its hold on those deposits, which were subsequently picked up by southwesterly winds. Today these winds hit the Sangre de Cristo Mountains, funnel through notches such as Medano Pass, and leave the sand grains behind. The winds intensify as they taper into the passes, inhibiting plants that might cover the dunes.

What, you may ask, keeps the dunes from marching up the side of the mountain and into the next valley? One reason is that creeks coming out of the Sangre de Cristos—joining together into Medano Creek—erode the sand from the east side of the dune field and deposit it to the south, where winds blow it back up onto the dunes. If you dig down from the crest of a dune a foot or so, you may find wet sand—the result of the high water table here, which also helps preserve the dunes' basic shape. (Indeed, the water table used to be so high that early Europeans approached the dunes by boat.) In part because of increased awareness of the importance of the entire watershed in maintaining these dune fields, on October 5, 2000, Great Sand Dunes became a national park and preserve, with expanded boundaries reaching high up into the Sangre de Cristo Mountains. Official designation will come with the imminent acquisition of the adjoining Baca Ranch.

## What to See and Do

This preserve protects most of the dunes in an unspoiled wilderness, but a strange wilderness it is: There's very little plant life, and the majority of wildlife is no bigger than insects or rats. However, six species of insects are unique to the dunes, and more may await discovery. Look out for the circus beetle, endemic to this site, which stands on its head when frightened. Kangaroo rats and other water-conserving rodents also live in the sand. More typical Colorado wildlife, from squirrels to bighorn sheep to black bears, inhabit the

Great Sand Dunes National Park and Preserve

nearby mountains and sometimes visit the edge of the dune field.

There are no trails here, but you can basically walk where you want. (Mountain biking is restricted to Medano Pass Primitive Road.) After parking at the Mosca Creek picnic area, most people head for **High Dune,** about a mile away. It's a tough mile of clawing through sheer sand in a variety of pitches, but the summit can be reached in about an hour. Don't worry if you decide to stop short of your goal though—you can always claim a private patch of dune from which to enjoy a great view.

Thrill seekers equipped with old skis or snowboards can be seen sliding down the hills. Kids, mean-while, delight in the freedom of being able to run amok in this wildland, while the grown-ups are happy to be able to keep the chil-dren in easy sight.

Though being on the dunes is the unique experience here, some visitors prefer to appreciate them from along Medano Creek, or from the mountains above. From Ponderosa Point, the 4.5-mile **Little Medano Trail** heads north through grasslands and forests along the edge of the dunes, paral-leling a high-clearance, 4WD road that eventually stumbles to the top of Medano Pass.

For a shorter adventure, the self-guided, half-mile **Montville Nature Trail** runs from near the visitor center *(trail guide available)* through an area burned in the spring of 2000. Another half-mile loop from the visitor center will introduce you to the area's natural and cultural history. ■

Aspens in autumn near Santa Fe, Sangre de Cristo Mountains

# Sangre de Cristo Mountains

■ South-central Colorado and north-central New Mexico ■ Year-round
■ Camping, hiking, boating, fishing, mountain biking, horseback riding, downhill
skiing, cross-country skiing ■ Contact Rio Grande National Forest, 1803 W.
Hwy. 160, Monte Vista, CO 81144, phone 719-852-5941. www.fs.fed.us/r2/
riogrande; or San Isabel National Forest, 1920 Valley Dr., Pueblo, CO 81008,
phone 719-545-8737. www.fs.fed.us/r2/psicc

FROM COLORADO INTO New Mexico, the Rockies plunge southward like a
forked stick, the west prong swelling as the massive San Juan Mountains
and the east fork remaining the long, lean, slightly independent-feeling
Sangre de Cristo Mountains. Between the two lies the peaceful San Luis
Valley. The Sangres are among the youngest of Colorado's mountain
ranges, containing ten peaks above 14,000 feet and more than two dozen
above 13,000 feet. The range begins near Salida, Colorado, and peters out
south of Santa Fe.

Just as the Sangres form a retaining wall that pockets millions of tons
of blowing sand at Great Sand Dunes National Park and Preserve, they
also created a barrier that protected 17th-century settlers in the San Luis
Valley. The towering range was a formidable obstacle to trade for the

Spanish, as well as later colonizers. Centuries before pilgrims arrived at Plymouth Rock, Ute, Comanche, Navajo, and Pueblo Indians lived in the region, later joining the Spanish in 250 years of tenuous farming in the San Luis Valley. Conquistadores from Mexico probed the range, regarding the mountains as the northern boundary of their political domain.

You might find the remains of an early Spanish stone fortress near the Crestone Needle (14,197 feet). An 1850s American expedition here came across a skeleton dressed in Spanish armor stashed in Sangre de Cristo Cave. Later, a 1940s team from the Colorado Museum of Natural History uncovered a cave littered with Aztec artifacts, believed stolen and hidden by Spaniards centuries ago.

Like other ranges in the Rockies, the Sangre de Cristo Mountains are an uplifted fault block. Sedimentary rocks here, including sandstone, shale, and limestone, overlie Precambrian granite and metamorphic rocks. Found along the upper reaches of the range are U-shaped valleys, glacially scoured lakes, arêtes, and bowl-shaped cirques—scars of the last ice age.

Unlike in the San Juan Mountains to the west, volcanism had minimal impact on the shape of the Sangre de Cristos. However, these mountains faced a rather different kind of fire. Ranching took hold in the 1860s and '70s, a period when more than a million head of cattle and sheep sauntered into these summer pastures, in the process nearly eliminating the native elk, bighorn sheep, and beaver—and wiping out the grizzly bear altogether. Between 1860 and 1910, much of the forest was deliberately burned off in order to enlarge summer sheep pastures, create charcoal, and make it easier to locate minerals. The magnificent aspen stands you see flanking the Sangres today are pioneers that sprouted after the fires cooled.

Despite this early development, today there are no asphalt highways, few chairlifts, no rail lines. Happily, much of the range seems destined to stay wild. Approved by Congress in 1993, the 226,455-acre Sangre de Cristo Wilderness protects much of the range's western slope, from roughly Poncha Springs to south of the Great Sand Dunes. More than 60 alpine lakes line the Colorado portion of the wilderness, where 400 miles of trail wind through forests of lodgepole pine and aspen (and, higher up, Engelmann spruce and subalpine fir). Here you stand a good chance of seeing everything from marmots to pine marten, coyotes to black bears.

## Sanguinary Sierra

The name of the beautiful Sangre de Cristo Mountains translates as the "blood of Christ"—a reference to the red glow that suffuses their cliffs and snowcapped peaks at sunset. Many assume this title came from the Spaniards; one story has a priest praying for a sign during the Pueblo uprising of 1680, only to look up and see the mountains glowing red. Current evidence suggests that the name surfaced in the early 1800s, perhaps bestowed by a zealous Christian sect of that era.

## What to See and Do

One of the best ways to appreciate the magnificent Sangre de Cristo Mountains is via the drive along US 285, which offers uninterrupted views of the saw-edged western slope. Along the way, be sure to shift your eyes from the white-capped peaks to the prairie now and then, where you'll almost certainly spy the distinctive white rumps of pronghorn (see sidebar on opposite page).

Though bagging a Fourteener draws many climbers to the Sangres, the following two easy hikes will let you sample this long, lean mountain range.

### Williams Lake

The 2.5-mile trail from the Kachina Chairlift at the famous Taos Ski Valley to Williams Lake offers a gentle walk through the quiet confines of a spruce-fir forest. The shallow lake sits in the inspiring folds of Wheeler Peak Wilderness, home to New Mexico's highest summit, Wheeler Peak (13,161 feet).

This is a good trail on which to observe how trees adapt to altitude; conifers that tower 40 feet in the valley may be greatly stunted at high elevations. This is a reaction to short growing seasons and harsh, pruning winds.

At its extreme, this stunted condition is called krummholz, a German word meaning "crooked wood." Here, small does not necessarily mean young. One tree, growing at 11,500 feet in Rocky Mountain National Park and measuring a mere 3 inches in diameter, was found to be 328 years old.

To reach the **Williams Lake Trail** (No. 62), take Colo. 150 to the Taos Ski Valley, watching for signs marking the Carson National Forest and the Wheeler Peak Wilderness. Follow Twining Road for half a mile, then turn left on Phoenix Switchback, driving for just over a mile to the sign for hikers' parking.

### Santa Barbara Trail

This lovely, gradually uphill walk of about 4 miles threads its way through a quilt of spruce, fir, and mountain maple forest, broken here and there by meadows embroidered with mats of harebell, groundsel, paintbrush, and asters. (From N. Mex. 75, take N. Mex. 73 S 1.5 miles, then left on FR 116 to parking lot by campground. Take Trail No. 24, opposite parking lot.)

Less than half a mile from the trailhead, the path joins the Rio Santa Barbara and the vegetation expands to include Oregon grape, ferns, thimbleberry, and willow. It's the willow, by the way, that makes this stream an inviting place for beavers.

The trail continues 1.2 miles into the quarter-million-acre **Pecos Wilderness.** Here it crosses the Rio Santa Barbara via a footbridge, entering an even more lush slice of forest. In 2.2 miles, just past the intersection with the **West Fork Trail** (bear right), a wonderful mountain meadow rolls out, framed by mountains and spruce-fir forest, and rich with harebell, yarrow, and false hellebore. The display is particularly beautiful during July and August. ■

Pronghorn

## Pronghorn

First comes a flash of white against a backdrop of brown and gray-green grasses. Then it dawns on you: This is a pronghorn, moving as fast as the prairie wind.

Pronghorn have been running for a long time, outpacing predators from saber-toothed tigers to wolves. Millions of years spent on the prairie have endowed the pronghorn with a light-boned, streamlined frame, powered by a large, highly efficient heart. When alarmed, the 80- to 110-pound pronghorn bounds off at 40 to 50 miles an hour, topping 60 miles an hour during short spurts.

These magnificent animals have large eyes and excellent eyesight, as well as a fur of hollow hairs that provides essential insulation. Horns top both the male and the female pronghorn; larger horns usually indicate a male.

Pronghorn once browsed on grasses and shrubs across much of North America, their numbers reaching 30 to 60 million. Sadly, their remarkable speed was not enough to outrun the bullets aimed at them. Nor was their nimbleness any match for fences, which greatly restrained their movement. By 1920, the pronghorn population had dwindled to an estimated 30,000, barely a thousand of that number in Colorado. Today, thanks to hunting bans, public awareness, and other conservation efforts, pronghorn in the state number about 60,000.

Good places to view the pronghorn in the Sangre de Cristos include the stretches of grassland from Poncha Pass to Saguache along US 285, and on US 40 between Limon and Kit Carson and from Craig to Elk Springs. In winter you can spot herds on either side of Kremmling, along US 40.

*Following pages:* Aspens in autumn, Sangre de Cristo Mountains

# Other Sites

The following is a select list of additional Southern Rockies sites.

## Colorado Plateau

### Kodachrome Basin State Park

Named after a National Geographic team that first used the relatively new film in the park in 1949, Kodachrome Basin State Park offers 2,241 acres of woodlands and colorful cliffs. The park boasts the world's only collection of "sand pipes," 67 chimney-shaped rocks that jut 170 feet skyward. The origins of these geological wonders are not well understood, but they offer breathtaking views as their colors change in waning sunlight. Contact the park, P.O. Box 238, Cannonville, UT 84718; phone 435-679-8562. http://parks .state.ut.us/parks/www1/ koda.htm

### Paiute Wilderness

Fifty-five square miles of majestic wilderness lie nestled in the northwest corner of Arizona, near the Utah-Nevada border. The Virgin Mountains dominate the area and feature scores of granite, gneiss, and limestone wonders. Deeply cutting through the heart of the mountains, several gorges conceal dazzling pools of crystal clear mountain water flanked by towering canyon walls. A strenuous climb up Mount Bangs, Paiute's highest point at 8,012 feet, offers a spectacular vista overlooking the entire area, with the Mojave Desert beckoning to the west. Contact the BLM Arizona Strip District Office, 390 North, 3050 East, St. George, UT 84770; phone 801-673-3545. www .az.blm.gov/rec/paiute.htm

## Utah High Plateaus

### Desolation Canyon

Despite the beautiful sandstone cliffs towering above the mighty Green River, the first explorers to this area named it "Desolation." However, Desolation Canyon today offers great rafting and kayaking through scenic rock layers that tell the story of this relatively young and colorful geological structure. Contact the Bureau of Land Management, P.O. Box 45155, 324 South State St., Salt Lake City, UT 84145; phone 435-636-3000. www.ut.blm.gov

### Otter Creek State Park

Ideal for a day on the water, Otter Creek State Park offers 3,120 acres on the shore of a freshwater reservoir. The park provides visitors ample opportunities for fishing and boating, modern conveniences for picnicking and camping, and the serene solitude of numerous nature trails and hiking paths. Contact the park, P.O. Box 43, Antimony, UT 84712-0043; phone 435-624-3268. http://parks .state.ut.us/parks/www1/ otte.htm

### Snow Canyon State Park

Red sandstone cliffs, lava flows, and twisted rock layers characterize Snow Canyon State Park. Although not as grand as neighboring parks, Snow Canyon provides a tranquil experience in the pure, crisp outdoors of southeast Utah. Scenic drives and short hikes are plentiful. Contact the park, P.O. Box 140, Santa Clara, UT 84765-0140; phone 435-628-2255. http://parks.state.ut.us/ parks/www1/snow.htm

## Wasatch Range & Uinta Mountains

### Bear Lake State Park

Formerly a meeting place for fur trappers in the early 19th century, Bear Lake is now visited more often by outdoor recreation enthusiasts. Co-owned by three states, Utah, Idaho, and Wyoming, Bear Lake is recognized by its aqua blue appearance, a result of calcium carbonates suspended in the water. A marina and beach make water-skiing, swimming, scuba diving, sailing, and fishing some of the more popular activities. Contact the park, P.O. Box 184, Garden City, UT 84028; phone 435-946-3343. http://parks.state.ut.us /parks/www1/bear.htm

### Ogden Nature Center

Founded in 1975, the Ogden Nature Center is committed to acquainting visitors with the environment through outdoor educational programs in the 127-acre wildlife sanctuary. Providing a refuge from urban development, the center houses hundreds of injured or orphaned birds and native plants and animals. Hands-on nature classes as well as many hiking trails are provided for children and adults. Contact the center, 966 West 12th St, Ogden, UT 84404; phone 801-621-7595. www .ogdennaturecenter.org

## Northern Colorado Rockies

### Colorado State Forest SP

Formerly a summer hunting ground for local Native American tribes, the 71,000 acres of Colorado State Forest retain the same natural beauty that they had hundreds of years ago. With a multitude of alpine lakes, forests, and mountainous peaks to choose from, visitors can enjoy the unadulterated splendor of the area by hiking, fishing, or camping. This state park captures the classic, unbridled image of the Rocky Mountains. Contact the park, 2746 Jackson County Road 41, Walden, CO 80480; 970-723-8366. www .parks.state.co.us/state_for est

### Lory State Park

This 2,400-acre park provides a wealth of opportunities for outdoor enthusiasts. Exhilarating hiking and mountain biking trails traverse the park. You can also try the Double Diamond Stables for horseback riding and a cross-country jumping course. The land is spotted with enough wildflowers, animals, and geological formations to dazzle the eye. Contact the park, 708 Lodgepole Drive, Bellvue, CO 80512; phone 970-493-1623. www.parks .state.co.us/lory

## Southern Colorado Rockies

### Arkansas Headwaters Recreation Area

This 80-mile stretch of the Arkansas River provides some of America's finest white-water rapids, including some Class V. Spend a day rafting, kayaking, canoe-

ing, fishing, or camping. Along the riverbanks, keep an eye out for bighorn sheep, ghost towns, massive granite canyons, and intriguing plant life. Contact the recreation area, P.O. Box 126, Salida, CO 81201; phone 719-539-7289. www.parks.state.co.us/ arkansas

### Gunnison Gorge National Conservation Area

President Clinton designated Gunnison Gorge, just downstream from Black Canyon of the Gunnison National Park, as one of the

nation's nine conservation areas in 1999. Free from any human blemishes, this 57,725-acre pristine area provides unbroken stretches for natural enjoyment. Gunnison Gorge boasts a unique double canyon system of layered black granite and red sandstone. Contact the BLM Uncompahgre Field Office, 2505 South Townsend Avenue, Montrose, CO 81401; phone 970-240-5300. www.co.blm .gov/ubra/gorgenca.htm

---

# Resources

The following is a select list of resources. Contact state and local associations for additional outfitter and lodging options. For chain hotels in the Southern Rockies states, see p. 283.

The USDA Forest Service operates campgrounds throughout the states' national forestlands. Call specific national forests for details or contact the National Recreation Reservation Service (877-444-6777. www.reserveusa.com). Information on some campgrounds can be found at the Great Outdoors Recreation Page (www.gorp.com).

Current information about road conditions is available for Arizona at 888-411-7623 or www.azfms.com; for Colorado at 877-315-7623 or www.co .blm.gov/conditions.htm; for New Mexico at 800-432-4269 or www.nmshtd.state.nm.us; for Utah at 800-492-2400 or www.dot.state.ut.us/public/trav eler_info.htm; and for Wyoming at 307-777-4375 or http://wy dotweb.state.wy.us/Docs/Roads /Roadtrav/roadtrav.html.

## ARIZONA

### Federal and State Agencies

Arizona Game & Fish Department
2221 W. Greenway Rd.
Phoenix, AZ 85023

602-942-3000
www.gf.state.az.us
Hunting and fishing licenses, and site information.

Arizona Office of Tourism
2702 N. 3rd St., Ste. 4015
Phoenix, AZ 85004
800-842-8257
www.arizonaguide.com
General resource for travel in Arizona, including camping and lodging.

Public Lands Information Center
222 N. Central Ave.
Phoenix, AZ 85004
602-417-9300
www.publiclands.org
Part of a national network which provides information and educational resources on state and federally managed public lands. Recreation permits may be obtained from the center.

U. S. D. A. Forest Service, Southwestern Region
517 Gold Ave. S.W.
Albuquerque, NM 87102
505-842-3292
www.fs.fed.us/r3
Source for maps and camping and trail information for national forests and grasslands in Arizona and New Mexico.

### Outfitters and Activities

Aramark Wilderness Adventurers
P.O. Box 717
Page, AZ 86040
520/645-3296

www.aramarkadvent.com
Hiking and boating tours, as well as rentals for the Grand Canyon area.

Canyon Trail Rides
P.O. Box 128
Tropic, UT 84776
435-679-8665
Offers horseback rides along the North Rim of the Grand Canyon.

### Outdoor Education and Resources

Grand Canyon Field Institute
P.O. Box 399
Grand Canyon, AZ 86023
520-638-2485
www.grandcanyon.org/field institute
Hiking, backpacking, and rafting excursions, plus classes and workshops in Grand Canyon National Park. Topics include geology, archaeology, Native American culture, photography, and art.

### Lodgings

Fredonia Chamber of Commerce
P.O. Box 537
Fredonia, AZ 86022
520-643-7241
Contact for information on lodging around Kaibab NF.

Grand Canyon Lodge
North Rim, AZ 86052
520-638-2611
www.grandcanyonlodge .com
Elegant rustic lodge on the edge of the North Rim. For

information on other lodging available in the park contact Amfac Parks and Resorts, Inc. (4001 East Iliff Ave., Suite 600, Aurora, CO 80014; 303-297-2757. www.amfac .com).

Jacob Lake Inn
  US Hwy. 89
  Fredonia, AZ 85712
  520-643-7232
  www.jacoblake.com
  Convenient to both Kaibab NF and Grand Canyon NP.

Kaibab Lodge
  Hwy. 67
  Fredonia, AZ 85712
  520-638-2389
  Located 5 miles north of Grand Canyon National Park. Open mid-May–mid-Oct.

## Camping

Many of Arizona's state parks allow you to reserve a campsite in advance for a fee. Call or visit Reserve America Reservations (800-444-7275. www.reserve america.com) for information and details.

## UTAH

### Federal and State Agencies

Utah Bureau of Land Management
  324 South State Street
  Salt Lake city, UT 84145
  801-539-4001
  www.ut.blm.gov
  Has information on recreation and travel on public lands throughout the state. Website provides links to resources for specific activities.

Utah Division of Wildlife Resources
  Southern Regional Office
  622 N. Main
  Cedar City, UT 84720
  435-586-2455
  www.nr.state.ut.us/dwr/dwr.htm
  Hunting and fishing information, regulations, and licenses.

Utah State Parks and Recreation
  1594 West North Temple
  Salt Lake City, UT 84114
  801-538-7220
  http://parks.state.ut.us
  Up-to-date information on state parks and visitor and use fees.

Utah Travel Council
  800-200-1160
  www.utah.com
  General information on travel resources, lodging, and attractions.

### Outfitters and Activities

Bicycle Utah
  P.O. Box 738
  Park City, UT 84060
  435-649-5806
  www.bicycleutah.com
  Clearing house of information on cycling and cyclists needs throughout Utah.

Bike Zion
  P.O. Box 272
  Springdale, UT 84767
  800-475-4576 or
  435-772-3929
  www.bikezion.com
  Rentals and tours in and around Zion National Park.

Canyon Trail Rides
  P.O. Box 128
  Tropic, UT 84776
  435-679-8665
  www.canyonrides.com
  Offers horseback rides in Bryce Canyon, Grand Canyon, and Zion NPs.

Canyonlands Tours/North American River Expeditions
  543 N. Main
  Moab, UT 84532
  800-342-5938 or
  435-259-5865
  www.oars.com
  Offers white-water rafting and wilderness tours in Canyonlands NP, as well as bicycle tours, educational and instructional programs, four-wheel-drive trips, hiking, backpacking, and climbing trips in the surrounding area.

Escalante Canyon Outfitters
  P.O. Box 1330
  Boulder, UT 84716

888-326-4453
www.escalanteoutfitters.com
Hiking and boating expeditions along the Escalante River.

Lin Ottinger Tours
  600 N. Main Street
  Moab, UT 84532
  435-259-7312
  Four-wheel-drive tours through the vast expanses of canyon country.

R&G Horse and Wagon Outfitters, LLC
  15 37 East 2750 North
  North Ogden, UT 84414
  801-782-4947
  Offers horse rentals, wagon rides, and guided horseback rides in Antelope Island SP.

Reflections on the Ancients
  P.O. Box 444
  Wellington, UT 84542
  800-468-4060 or
  435-637-5801
  Guided rock art tours in the San Rafael Swell area.

Tag-A-Long Expeditions
  452 N. Main Street
  Moab, UT 84532
  800-453-3292 or
  435-259-8946
  www.tagalong.com
  Educational programs, four-wheel-drive trips, hiking, backpacking or climbing, river running, and skiing tours throughout the canyonlands region.

Utah Guides and Outfitters
  P.O. Box 21141
  Salt Lake City, UT 84121
  www.adventuresports.com/wwraft/ugo
  UGO is the industry trade association for Utah river outfitters. UGO can provide lists of outfitters operating on Utah rivers.

### Outdoor Education and Resources

Canyonlands Field Institute
  P.O. Box 68
  Moab, UT 84532
  435-259-7750
  www.canyonlandsfieldinst.org
  Conduct field trips and programs about the Colorado Plateau

environment and history.

Four Corners School of
Outdoor Education
P.O. Box 1029
Monticello, UT 84535
435-587-2156
www.fourcornersschool
.org
Educational travel and
research trips open to the
general public.

## Lodging

### Colorado Plateau

Grand County Travel
Council
P.O. Box 550
40 N. 100 E.
Moab, UT 84532
800-635-6622 or
801-259-8825
www.discovermoab.com
Source of lodging infor-
mation around Arches and
Canyonlands NPs. Also a
good source for books
and maps.

Springdale Chamber of
Commerce
P.O. Box 331
Springdale, UT 84767
435-772-3757
Source of information on
lodging in the Zion NP
area.

Zion Lodge
Zion National Park, UT
84767
435-772-3213
An historic lodge features
rustic, old-style cabins, as
well as motel rooms, for
the modern traveler. Call
either the lodge or the
concessionaire (AMFAC
Parks and Resorts, 4001
East Iliff St., Suite 600,
Aurora, CO 80014; 303-
297-2757. www.amfac
.com).

### Utah High Plateaus

Bryce Canyon Lodge
Bryce Canyon National
Park, UT 84717
435-834-5361
www.brycecanyonlodge
.com
This property has been
restored to its original
1920's rustic elegance.
Cabins offer a peaceful
return to nature and a
short walk to the canyon

rim. Call either the lodge
or the concessionaire
(AMFAC Parks and
Resorts, 4001 East Iliff St.,
Suite 600, Aurora, CO
80014; 303-297-2757.
www.amfac.com).

### Wasatch Range &
### Uinta Mountains

Cache Chamber of Com-
merce
160 North main
Logan, UT 84321
800-882-4433 or
435-752-2161
Information on lodging
opportunities near Logan
Canyon.

Flaming Gorge Lodge
155 Greendale
US 191
Dutch John, UT 84023
435-889-3773
www.fglodge.com
Motel and condo unit
accommodations with
fishing guide services and
boating rentals.

Red Canyon Lodge
435-889-3759
www.redcanyonlodge.com
Log cabin rentals on
shore of small lake near
Flaming Gorge. Open daily
April through October
and weekends through
the winter.

Spirit Lake Lodge
760 West 2000 North
Vernal, UT 84078
435-781-8884 or
435-783-2339
Lakefront lodge and nine
cabins. Offers horseback
riding, boating and fishing.

Utah County Convention &
Visitors Bureau
51 S. University Ave.,
Suite 111
Provo, UT 84606
800-222-8824 or
801-370-8393
Information on lodging
along the central Wasatch
Front area.

## Camping
For a list of private campgrounds around the state,
contact the Utah Camp-
ground Owners Association
(801-521-2682).

Many of Utah's state parks

allow you to reserve a
campsite in advance for a
fee. Call or visit Reserve
America Reservations (800-
444-7275. www.reserve
america.com) for informa-
tion and details.

## COLORADO

### Federal and
### State Agencies

Colorado State Parks
1313 Sherman St., Rm 618
Denver, CO 80203
303-866-3437
www.parks.state.co.us
Up-to-date information on
state parks, fees, activities,
and camping information
and reservations.

### Outfitters and Activities

Academy Riding Stables
4 El Paso Blvd.
Manitou Springs, CO
80904
719-633-5667
Offers horseback riding in
Garden of the Gods.

Challenge Unlimited
204 S. 24th St.
Colorado Springs, CO
80904
800-798-5954 or
719-633-6399
www.bikithik.com
Offers cycling tours and
bike rentals for the Pikes
Peak area.

Colorado River Outfitters
Association
P.O. Box 1662
Buena Vista, CO 81211
www.croa.org
303-280-2554
This organization provides
information on outfitters
for Colorado's 13 river
systems. Includes fishing,
white-water kayaking, hiking, mountain biking,
camping, and horseback
guides.

Dvorak's Kayak & Rafting
Expeditions, Inc.
17921 U.S. Hwy. 285
Nathrop, CO 81236
800-824-3795 or
719-539-6851
www.dvorakexpeditions
.com
Offers raft, kayak, and

canoe guided tours, as well as fishing expeditions.

Hi-Country Stables, Inc.
330-442-0258 (winter)
www.hicountrystables.com
Guided horseback riding tours (anywhere from 2 hours to full day) in Rocky Mountain NP. Two locations: Glacier Creek Stables (970-586-3244) and Moraine Park Stables (970-586-2327).

Mountain Spirit Adventures
P.O. Box 26
Salida, CO 81201
719-530-0914
www.coloradovacation.com/tours/spirit
A small, personalized backcountry guide service that will show you the best of the Colorado Rockies with hiking and snowshoe tours, or kid's hikes.

The following offer information about Hut-to-Hut backcountry travel, be it skiing, cycling, or hiking: Summit Huts and Trails Association (P.O. Box 2830, Breckenridge, CO 80424; 970-453-9615. www.huts .org); Tenth Mountain Division Trail Association (1280 Ute Avenue, Suite 21, Aspen, CO 81611; 970-925-5775. www.huts.org); and San Juan Hut to Hut System (P.O. Box 1663, Telluride, CO 81435; 970-728-6935).

## Outdoor Education and Resources

Beidleman Environmental Center
740 W. Caramillo
Colorado Springs, CO 80907
719-578-7088
www.colorado-springs .com/parksrec/places/bei dlman.htm
Year-round environmental programs geared to all ages.

Crow Canyon Archaeological Center
23390 County Road K
Cortez, CO 81321
800-422-8975 or
970-565-8975

www.crowcanyon.org
Research and educational programs highlight prehistoric Native American cultures.

Environmental Learning Center
College of Natural Resources
Colorado State University
Fort Collins, CO 80523
303-491-1661
The center has a 200-acre preserve and "open classroom" programs, plus nature trails and wildlife viewing opportunities.

Rocky Mountain Field Seminars
Rocky Mountain Nature Association
P.O. Box 3100
Estes Park, CO 80517
800-816-7662 or
970-586-0108
www.rmna.org/bookstore
Seminars on natural and cultural history, geology, biology, photography; all age levels.

## Lodgings

### Colorado Plateau

Far View Lodge
P.O. Box 277
Mancos, CO 81328
800-449-2288 or
970-529-4421
Far View Lodge sits on a high shoulder of the Mesa Verde within the national park. Open late April through October.

### Utah High Plateaus

Alexander Lake Lodge
P.O. Box 900
Cedaredge, CO 81413
970-856-2539
Turn-of-the-20th-century lodge provides modern cabins and camping near Grand Mesa.

Grand Mesa Lodge
2825 Hwy. 65
Cedaredge, CO 81413
970-856-3250
Located in Grand Mesa National Forest, this resort features cozy cabins and a motel overlooking beautiful Island Lake.

Mesa Lakes Resort

P.O. Box 230
Mesa, CO 81643
970-268-5467
Perched at 9,800 feet in Grand Mesa National Forest, the resort provides scores of family activities interspersed among seven mountain top lakes.

Spruce Lodge
P.O. Box 1048
Cedaredge, CO 81413
970-856-6240
A quaint, historic lodge with modern conveniences and turn-of-the-20th-century charm. Near Grand Mesa.

### Northern Colorado Rockies

Bed and Breakfast Inns of Glenwood Springs
6471 County Road 117
Glenwood Springs, CO 81601
970-945-4004
www.glenwood-springs-inn.com
Provides B&B recommendations in the Glenwood Springs area.

Contact the Estes Park Area Chamber Resort Association (970-586-4431 or 800-443-7837. www .estesparkresort.com) for lodging opportunities around Rocky Mountain National Park.

### Southern Colorado Rockies

Durango Area Chamber Resort Association
111 South Camino del Rio,
Durango, CO 81302
800-525-8855 or
970-247-0812
www.durango.org
Provides information on lodging in the San Juan Mountains.

Ouray Chamber Resort Association
1230 Main Street
Ouray, CO 81427
800-228-1876 or
970-325-4746
Provides information on lodging in the San Juan Mountains.

Red Crags B&B

302 El Paso Blvd.
Manitou Springs, CO
80829
800-721-2248 or
719-685-1920
http://redcrags.com
Victorian-era B&B with
views of Pikes Peak. Once
frequented by Theodore
Roosevelt.

Strater Hotel
699 Main St.
Durango, CO 81303
970-247-4431
www.strater.com
Century-old Victorian
hotel in historic down-
town; 93 antique-filled
rooms.

## Camping

For a list of private campgrounds around the state,
contact the Colorado Association of Campgrounds,
Cabins and Lodges (888-
222-4641 or 303-499-9343).

Many of Colorado's state
parks allow you to reserve
a campsite in advance for a
fee. Call or visit Reserve

America Reservations (800-
444-7275. www.reserve
america.com) for informa-
tion and details.

## Hotel & Motel Chains in Arizona, Colorado, New Mexico, Utah, and Wyoming

Accommodations are avail-
able in all states unless otherwise noted.

Best Western International
800-528-1234

Choice Hotels
800-424-6423

Clarion Hotels
800-252-7466

Comfort Inns
800-228-5150

Courtyard by Marriott
800-321-2211
Except Wyo.

Days Inn
800-325-2525

Econo Lodge
800-446-6900

Embassy Suites
800-362-2779

Fairfield Inn by Marriott
800-228-2800

Hilton Hotels and Resorts
800-445-8667
Except Wyo.

Holiday Inns
800-465-4329

Howard Johnson
800-654-2000
Except Wyo.

Hyatt Hotels and Resorts
800-223-1234
Except Utah and Wyo.

Marriott Hotels and
Resorts
800-228-9290

Motel Six
800-466-8356

Quality Inns-Hotels-Suites
800-228-5151

Ramada Inns
800-272-6232

Red Lion Hotels
800-547-8010
Except N. Mex. and Utah

Sheraton Hotels and Inns
800-325-3535
Except Wyo.

Super 8 Motels
800-843-1991

# About the Authors/Photographer

Before **Gary Ferguson** began his writing career, he worked as a U.S. Forest
Service interpretive naturalist in Idaho's Sawtooth National Recreation Area.
He is the author of 14 books on nature and science, including *New England* in
this series and *Through the Woods: A Journey Through America's Forests,* which won
a Lowell Thomas Award. Ferguson has appeared on more than 100 radio and
television programs across the country; his essays on nature can be heard on
National Public Radio.

Nonfiction writer **John Clayton** specializes in issues affecting both human and
natural communities in the rural West. The author of *Small Town Bound,* he writes
regularly for *Montana Magazine,* the *Chronicle of Community,* and *High Country
News.* He and his dog live in central Montana.

Writer and naturalist **Maureen Keilty** explores the canyons and mountains of
the southern Rockies from her home in Durango, Colorado. She is the author
of several guides to the region, including *Best Hikes with Children in Colorado.* Keilty's
outdoor adventure articles have appeared in a variety of regional and national
publications, including the *Denver Post, Los Angeles Times,* and *Rocky Mountain News.*

A travel and natural history photographer based in Arizona, **George H. H. Huey**
has a passion for the visual interpretation of remaining wildlands. His subjects
range from western landscapes to natural details to international destinations.
Huey's work has appeared in dozens of magazines, including *Audubon, Islands,
NATIONAL GEOGRAPHIC, Outside,* and *Time.* His books include the *National Geographic
Guide to America's Outdoors: Southwest, Channel Islands National Parks,* and *Grand
Views of Canyon Country.*

# Index

**National Geographic Guide to America's Outdoors: Southern Rockies**
by Gary Ferguson, John Clayton, and Maureen B. Keilty
Photographed by George H. H. Huey

**Published by the National Geographic Society**
John M. Fahey, Jr., *President and Chief Executive Officer*
Gilbert M. Grosvenor, *Chairman of the Board*
Nina D. Hoffman, *Executive Vice President,*
  *President, Books and School Publishing*

**Prepared by the Book Division**
Elizabeth L. Newhouse, *Director of Travel Publishing*
Allan Fallow, *Senior Editor and Series Director*
Cinda Rose, *Art Director*
Barbara Noe, *Senior Editor*
Caroline Hickey, *Senior Researcher*
Carl Mehler, *Director of Maps*

**Staff for this Book**
Jane Sunderland, *Book Manager*
Mary Luders, Jim Lynch, *Editors*
Susan K. White, *Designer*
Molly Roberts, *Illustrations Editor*
Sean M. Groom, Victoria Garrett Jones, Elizabeth A. Lenhart, *Researchers*
Lise Sajewski, *Editorial Consultant*
Matt Chwastyk, Jerome N. Cookson, Sven M. Dolling,
  Thomas L. Gray, Joseph F. Ochlak, Nicholas P. Rosenbach,
  Gregory Ugiansky, National Geographic Maps, Mapping Specialists,
  XNR Productions, *Map Edit, Research, and Production*
Tibor Tóth, *Map Relief*
R. Gary Colbert, *Production Director*
Janet Dustin, *Illustrations Assistant*
Julia Marshall, *Indexer*
Larry Porges, *Program Assistant*
Deb Antonini, Andrew Emmett, *Contributors*

Gregory S. Holden, Colorado School of Mines, *Consultant*

**Manufacturing and Quality Control**
George V. White, *Director;* John T. Dunn, *Associate Director;*
Vincent P. Ryan, *Manager;* Phillip L. Schlosser, *Financial Analyst*

**Library of Congress Cataloging-in-Publication Data**
Ferguson, Gary, 1956-.
  Guide to America's outdoors: Southern Rockies / by Gary Ferguson, John Clayton, and
  Maureen B. Keilty; photography by George H. H. Huey.
    p. cm
    ISBN 0-7922-7749-X
    1. Rocky Mountains—Guidebooks. 2. National parks and reserves—Rocky Mountains—
  Guidebooks. 3. Outdoor recreation—Rocky Mountains—Guidebooks. I. Clayton, John, 1964-
  II. Keilty, Maureen, 1952- III. Huey, George H. H. IV. Title
    F721.F47 2001
    917.8804'34—dc21                                                              2001018046
                                                                                   CIP